IRON MEN

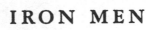

IRON MEN

BUCKO, CRAZYLEGS, AND THE BOYS RECALL THE GOLDEN DAYS OF PROFESSIONAL FOOTBALL

STUART LEUTHNER

DOUBLEDAY

NEW YORK • LONDON • TORONTO • SYDNEY • AUCKLAND

Published by Doubleday, a division of
Bantam Doubleday Dell Publishing Group, Inc.,
666 Fifth Avenue, New York, New York 10103

Doubleday and the portrayal of an anchor with a dolphin
are trademarks of Doubleday, a division of
Bantam Doubleday Dell Publishing Group, Inc.

Library of Congress Cataloging-in-Publication Data
Leuthner, Stuart.
Iron men: Bucko, Crazylegs, and the boys recall the golden days of professional football / Stuart Leuthner. —1st ed.
p. cm.
1. Football players—United States—Biography. I. Title.
GV939.A1L46 1988
796.332'092'2—dc19
[B] 88-9555
CIP

ISBN 0-385-23977-7

PRINTED IN THE UNITED STATES OF AMERICA
September 1988
FIRST EDITION
BG

ACKNOWL-EDGMENTS

ONE of the questions I'm often asked is how I go about finding the people I talk to. There are many ways; friends, a chance article in a newspaper or magazine, a scrap of overheard conversation. Then sometimes you get lucky and find somebody like Anne Mangus. Anne is the librarian at the Football Hall of Fame and I contacted her when this project consisted mainly of a few three-by-five cards. She suggested I send her my list of prospective ex-players and I soon received more than I had hoped for. Phone numbers, addresses, reprints of articles, and, maybe more important, insight into the players themselves. Anne made my research a great deal easier than it could have been, and I want to thank her and her colleagues at the Hall of Fame for their valuable assistance.

There were also the countless fans I questioned about their favorite players from the past. Certain names started to occur more often than others and these patterns helped me with my final suggestions. Please don't hate me if one of your number one picks isn't here. I would have liked to talk to them all, but time and space intervened. John Cameron and Don McAuliffe were most helpful, suggesting names of men they played with or against. Bobby Ingham and the rest of the O'Brians' regulars added their two cents' worth. Richard Titsch brought his football know-how to the initial interviews and helped get me started on the right track.

On the editorial side, Margaret Unser Schutz is more than a transcriber. Her accuracy and enthusiasm for the material helped shape the final manuscript. David Gernert is a first-rate editor. His direction is subtle but extremely thoughtful. Lucy Herring kept little problems from becoming big ones.

Also deserving mention are Ken Carlson, Jim Gibbons, Mary

Hess, Dan Edwards of the Pittsburgh Steelers, Bobby Layne, Vicki Christensen, Sam Meredith, Ken Vose, Rocco Pirro, Nick and Mark Baratta, Jan Dodrill, and Dewey Graham. Jim Gallagher of the Philadelphia Eagles, himself a part of this book, went far beyond just helping me with his memories. And lastly, special thanks to Carolyn Jensen. She doesn't even like football, but without her selfless support this book would probably still just be an idea.

CONTENTS

CONTENTS

INTRODUCTION

Professional football is a great show. It's dead on the level, you can't fake it.

—Johnny Blood McNally

I grew up in Buffalo and when the All-American Conference went out of business, and with it the Bills, the Cleveland Browns were the closest thing we had to a home team. Rooting for the Browns was similar to being a Yankee fan; they always seemed to win. Otto Graham would drop back, survey the field at his leisure, and then throw a pass to Mac Speedie or Dante Lavelli. Touchdown.

It wasn't long before I realized that Graham was able to spend so much time in the pocket because Marion Motley was knocking down anyone who had designs on his quarterback. Gail Bruce, an end who played for the 49ers, was one of those players trying to dismember Graham. "You rush Graham and put on a move and beat your man, and there's Motley waiting for you. Next play, you beat your man with a different move, and there's Motley, waiting again. Pretty soon you say, 'The hell with it. I'd rather stand on the line and battle the first guy.' "

When he wasn't protecting Graham, Motley was gaining a lot of yards—he had a 5.7 career rushing average—catching a few passes, and playing linebacker. Marion Motley has been called the greatest all-around player who ever played the game. And yet, when was the last time you heard his name?

Professional football has a short memory. Several weeks ago I was watching a game and was pleasantly surprised to hear one of the announcers compare a runner's style to Bronco Nagurski's. I was astonished when his cohort in the booth asked, "Who?" Can you imagine Joe Garagiola asking, "Who's Lou Gehrig?"

INTRODUCTION

Watch a baseball game and chances are that sometime during the broadcast you're going to hear about "Diz" or "Whitey" or some great play that Minnie Minoso made in the second game of a doubleheader in 1951. Names, facts and statistics are the stuff that baseball is made of. Pro football's history isn't anywhere as long as baseball's—the National Football League didn't come into existence until 1920—and the game is much more open to modification. You only have to look at the equipment worn today to see how the game has changed since the 1950s. Today's players are starting to look like something out of *Rollerball* or *Mad Max.*

With all the hype and promotion, it's easy to forget the people who helped create the modern game of football. Every year Super Bowl week becomes more of an extravaganza, and the accompanying media blitz more insufferable. It's a far cry from the time when pro football was a byline on the sports page. The men in this book played first because they loved the game and second because it seemed like a good way to put a few bucks in the bank. Pro football certainly wasn't looked upon as a career. And yet their blood and sweat created a national passion where season's tickets are contested in divorce settlements and Super Bowl tickets anywhere near midfield go for $2,000.

Joe Schmidt told me, "Maybe people just don't give a damn about our time." That may have been true a few years ago, but interest in pro football's past seems to be on the rise. Television halftime shows now feature documentaries on players from the past and magazines are appearing that focus on the history of the game. And last year over 200,000 people visited the Football Hall of Fame. Located in Canton, Ohio, this museum's displays honor the exciting characters who helped invent the game. Bert Bell's desk, a Washington Redskins' Band drum and headdress, Ernie Stautner's jersey . . . it's all there. The Hall of Fame is a fitting tribute to the men who helped make professional football the most popular sport in history.

Meeting and talking to these people was an experience I will always remember. Marion Motley picked me up at the airport in a

Datsun, a two-door. Getting in and out, he seemed to fold and unfold—he fit, but I don't know how. Walking into Jim Ricca's office and finding a row of handmade dollhouses. "If Rosie Grier can do needlepoint, I can build dollhouses." Doak Walker, a three-time All-American and Heisman Trophy winner, telling me, when I asked him how he did in college, "Oh, fine." A very unpretentious man. Not knowing what to expect from Ed Sprinkle, known as the "meanest man in football" and finding him to be not only congenial, but almost shy. Trying to spot Jim Ringo in the middle of a group of contemporary Buffalo Bills. He's in the Hall of Fame and played for Vince Lombardi? Shouldn't he be bigger?

This book is not a lament about the "good old days" by a bunch of grizzled, aging athletes. These men played at a special time and place. While they might be envious of the salaries being paid today, they realize that each man lives in his own time. A game was in the process of becoming a national obsession, and they were at center stage while it was happening. No one has to tell them they played a hell of a game.

—Stuart Leuthner, 1988

We were Wops and Polacks and Irishmen out of Flatbush, along with one mad dreamer out of the cold, cow country up yonder, and though we may not have had the background, or the education, to weep at Prince Hamlet's death, we had all tried enough times to pass and kick a ball, we had on our separate rock-strewn sandlots taken enough lumps and bruises, to know that we were viewing something truly fine, something that only comes with years of toil, something very like art.

—From *A Fan's Notes*, © 1968 by
Frederick Exley, Random House.

PART

I

FOOT SOLDIERS

FOR THE GOOD OF THE TEAM

ANDREW ROBUSTELLI

END

Los Angeles Rams 1951–55

New York Giants 1956–64

If we had a smart-mouthed kid on the squad, Andy would take him alone in a corner and when they came back the kid would be shaking and he'd call everybody "sir" for the next year or so.

—Alex Webster

PEOPLE sit down with Andy Robustelli and they want to talk football with me. I don't want to talk football because it's usually boring. Andy Robustelli isn't just an ex-football player, he's a creative, intelligent marketing person. All I have to do is look around this office and I know that. If there's one thing you learn from football, it's perception. How do you prepare for a game? Based on what you saw the other team do in the past, that's how you're going to proceed in the future. You want to benefit from what you've seen happen before and take advantage of it. The same thing works in business.

In 1987, when the Giants were in the Super Bowl, I probably

could have made more money than I did in my whole first year of pro football, going on television talk shows and such. You couldn't get me to stand in a booth and sign autographs if you gave me $5,000. I've lost a hell of a lot of business because I wouldn't prostitute myself. The recognition value of my name is useful, there's no question about that, but I've never flaunted my name and reputation as a football player. We probably have eighty people working in this complex, and not one of the accounts that we have in house was solicited by me. I don't have to go out and have a beer with a guy or go on a vacation to get business. Not that I'm above anything, but I don't owe anybody and nobody owes me. When one of our people picks up the phone and talks to Howard Cosell or Arnold Palmer, although I've met them, it's strictly a business relationship. I guarded myself while I was playing, so I didn't become an athlete who used that athlete's reputation to survive. I let professional football become a stepping stone for my future and broke my ass to get it.

After my last game, I took off my football shoes, put them in a sack, and came to work. I'd been building the business while I was playing, so I didn't have one day of unemployment between football and after football. The first year that I was in pro football, I was with the Los Angeles Rams and we won the championship. My share was $2,100.49, and I took that money and went into business and I've been in business ever since. When people ask me what we do here, it's pretty tough to answer because we do a lot of things. We're basically a travel business, but we also do a lot of corporate services, promotion, sales incentives, and special events like the Super Bowl and America's Cup. We currently have fourteen travel offices and a meeting center where we can accommodate 100 people for sales meetings, whatever. We also do our own video presentations for our sales people, create contests for clients, have a little hotel in the West Indies and some property in the Dominican Republic and Puerto Rico. You can see that we've kind of spread our wings.

I came from a poor family. We lived in Stamford, Connecticut, in a cold-water flat. There were four black families in the apartment building. My mother and father both worked; she was a dressmaker and he was a barber. It was pretty tough for them because my father came over from Italy and it was hard for a guy like that to earn a living for his wife and six kids. I've told my kids how, when we were kids, we'd go out in the backyard and take snow and mix it with jelly. That was our "ice cream." They, of course, look at me like I'm nuts.

My mother and father were very religious people, dedicated to the church and their family, and I think they brought us up with very strong values. I was always a devil when I was young, but I always worked to pick up a few bucks here and there and, although I came close, I never really got into too much trouble. We knew better because our parents were really strict. If a teacher said something to one of us at school, we never went home and told our mother because we'd have gotten it twice.

We played football and baseball in the street from the time I was five or six. There was a trade school in our town where people would go to night school and the light would shine out on a little patch of ground. That was our field. We'd take a stocking and fill it with rags for a ball, and almost every night for two or three years that was where we'd get our football in. My first organized football experience was with a couple of church C.Y.O. teams, and I only played one year of high school ball because I really wanted to play more for the church than I did for Stamford High School.

After high school, I went to LaSalle, a little military academy on Long Island. I wanted to join the service, but I was only seventeen and my mom wouldn't let me, so I played football that fall at LaSalle. When I turned eighteen, I volunteered to go into the Navy and told my mother I was drafted. I was a water-tender third-class on a destroyer escort, the *William C. Cole,* and we were all over the South Pacific. The most extensive fighting we saw was off of Okinawa. We were there for about six months.

When I got back from the war, my high school coach, Paul

Kuczo, wanted me to go to Villanova because that's where he went to school. He talked to Jordan Oliver, the coach at Villanova, and Oliver said I'd need a year of prep school to get in. I didn't want to do that, and a couple of my high school buddies had decided to go to Arnold College so I went along with them. The school is located in Milford, Connecticut, and it's now a part of the University of Bridgeport. We were a pretty serious group of students because you're talking about people twenty-one, twenty-two years old. We had traveled around the world and seen a little bit more than some kid just coming out of high school. The government was paying us fifty bucks a month on the G.I. Bill, and that's the only money we had. I couldn't even get home on the weekends because none of us had the nickels for the tolls on the highway. Most of us worked while we were going to school, and nobody was going to Arnold because he was going to be a professional football player—that's not the kind of school it was. We played mostly other teachers' colleges —New Britain, Adelphi, Wagner, teams like that. It wasn't big-time football, or anything like that, but I played some pretty good football and baseball at Arnold and was the captain of the football team for three years.

I enjoyed playing football but never thought about a career in pro ball until my last two years of college, when I started to get letters from teams asking me if I'd be interested in playing pro football. They said I'd have to build my stats and get recommendations from the coaches. This was all through the mail. I never actually talked to anybody, and I was shocked when I was drafted by the Rams.

Supposedly Lou DeFillipo, who played for Fordham and was scouting for the Rams, saw me in a game and told the Rams they should think about drafting me, but I talked to a fellow by the name of Eddie Cotell, who also did a lot of scouting for the Rams, and asked him, "How the hell did you ever find me?" He said, "Well, when we get down to the eighteenth and nineteenth pick—I was drafted nineteenth—we're drafting on speculation, and any guy who can block nine or ten punts like you did in one season has got to have something. That's why we drafted you."

Actually I think I would have possibly been a better baseball player than a football player. I tried out with the baseball Giants after I got out of college and was catching batting practice at the Polo Grounds the day Willie Mays came into the major leagues. They wanted to send me to Knoxville, which was in Class B, and I had to make up my mind to either go to Los Angeles and try out for the Rams or go for baseball. I felt that if I made it, I'd make it quicker in football because I was twenty-five years old, which is pretty old to be bouncing around in the minor leagues.

The Rams wired me money to report to camp, and I took the train out to the Rams' training camp in Redlands. In those days it was tough to make a team because they only had thirty-three players, so there were only two or three spots open each year on each team for the whole mess of kids coming out of school. The teams were also reluctant to replace somebody. Today you can replace ten guys and get away with it because you've got so many players, but in those days if you replaced just a few, you were losing a lot of experience. In fact, when I went with the Rams in 1951, they were in a period of transition, and I think there were fifteen rookies on the team. We were kind of written off for winning anything that year but ended up winning the championship.

They didn't really ignore me, but the veterans didn't go out of their way for me either. I'm not that much of a gregarious kind of guy. I don't like to make a lot of small talk, so I don't make a lot of friends. I was very homesick and discouraged; in fact, I didn't unpack my bags for two weeks. Joe Stydahar was the Rams' coach, and I went in to see him and told him I wanted to go home. Joe was a tough guy and he said, "You son-of-a-bitch, you go home and your wife will kill you. If you don't have the moxie to stick it out, you'll never amount to anything. Promise me you'll stay another week, and we'll decide whether or not you're good enough to play with us."

You were talking about some real classy ball players on the Rams at that time. I had always considered myself a pretty good offensive player until I saw Crazylegs Hirsch, Tom Fears, and Bob Boyd. Crazylegs was probably the premier end in the league, along with Fears, and Boyd was just about the fastest. I knew I wasn't going to beat them out, so I decided to go all out and try to make the defense.

Evidently I did all right because after the second game of my rookie season I started. I missed one game toward the end of that season and never missed another game for fourteen years. At that time pro football was really opening up. The formations right after the war were still variations on the single wing, which is a power way to play football. The Rams started to bring in a lot of variations which were kind of against the grain—man in motion, all of that stuff—and that was the beginning of what pro football is today. The war caused a break in tradition, and people had to face a lot of new things. Everybody wanted new cars, new houses, new everything, and football changed along with everything else.

When I played with the Rams, I was probably a more spectacular player. I played with a little bit of reckless abandon. But I don't think I was as good a player as I was when I started to learn why and how I was doing things. When I got to the Giants and Tom Landry's defense, it was somewhat different. Everything was all coordinated, and it wasn't the kind of setup that could make you a superstar, it made you a part of a unit. We were good and we knew it. At that time the defense still didn't get that much credit and our pride came from knowing that we could get the job done. We were tough individuals and we knew how to work with each other. I was on a television show last year with Jim Katcavage and we were talking about those days and a game where he wanted to come out because he said his shoulder hurt. We didn't want to hear it and all of us were getting on him, "What the hell is this crap? You want to come out because your shoulder hurts? You play." He kept moaning and groaning, and we just kept after him and wouldn't let him out of the game. It turned out that he played almost the entire game with a broken shoulder. That's tough.

The reason I left the Rams was that my second daughter was close to being born. I called Sid Gillman, who was coaching the Rams at that time, and asked him if I could stay in Connecticut for three or four days. He told me something to the effect that I'd better get my ass out there or they were going to do something about it. I told him that I wasn't going to come, and he told me that he'd fine me for every day I was late. That got me mad, and I told him that I wasn't coming for sure. He told me to do what I had to do and he'd do what he had to do. Two or three days later I got a call from Well Mara, president of the New York Giants, and he asked me, "If we're able to get you from the Los Angeles Rams, would you consider playing three or four more years with the Giants?" I knew I had been traded and that was a real blow, being traded to the Giants. Even though I lived in Connecticut and always felt I wanted to play where I thought things could be better for me, for my business and family, when the day came and the Rams said they didn't want me, I felt abandoned and depressed. In a situation like that, you feel the whole world's against you.

As I said, I had been preparing myself to leave football right along, and I never really expected to stay in it as long as I did. Fourteen years is a long time to play and I was thirty-nine years old when I quit. I retired at the end of the 1964 season and started to work full-time at my travel business. The Giants fired Al Sherman in 1969, and I was a little disappointed that I didn't get the job as head coach. I don't know if I felt I should have gotten it, but I didn't think I was given the recognition that I deserved. What the hell, I had been the captain of the team and coached the defense for the last four years I played. I've always thought I could have been a good head coach and still do, but I never got the chance to prove it.

The Giants called me up after the 1973 season and offered me the job as the director of operations. They hadn't had a good season, and I think they were having a problem with Randy Johnson, their quarterback. He went home, or something like that, and I called Tim Mara to see if he wanted me to go down and try to talk to the kid. That might have been what put a seed in his mind because it was a month or so later when they called me and wanted to know if I wanted the job.

I told them that I'd come back, but I wasn't coming back into football permanently because I didn't want to leave my business. We had just built our new office in Stamford, and I had to turn the business over, and that was very tough to do. But I knew that the Giants were in bad shape, and if I could do something to help that situation, that's what I wanted to do, for the good of the team. I told Well, "I'll try it for a couple of years and be as honest with you as I can. I'll tell you what you need, and then I'm going to leave." I stayed there a couple more years than I wanted and gave everything back to pro football that I ever got out of the game. Every bit of enjoyment that I ever got out of sports, I gave back. It was a tough time.

I think both Wellington and Tim Mara are decent guys. The Giants have a character that could only come from the owners, and it wasn't a question of my having a battle with them, as a lot of people have indicated. I don't really want to go into it because I don't think it would serve any purpose, but it was a situation where Wellington had to do something besides being completely involved with football and Tim had to realize that he had to become more involved with the team. Both of them could then understand what it means to be part of an organization. At that time the owners were set in their traditional ways. It had worked for them up to that point and they just didn't realize that you couldn't do everything yourself anymore. You had to hire other people and let them accept the responsibility. When there were twelve or fourteen teams, and those teams were relatively small, the game had settled into a very nice pattern and owners could do things like call each other and say, "I've got a pretty good kid—do you want him? Next time I need a guy, I'll let you know." That kind of thing.

Now you had more teams that were constantly fighting for the marketplace, and it wasn't enough to just settle back and put things in a file. You had to have it in a computer, you had to have the strength coaches, all the new ideas; and I told them as soon as I got there: "The first thing you have to do to improve this team is to get rid of me. If you're going to build for the long haul, you can't have a short-term guy running the organization or supposedly running it. You also have to realize that if you have 'yes' people working for you, you're not going to accomplish anything. You've got to start setting up your business so somebody calls the shots."

I think if there was anything that I did accomplish, it was the fact that someone could come into the Giant organization and be able to point some fingers and say, "This is not the way to do it and I disagree with you totally." That had never been done before and I think that by the time I was finished, they knew they weren't structured the way they should be and probably indirectly caused the whole organization to turn into what it is today.

One thing I am still angry about, and let me be diplomatic and call somebody a bastard without actually calling him a bastard. There were things that several sportswriters said that really upset me. They wrote that I wasn't really concentrating on the Giants, I was worried about my own business. Hell, that was the only thing that I had going for me, that I always had my own business to come back to. During some of the confrontations, I always had the psychological wedge to say, "Hey, you don't like what I'm doing? Let me get the hell out of here. I'll go home and be a lot happier than I am here." Another guy wrote an article one Sunday about George Young and he said I "retired." Well, that's bullshit. If you want to say I got fired, pick up the phone and ask me, "Did you get fired from the Giants?" I'd say, "No." I don't have anything to prove to anybody, but if you don't bother to really ask the people involved, then you have no right to be cute. That's why I don't read articles about athletes because so much of the reporting done about sports today, and even in my time, is negative. If there's something good to say, they'd rather not write about it.

Today all they write about are the athletes who get involved with drugs, that sort of thing, and how much money they're making. We never talked about money with each other, and today every player seems to run around and check with everybody else to see how much they're making, and then he goes to see his agent and tells him he's not making enough. I never lifted a weight in my life and never took anything artificial. No pills, no anything. In fact, I used to go to my own doctor when I was playing. Some of the guys in my day drank, but there weren't too many of them that had a real problem. The coaches used to deal with it in their own way when the guys went out and drank a little too much. They had what they called a "roll drill," and they'd have you lie down and roll over and over, the whole length of the field, until you puked your guts out. In effect they were saying, "Okay, you want to go out and drink, go ahead, and tomorrow we'll have another roll drill."

Last week I watched the Giant–Washington game. The minute the game was over, the announcer came on and started to talk about the point spread. When he was through, you had a Miller High Life commercial, followed by Budweiser. In fact, it seemed that the whole show was sponsored by beer companies. Now, the first thing we do is criticize kids for drinking and athletes for gambling. There's a lot to be said about the decent things that sports stand for and the good that comes out of participating in athletics. It's time for a lot of us who have participated and upheld sports to start re-evaluating what professional sports has become and what it's doing to us—what we're doing to professional athletes or anybody involved with athletics, for that matter. Look at what goes on in Little League. I'm not so sure that half the parents in this country don't give a damn about their kids. They only seem to care about themselves.

If there's a player that stands out in my mind today, it's Walter Payton—the kind of player who's played for twelve or thirteen years, has not been a problem to his team, is a credit to the game of football. I don't know what a player should be, but I think a guy like Payton comes close. He plays hard and plays hurt and never complains. He does everything he can for the team, the whole team, and I think that's the kind of guy who should be recognized as the better player. He's the kind they should write about, but maybe I'm just old-fashioned. Maybe it's stupid to be as honest as I am about things. But if you start watching everything you say, start being careful of how it sounds, you'll never say anything at all.

WHO'S THIS GUY VINCE LOMBARDI?

JAMES RINGO

CENTER

Green Bay Packers 1953–63

Philadelphia Eagles 1964–67

The woods are full of performers. I want champions.

—Vince Lombardi, talking about Jim Ringo

IT was my first year with Green Bay, and we opened up against the Cleveland Browns. I was a twenty-one-year-old kid and I had to play against Bill Willis. He was all over me. Later that year I had to go up against Les Bingaman of the Lions. Hell, he was twice as big as I was. We played the Eagles, and "Bucko" Kilroy lined up over top of me on an extra point. That son-of-a-bitch hit me so hard, the ball hit me in the ass. Alex Wojciechowicz, Arnie Weinmeister, Chuck Bednarik—there were any number of those guys playing in those days. You'd go to Chicago and there would be Ed Sprinkle waiting for you. If I told one of those kids I'm coaching today that I played against Hardy Brown, he'd say, "Who the hell is Hardy Brown?" That guy would put you right on your ass. Those players taught you in a hurry that if you were going to play in this business, that was the kind of football you had better be prepared to play.

It started to clean up when I retired, but there wasn't a game when we didn't get into a fight. That was something you knew before you even went on the field. Today, with the camera close-ups and the announcers, all of that, they don't want any extra activity. It's entertainment and the league doesn't want fights because it takes away from the game. They've dressed the NFL up a little bit, but it's still a contact sport. I don't care who you are. YOU sit in the locker room on Sunday morning and you know what you're going to be doing for the next sixty minutes. There's no ducking it. The amazing thing is that they ask you to come out of that game and be a normal, sane human being—be a violent person like that, and walk out of the locker room with a smile on your face and be a good husband, father, and neighbor. I battled my butt off out there for survival. If you took the same mayhem that is created out on that field down to some street corner or in a bar, they'd lock you up for twenty years.

There isn't a ball player that's played in this business who didn't know what he was doing when he signed his contract. If you sign the contract, goddamn it, you sell your body. It's as simple as that. Do you think that today a kid still doesn't sell his body? I will probably get my butt in trouble, but I don't care. I'm a coach. If you're a player, you put a price on your body, and if I want it, I'll buy it. You can do a service for me, a physical service—now what do you want to get paid for that service?

My rookie year those guys tore me up. I got my cartilage torn, my hand broken, my cheekbone cracked, and Gene Ronzani, the head coach, told me I'd better go home before I got killed. The Packers sent me home around Thanksgiving, and I lifted weights and did everything I could so I could play in the business. When I came back the next year, I asked Dave Hanner to work with me. Hanner was a pretty good defensive tackle, and the only reason he didn't get more recognition was because of Green Bay's record at that time. I got together with Hanner, and he let me fire off on him all week. I told him, "Anytime you get a chance, take a shot at me. I want you to beat the hell out of me," and that's exactly what he proceeded to do. Dave taught me that because I was small, I had to be quick. He taught me not to come off the ball to high or too low. And he taught me how to cut down a tackle because—and I never forgot that—a tackle lives on his legs. Dave Hanner helped me become a player in the National Football League. I wouldn't have survived if I hadn't done it that way.

You talked to Chuck Bednarik? He lived in Bethlehem, Pennsylvania, and I grew up right near there in Phillipsburg, New Jersey. We used to play his high school, and he was a hell of a player even then. In the area I grew up in, you went out for football. You didn't worry about baseball or basketball. It was an honor and privilege to play on the high school team. Football was a ticket for me to a college education because my parents couldn't have afforded to send me. It was just about the only way a kid like me could get out of Phillipsburg. My father, God bless him, worked at Ingersoll-Rand, and that was where most of the people in town worked. That's not what I wanted for myself.

I graduated in 1949 and went to Syracuse University. A lot of people in my hometown thought that was a mistake because they told me I wouldn't make it at Syracuse. Not because of the football, but because I didn't have the gray matter to cut the courses. They'd look at me, and you could tell that they thought it wouldn't be long before I was back home. One man who had confidence in me was my high school line coach, Wiz Rinehart. Wiz was the one who suggested I move from fullback to center. He told me I could make it at Syracuse, and Wiz was the one I chose to induct me into the Pro Football Hall of Fame.

At that time Syracuse was playing schools like Lafayette, Colgate, and Cornell. You couldn't say they were playing major league football. It was, however, the best I could handle at that time. I never wanted to go to a major football school because I was afraid I'd be gobbled up. Hell, I was just about gobbled up at Syracuse. At that time Ben Schwartzwalder was starting to put his ball team together. He brought in about twenty-five or thirty players, and four of us managed to graduate. He was looking for football players, but the university was looking for students. College wasn't anything like it is today. Those professors didn't care if you played football—you were expected to get the marks. Eventually, as his record shows, Coach Schwartzwalder was able to come up with the right combination. He was a good man and had been in the 82nd Airborne in World War II. He'd made several jumps and knew what life was all about. He was a very, very tough coach who sent a lot of people into pro ball.

During my senior year I hurt my knee. Then we went down to the Orange Bowl and got the hell beat out of us by Alabama, 61–5. We were completely mismatched. I was married by then and on the trip back to Syracuse wondered what the hell I was going to do with the rest of my life. There was a telegram waiting in my mailbox that said I had been drafted by the Green Bay Packers. Hell, I didn't even know where Green Bay was. I had to look it up on a map. I had my knee operated on and went to see the old man, Coach Schwartzwalder, with a cast on my leg. I asked him what he thought about me playing in the pros. He said, "Well, you'll never know unless you try it."

It was an experience in itself going to training camp that first year. Hibbing, Minnesota, was so far back in the woods that by the end of the first week the sheep were starting to look good. I walked into the equipment room and had to pick a left shoulder pad from one pile and a right one from another. I managed to patch myself together and thought, "So this is professional football. We had better equipment at Syracuse."

I spent a week and a half up there and we didn't run a play. All we did was run down on punts and hit each other. There were seven centers in camp, and they were all bigger than I was. I didn't see how I was going to make the team because they were only going to keep one. Everybody was very rough. I came from a neck of the woods where people are tough, but not like that. Those guys were going to kick the hell out of you because you were going to take somebody's job. I was always getting into fights. One day a kid by the name of Bob Kennedy—he was a high draft choice from the University of Wisconsin—left, and I went with him. His family lived in Rhinelander, Wisconsin, and there I was, a thousand miles from home with twenty-eight cents in my pocket. I sat there for four days and finally borrowed some money from Bob so I could get home.

By the time I got home, it was common knowledge that I had left camp and my wife was waiting for me. She said, "What a hell of a way to do it, quit." My father was also very upset, and my father-in-law was even more upset. He was interested in the amount of money I was making—$5,200. I think he was afraid I might turn into a bum and not take proper care of his daughter and grandchildren. I could see that I wasn't going to have any fun in Phillipsburg, so I called up Chuck Drulis, one of the assistant coaches at Green Bay, a pretty damn good guy, and he told me to come back up.

There was an old cliché in those days about Green Bay being the doormat of the league, and it wasn't far from the truth. There was always a bus going and another one coming. That first year we played Pittsburgh and they had a back named Ray Mathews. He caught a pass and they beat us, 21–20. We had Monday off, and when I walked out on the field Tuesday, there were fifty new guys standing there. In those days any time you wanted to change the personnel on your team, you could do it in a matter of a day. If you picked up your check and there was a pink slip in the envelope, you were gone. No contracts, no injury clauses, none of that. Things have changed drastically and all for the better.

In 1958 we were 1–10–1, and I wasn't very happy. I thought I was getting to be a pretty good football player and it was hard for me to get a $300 raise. My wife didn't want me to play in Green Bay anymore because it was a small community and too many people knew your business. I was home in New Jersey during the off-season and got a call from Vince Lombardi, the new head coach. "You better get your behind up here. I want to talk to you." I thought to myself, "Who the hell does this guy think he is? Who's this guy Vince Lombardi?" We knew he came from the Giants, but nobody knew who an assistant coach was in those days. Before I left for Green Bay, my wife told me, "Now, don't do anything foolish."

When I got to Green Bay, I went out to the old Packers' office and met this dynamic person sitting behind one of the biggest desks I've ever seen in my life. We were sitting there shooting the bull about the Green Bay Packers, and he's telling me he's going to do this and going to do that. I made the unfortunate mistake of telling that man, "Vince, I've heard that same story two times before from two different coaches." He hit the desk so hard that an ashtray flew up in the air and broke into a million pieces. At that point I started to call him "Sir." I had made up my mind on the plane to ask for a $2,500 raise. Once he heard that, I figured I'd be playing for somebody else. When Vince got done, I was making $19,000. He practically gave me the kitchen sink. He wanted me on his team, and it was the first time I really felt appreciated. Vince told me, "We will be winners here," and when I left that office, I believed him. My only problem was telling my wife we'd be going back to Green Bay.

I started to really believe when Vince took us out to our first training camp. A sportswriter from Chicago came down to cover the camp, and he called it the "Green Bay Packers' Concentration Camp." Vince ran the camp himself, and he didn't care what anybody thought—he just wanted a winner. He had that grass drill of his. We'd be running in place, and when Vince yelled you had to drop down to the ground and then spring up and keep running in place. The most I remember is going down eighty times and then I lost count. I asked him about it one time, and he said it was designed to make us submit. Completely give in. Camp was so grueling, by the time you finished you were going on pure manpower. Vince tore you down, all the way down, and then brought you back up, his way.

One of his philosophies was for us to attack a man at his strengths. Once he was vulnerable, the weaker points would come more readily. That's the way we attacked, too, as a team. When we played the Colts, we came up against Big Daddy Lipscomb, who was the premier defensive tackle at the time. We went after him. Hence the rest of the Baltimore defense was more likely to quickly become demoralized.

The fact that the Packers had been so bad was also one of the things that really ended up helping Vince. They had gotten some tremendous draft choices during those years, and he didn't really change a thing as far as personnel was concerned. Bart Starr, Fuzzy Thurston, Paul Hornung, Gerry Kramer, Ron Kramer, Max McGee—we really had some talent on that team. Lombardi's first year we were 7–5–0. When we won our first four ball games, nobody believed it. Then we had a lull in the season, but we were slowly finding out who we were.

In 1960 we backed into the championship game and played Philadelphia at Franklin Field. We were riding high, but the Eagles were a much more experienced team than we were and we lost the game very foolishly, 17–13. We were in the dressing room after the game with tears in our eyes. Before Vince let the press in, he said, "This is the last time anything like this will happen to us. After today we will be world champions. Now, dry your tears. Our football team doesn't cry because we lost with class." Vince kept us together, and from that time on it's history.

There was no way I could talk contract with Lombardi. Hell, I'd go in looking for a thousand-dollar raise, and by the time he got done talking to me, even though I went to the Pro Bowl, even though we were a championship team, I felt as if I should pay him for the privilege of playing at Green Bay. As much as I liked and respected Vince Lombardi, I was there before he got to Green Bay. He didn't make me. I was already a decent player. Vince did some good things for me, but I also knew that I was a thirty-one-year-old center. The only thing I was going to gain from being a Green Bay

Packer was what I was worth on the field. We weren't going to get any endorsements because of the type of community we played in. With the number of new teams in the league and the fact that the American Football League was starting up, I knew that if I didn't take my shot then, I'd never do it.

There's this legend that I walked into Vince's office with an agent to talk about my contract. He became so upset that he went into the other room, and when he came out I was playing for the Eagles. That agent story isn't true. I would like it to have been true because it's become such a great legend, but it's not. It started in Jerry Kramer's book, *Instant Replay,* and I remember talking to Jerry and saying, "Jerry, that story is just not true." Maybe that's the story that Vince told to show how tough he was.

What I did do was go in to see Pat Peppler, the Packers' assistant GM, and asked him for a raise. I told him that I wanted to be traded if I didn't get the money I wanted. Pat went to Lombardi and told him that I wanted to be traded if my contract demands weren't met. A while later, Pat called me back and told me I had been traded to Philadelphia. I didn't see Vince in person for another five years after that happened. We ran into each other when I was coaching for the Bears and he was with Washington. It was a very emotional moment. We embraced, and he told me, "You're where you belong, Ringo . . . . but remember, this is a tough business."

At first, leaving Green Bay was a shock, but eventually I realized it was for the best. I was from the East Coast, and if I could play a few more years in Philadelphia, I would be able to work on getting my life straightened out. It would be a lot easier to get a half-decent job because at that time you couldn't really make business contacts in Green Bay.

It was a hell of a difference going from the Green Bay Packers to the Philadelphia Eagles; from a championship-caliber team to one that wasn't doing that well. Playing wasn't much fun and football became just plain hard work. It just wasn't the same when you didn't have a good shot at winning the championship. The Eagles had lost a lot of people from the championship team of the '60s and the ones who were there were getting old. They still had a few guys like Pete Retzlaff, but there just weren't enough of the great ones. We did manage to win our fair share and I enjoyed playing for Jerry Wolman. It's a shame that he got himself in a financial bind because I think he would have been one of the great owners in this business. He had empathy for his players and their problems. Jerry came up the hard way and understood a lot of things other guys didn't.

After four years at Philadelphia, I quit because my age was starting to get to me. I realized I was playing against fellows who were a lot younger than I was. We weren't going for a divisional title or anything like that, and at thirty-five years of age I felt it was time for Jim Ringo to put away his uniform and get on with his life's work. It was hard, don't get me wrong. I think retiring is the most traumatic thing a ball player ever does. Football is something you've been playing since you were nine years old. I tell these kids I coach today that they can't play forever, but they don't believe me. Hell, when we were playing we thought it would last forever, and I guess everybody has to learn for themselves. Paul Wiggin and I were at the Pro Bowl one year, and we were near the end of our careers. Neither of us would take off our sweat clothes because we had such bad bodies compared to those young kids who were just coming up.

Jerry Wolman was in the construction business, and I was working for him while I was playing in Philadelphia, but after I retired I realized the only thing I wanted to do was get back into football. Coaching was the closest thing to playing, so the next year I went with the Chicago Bears as the offensive line coach. Would you believe it? That year we went 1–13. Ball players come out and they think they know a lot about the game. Until you get into coaching, you don't realize how ignorant you are. Thank God for people who were in the business like Abe Gibron. He had been coaching the offensive line and when I came moved over to the defense. Abe took me under his wing, and he's a great person with tremendous football knowledge. Abe is typical of the kind of guy who has contributed a lot to the game and received very little credit.

There wasn't a whole lot of material at Chicago. We had Gayle Sayres, of course, but he had gotten hurt the previous year. The Bears were struggling the whole three years I was there, and then I had the great fortune to go to Buffalo. Lou Saban hired me and told me, "Take a look at these films. We've got this Heisman Trophy winner by the name of O. J. Simpson. Let me know what you think about him." I kept trying to find number thirty-two. I'd see him as an outside receiver, then a decoy on the other side of the formation, and every once in a while I'd see him run with the football. After I looked at four or five cans of film, I told Lou, "This is one hell of a back." I was there all through O.J.'s career, and he brought a tremendous style to professional football. Not only on the field. My wife and I used to sit in the parking lot once in a while after a game and watch him. There might be 150 kids out there, and he stayed until the last kid got his autograph.

When Lou quit, they offered me the head coaching job. We all have that ego in ourselves and it was a great example of the Peter Principle at work. I thought I was ready for the job and found out that I just didn't have the experience. That job isn't just X's and O's. You have an owner, a general manager, an accounting department, the players, the media, and the fans coming at you from every direction. Get on the sidelines sometime when your team is losing at home. Don't look at the field—turn around and look at that angry crowd of people. The hate, the obscenities; God Almighty, if they could come down on the field and beat the hell out of you, they would.

The worst fans I've ever seen were in Philly. They hated Joe Kuharich's guts. He could just about get on and off the field. When we'd come out to warm up, the planes would start to fly by, towing banners, and more banners would go up in the stadium: JOE MUST GO. One guy even quit his job for a year so he could make JOE MUST GO buttons. Those were scary fans.

I lasted two years as head coach of Buffalo, 1976 and 1977, and then went up to New England for four years as an assistant coach, put in one year with the Rams, and then a couple of years with the Jets. My family stayed in Buffalo, and I kept in touch with Ralph Wilson, the owner of the Bills, because I wanted to end my career in Buffalo. I came back here in 1983 as offensive coordinator and I'm proud to be here today. Buffalo is a well-kept secret. They've done a tremendous job with the organization. Marv Levy is a real class coach and I'm very happy in the position I have. As long as the Buffalo Bills treat me as they have in the past, I'm very happy to stay here.

Coaching today isn't really that difficult because players respect the coaches. They never lose that. The only time you might lose their respect is when you don't know what you're doing. It's just like anything else, especially if you're coaching a veteran player. He knows immediately if you're in over your head. At that point you better know how to back up because otherwise you'll lose that person's confidence.

Somebody asked me a while back, "What do you think the biggest difference is between the time you played and now?" I think the biggest difference is that everything today is taken away from the ball players. Coaches are calling all the plays from the sidelines. Defenses are called by the coaches. They have people up in the press box and television monitors all over the place. Instant replay tells you yes or no. They want the players to be robots, but the game still belongs to the men who play it. Out there on the field, that's where men play football. I think I came into pro football during the changing of the guard. You wouldn't want to try to call a play for Bobby Layne. Hell, no.

It wasn't until after I started to play in Green Bay that I realized the traditions that existed between certain teams, the great football players that had come before me. I was hearing what a great player Don Hutson was when we were in the championships. I walked into a drugstore, and when I got upset about it those guys told me,

"What are you getting so upset about? Fifteen or twenty years from now, we'll talk about you." You didn't have to ruffle your own feathers if you were in the business in my time. People knew who you were. The media didn't cover the game because pro football was just a byline. The announcers and sportswriters didn't make you. Your satisfaction came from the respect of the opponents you played against. Another thing. Nobody had any extra cash in those days. Sometimes we didn't even know if we were going to get paid. Nothing was said, but you could feel it. When you're traveling in DC-3's flying at fifteen hundred feet, you knew there wasn't a lot of money in the bank.

Football is a game, more so than many others, where you have to operate as a team. Everybody relies on everybody else, including the coach. I was very lucky to play under Vince Lombardi. His philosophy of the game was that you should love to run and love to hit. If you didn't want to do that, you'd better quit. He made a lot of boys grow into men. He helped a lot of people reach stardom who might not have made it otherwise. When Vince was with the Packers, he wasn't just known in this country, he was known all over the world. My brothers were in the service at that time, and they used to read as much about Vince in Japan and Germany as we did here. He took a group of football players and made us into a real team. I'll never forget those players and I'll never forget him. Vince said one time, "You have a love for your teammates that is different than what you have for a woman or anything else."

CYCLOPS

JAMES RICCA

TACKLE

Washington Redskins 1951–54
Detroit Lions 1955
Philadelphia Eagles 1955–56

Jim Ricca's spirit is typical of the Redskins. The kid who wasn't supposed to have a ghost of a chance of making good stayed on to confound the critics and haunt the opposition. It's a winning spirit, the kind Washington fans have waited for since 1945.

—Lewis Atchison, Washington *Evening Star*

Parker couldn't sit still. He jumped up, grabbed a piece of chalk and went to work on the blackboard a short step from his desk . . . He made a big *circle in the middle of the defensive line. "That's Jim Ricca . . . our little Les Bingaman," he explained. "No worries about Jim. He's had four years in the league. He'll go 279 now . . . he's over six-four. Strong and fast for his size . . ."*

—Lyall Smith, Detroit *Free Press*

JAMES RICCA

THE first game that I actually started for the Redskins was during preseason against the Bears in Kansas City. I was absolutely scared stiff because I was going to have to play against "Bulldog" Turner. My God, the man was playing pro football when I was in grade school. Just that name, "Bulldog." Wayne Millner was an assistant coach with the Redskins. He was a hell of a player in his time and is in the Hall of Fame. Wayne always thought I wasn't geared up enough before a game. He never realized that some people can be geared up without showing it and he would sometimes get me so overgeared that my arms would be going in all directions. All week long before we played the Bears, Wayne was telling me, "This guy Turner is just a big slob. He's chicken, over the hill, and if you hit him the first play of the game, you'll own him for the rest of the afternoon."

The Bears got the ball for the first time and Bulldog lines up in front of me. When the ball was snapped, *boooom,* I hit him my best shot in the head. I had a hell of a ball game and I think it helped me make the team. After the game was over, I was walking around the locker room, feeling like Mr. NFL. "Hey, if Bulldog Turner's the best they've got, I own this league." When I came out of the locker room, Bulldog was waiting for me. He said, "You're a hell of a rookie, kid. After you hit me, I didn't know where I was for three and a half quarters." Then he said, "We'll play again someday," turned around, and left.

Later that year we played the Bears in old Griffith Stadium in a regular season game and Bulldog turned me every which way but loose. He never hurt me; I never even got dirty. He just outfinessed me. Did you ever miss a step when you're going down the stairs and have that feeling that nothing is there? That's how it was with Bulldog. I'd wind up and fire off on him, but he wasn't there. Then I'd try to play him cozy and he'd play me cozy. The two of us would be standing there looking at each other and that's all the time his quarterback needed to throw the ball. If I chose a side, he'd give it to me. It went on that way all afternoon and after the game I told my father, "That guy never hit me." Dad said, "Son, you better watch the referee because somebody out there was sure beating the hell out of you."

Paul Brown was another guy who could really do it to you. We were always trained that if you saw a guard pull out, and nobody blocked you, there was a trap coming from the other side and you should turn and face it. When we played Cleveland and the guard pulled and you turned and faced that way, the tight end would come back from the other side. He'd usually knock your butt off because you had your back to him. That had nothing to do with my bad eye because Brown would catch a lot of people with that move.

I was born with no vision in my right eye. I do, however, have great hearing on that side. God's good to you in that way. As soon as I heard anything coming, I used to swing my arm up. That usually kept everybody away from me. I don't think anybody actually tried to take advantage of me, but I did move to the right side of the line so I could look down the line. The only one who said anything about it was Joe Kuharich. He kept me out of the College All-Star game and later traded me to Detroit because of my eye. My favorite coach of all time! Kuharich was the coach at San Francisco University and I was selected for the game. Dick McKann, the Redskin G.M., who is dead now, was a good friend of mine and he told me Kuharich kept me out of the College All-Star game because he said that somebody with only one eye couldn't play the game. As soon as he became the Redskins' head coach in 1954, I was through as far as Kuharich was concerned. He wanted Dick Modzelewski to play my position, middle guard, and me to play tackle, Dick's position. He told Dick that he would never be a tackle in the NFL and, of course, Dick ended up being one of the iron men of pro football. I still hold grudges, but only if people were unfair.

Buddy Parker was another one—as far as I'm concerned, the total jerk of all time. George Wilson was his assistant at Detroit. George later went to Miami and he was the brains behind Parker. After every game Buddy would get himself all worked up and pick on somebody. No matter what, that was just his style. I thought it was very degrading and knew if he ever did it to me there was going to be trouble. That Italian background of mine—lots of pride. Sure enough, he started looking for me after a game and George told me to hide. Buddy caught up with me on the plane ride back to Detroit and started in on me. I told him, "Don't you dare talk to me like that." He said, "I will if I want to." We went back and forth and finally he said, "I'll fire you." I said, "You don't have to. I quit."

The general manager, Nick Kerbawy, called the next morning and said, "Buddy put you on waivers, but we took you off. Let's forget about it." I said, "Do anything you want. I don't want to play here anymore." There were a couple of reasons why I didn't want to stay in Detroit. One. I didn't want to listen to all that crap from Parker. Number two. I had a wife and three kids living in a hotel in Detroit and paying for a house back in Washington. I was spending as much at the diaper laundry as I was making. Philadelphia picked me up and I spent two years playing there until I retired.

The only record I probably hold in the NFL is playing for the most coaches in a single career. In fact, I never had the same head coach two years in a row. At Washington I had Herman Ball, "Curly Lambeau," Dick Todd, and Joe Kuharich. Buddy Parker in Detroit and Jim Trimble and Hugh Devore at Philadelphia. I happened to like Herman Ball the best. He wasn't a real personality, nothing like Shula or Lombardi, but he had great football knowledge. Dick Todd was also an excellent coach, but he was very short-tempered and couldn't get along with George Marshall.

I grew up in Brooklyn, but I was actually born in Rockville Center, Long Island. My mom and dad were on a Sunday drive and I started to come on, so they rushed my mother to Jewish Memorial Hospital. They circumcised me and I always tell people that I've been half-Jewish ever since. My dad worked for the State of New York and his original job was with the Home Relief Program during the Hoover administration. He worked for the Department of Welfare for fifty-two years and was sort of a crusader. Most of the programs he started in New York are now part of the national welfare programs. He was also a politician and ran for any number of offices. The problem was that he was an Italian-Catholic Republican running in a Jewish-Liberal Democratic neighborhood. He used to get swamped, but he never gave up until he passed away.

My dad was never active in sports, but a couple of his brothers played baseball in the old days. One of them, my uncle Joe, played at the University of Pennsylvania and I grew up with all his stories about playing against the Carlisle Indians and Jim Thorpe. Being a big kid, I went right into football in my freshman year at Boys' High in Brooklyn. The coach, Wally Muller, is one of the greatest men I know. He's still alive today and was a great influence on my life. Wally was just a little teeny guy and we used to call him "Little Knute." He'd never played football himself, but he was very inspirational. He taught Spanish and when the football coach had a heart attack, he substituted for him the rest of that year. Wally ended up staying there for fifty-two years as head coach. An excellent teacher and, more than that, like another father to his players.

In high school we used to play what Wally Muller liked to call the "GBR formation." Grab the ball and run. That's what made him a great coach, he adapted to the material that was on hand. My first two years we ran the single-wing and split-T. My last year we used a modified punt formation. He used to love to find little quick left-handed wingbacks. In the old single-wing, the left-handed pass was a tremendous weapon.

I graduated from Boys' High in 1947 and was fortunate to have a father smart enough to say, "Remember, son, your mind is going to have to carry you a lot longer than your legs." He insisted that I choose a school based on the education I was going to get, not football. I was lucky enough to win the *Sports Forum* magazine high school player of the year award. It was unheard of for a lineman to win anything and because of that I was well sought after. I was also six four and 260 pounds coming out of high school, plus I was nineteen. In New York we managed to fool around enough to stay in school for an extra year. Out of all the schools in the nation I selected Georgetown. I had never heard of the school, but I had heard of Fordham and knew Georgetown was also run by the Jesuits. Since I didn't want to stay at home and Washington wasn't that far away, it seemed like a good choice.

It was tough at Georgetown because in those days you had to hide the fact that you were an athlete. I went to the School of Foreign Service and the instructors would call on me every single day, no matter what. At that time the Jesuits were actually the owners and operators of the school and they had a lot of pride in the level of education. They had so much pride that it took me five and a half years to get out of there. I haven't been sorry one day since and I'm very grateful for the education I got at Georgetown, even though at the time I thought it was terrible.

When I started to play college ball I ran into another great man, Maurice "Mush" Dubofsky, a big loud Jewish guy coaching football at a Catholic University. Mush was a great defensive coach and way ahead of his time. My second year with the Redskins, Curly Lambeau took over as head coach and he started fooling around with a new defense. Everybody at that time was playing what they called the "Oklahoma" or "Eagle," 5–4. Since people couldn't run against it they started to pass. Now the pendulum was starting to swing and since you had to stop the pass, how do you do that? In the 5–4, the middle guard would hit the center and the two tackles would pinch in. The middle guard was totally wasted because he didn't have anywhere to go and that basically eliminated those three men from the pass rush.

Curly came to me one day and said, "I think you're fast enough to drop back in a third-and-eight situation and almost become another linebacker." We started working on that and I'd see something wrong and say, "No, Coach. When that happens, we should do this." That went on for three or four days and he called me into his office. He said, "You're upsetting me. You're saying things at practice and you're upsetting me because you're right. How do you know so much about this defense?" I told him that I had played it for three years under Mush Dubofsky at Georgetown. Mush actually wrote a book called *Everybodys' Football,* in which he explained the three- and four-man line. That must have been 1947 or 1948. Pretty soon everybody was playing the four-man line and in a way that was my downfall. Now they could bring in a guy who wasn't quite as big and a little bit faster and do away with the middle guard completely: the Sam Huffs, Joe Schmidts, and Chuck Bednariks. First thing you know, I'm a tackle again. When Sam Huff went into the Hall of Fame, I told him that if it weren't for me, he'd never have made it because I created that position for him.

While I was at Georgetown, we had an excellent team, but we never really got any kind of recognition. We went to one Sun Bowl and a couple of the guys tried out for the pros, but none of them made it. Actually, I came along at a bad time to go into pro ball. When I started at Georgetown, there was no freshman rule because it had been done away with during World War II. I played three years and when I got to be a senior they brought the rule back and said I was ineligible, having already played three varsity seasons. We fought like crazy, but couldn't get any satisfaction. In the meantime I had been drafted by the old New York Yankees of the All-America Conference. They offered me a lot of money and I thought I had it made. But then the league said, "You're class hasn't graduated, so you can't sign." That's the rule Rozelle is trying to change now. I was caught betwixt and between, so I didn't play that year and coached for St. Johns High School here in Washington. My son is now the athletic director and head coach at the same school.

At the end of that year, I had Pete Haley, who was my father-in-law at the time and a well-known sports person in the Washington area, call George Marshall, the owner of the Redskins, to ask him for a tryout for me. Marshall used to come to one or two Georgetown games a year and remembered I had a great day against Villanova. The Redskins took me to training camp that year, 1951, and listed me as a tackle. They had ten tackles: six returning veterans, three high-draft choices who were All-Americans, and me. I wondered where the hell I was going to fit in. I went through the entire training camp with the coaches yelling at me, "Hey, you, number 75. Come here," because none of them knew my name.

I thought I had a good training camp and then we went out to the West Coast to play Los Angeles in our first preseason game. We got beat, 58–14, and fifty-seven of the fifty-eight guys on the squad got to play. Guess who didn't get in the game? Me. The next week we went up to play San Francisco and we were losing, 21–0, at halftime. Again, I didn't get to play. George Preston Marshall came into the locker room at halftime and he was carrying on and screaming at everybody. He spots me and says, "And you, you big guinea, you stink. I don't know why I ever signed you." I told him that the only thing I did that afternoon was warm up and he said, "You haven't played? Well, you're going to play, goddamn it." They read the lineup for the second half and I hear, "Ricca, middle guard." I had never played middle guard in my life and I was just petrified. I ended up making twenty-two tackles in the second half and the next day the headlines in the paper said: 49ERS WIN FIRST GAME. RICCA WINS SECOND GAME. I will finally admit it to the world. The only reason that happened was because I was scared to death and nobody was going to touch me. Their guys, my guys, I hit anybody that came near me. The guy who was playing my position had been with the Redskins for five years, but I got the job.

My relationship with George Marshall was excellent because he always felt that he had discovered me. That made it hard for me with the other guys, especially when he would walk in the locker room and say, "Hi, Jimsie." Marshall, George Halas, Art Rooney—they were incredible characters and there wouldn't be an NFL if it hadn't been for those guys. Marshall brought Sammy Baugh to Washington and created the forward pass, so to speak. The first year I played with Sam they called us "the basketball team" because we passed twenty times a game. Today they throw that many passes in a quarter.

When Sam was the quarterback, it was great because as soon as he got the ball, it was gone. He was like Dan Marino. Later on we had Eddie LeBaron and Jack Scarbath and they'd be back there doing all sorts of tricky stuff with the ball and we'd be yelling, "Look out!" as the guy went by. When we were playing the Colts, they had Gino Marchetti, Artie Donovan, Don Joyce—they just brought them in one right after another. You'd think, "Which one of these guys am I supposed to hit?" You'd take one and the other one was gone. We'd be yelling, "Coming right! Coming left!"

The Redskins were the first team to have an alumni association. The alumni promoted the Redskins, helped sell season tickets, and also helped the players get off-season jobs. Marshall asked the guys who were established in Washington to help the other guys get involved. He cared about his players, but again, it was a lot different in those days. Five of us went to see him once about getting more money. It was almost a union situation and he wasn't going to have any part of it. He told us, "Get out of here. It's my money and nobody is telling me what to do with it." Two of those guys later got cut, two got fined, and I got scolded. Again, his boy.

He was always coming up with charity games for us to play, which we didn't get paid for. We used to gripe, but the team couldn't have survived without things like that. There was no television to speak of, no big bucks coming in, and he had to do anything he could to bring in revenue. We would have our pictures on bubble gum cards. The players would get two dozen packs of bubble gum cards and Marshall got the money. If you got assigned to a speaking engagement and Marshall got paid, you never got a cent. There were only three or four of us living in the Washington area during the off-season and I can't believe how many things we were signed up to do. All free, of course, but I always thought it was good for my future, getting the exposure. When I call today and try to get some of these players to speak, a relatively unknown Redskin costs you

$300. The next level up, $500. And a quarterback? That can cost you $3,000. It's a different world.

Of all the teams I played for, the Redskins fed you the best. They also had the best doctors and equipment. One team—and I won't go into it—the team doctor was a dentist. I was amazed when I went to Detroit. They were the world champions and you couldn't find a jock to fit you. At Washington we had the finest shoulder pads, helmets, and Marshall bought us our shoes. No other team in the league did that. When I got to Detroit, I called Kelly Miller, the equipment manager at Washington, and asked him to send my shoes. He sent all of them, not only the ones I had worn, but the three new pairs that were waiting for me. Shoes were thirty-five or forty bucks a pair and that was a lot of money when you were making ten thousand dollars a year.

Detroit was something else. We had Bobby Layne and all those guys and a lot of them couldn't walk straight most of the time, including Buddy Parker. It was amazing. Layne would get in those huddles and say, "You do this and you do that," and it would work. Forget about all this scientific football. Parker decided that I couldn't play with one eye and when I got to Philadelphia I replaced Bucko Kilroy. He had gotten hurt and there was an article with pictures of both of us. It said: FOOTBALL'S ROUGHEST PLAYER REPLACES FOOTBALL'S DIRTIEST PLAYER. I was considered very rough but never dirty and, as far as I'm concerned, Bucko was just a hard hitter. I was always accused of having two personalities: one on the field and another off the field. I'm convinced that it wasn't guts or courage and I also don't think it was the fear of getting hurt. It was the fear of looking bad, being embarrassed by somebody. The people I played with in Philadelphia were great. Bucko, Mike Jarmoluk, Norm Willey was there, Tom Scott, Frank Wydo, who is dead now, all super guys.

My last year was 1958. I was injured during preseason and played with a bad knee in the first two league games. They had moved me to offense and when I went to see the coach and told him I wanted to go back on defense, he told me that they were all set. Every time we got into a short yardage or goal line situation, they would send me in. I'd be sitting there, all stiff, without any warmup and every time I went in I hurt the knee again. My wife and kids were down in Washington and I was starting to feel like a piece of meat. We played Washington in Philadelphia and I went over to see Marshall and asked him if I could ride back to Washington with the team. It was great, seeing all my buddies, and that Monday was my birthday. I was having my birthday dinner and the phone rang. It was the Eagles, wanting to know where I was. I told them I wasn't going to come back. Vince McNally called me later that night and told me they had put me on waivers. He sent me half a year's pay, which was unheard of in those days.

I spent that year on crutches and toward the end of the season Kuharich, who was now the head coach at Washington, called me up and asked if I could play. They were running out of everybody. I told him that I would try to help them out if they could pull a trade for me. I'm just crazy, I guess. He called back and said, "They want our second-string quarterback for you." Philadelphia held out for more than I was worth because they figured we had something going and that was the end of my football career.

My second career was well established and I went right out and coached a C.Y.O. team to get football out of my system. We had a little eighty-five-pound team and went all the way and won the championship. At that point I was also starting to make some money, which I hadn't before that. Everybody thinks because you played in the NFL you're a fat cat. I was in the automobile business and worked myself up to general manager. At one point somebody came up with the idea of me doing a radio show, "Time Out for Sports with Jim Ricca." One thing led to another and pretty soon I was doing eight shows during the day and two call-in shows at night. When my kids got older and started to play ball in high school, I got out of the automobile business completely, so I could go to their games, and went to work selling for a radio station.

While I was at the car agency, I had been writing copy and one off-season I sold printing. Advertising always seemed like an interesting business, so I went to work for an agency in Chicago. I spent two years with them and opened my own company here in Washington in 1968, Jim Ricca & Associates. We're considered by many people to be the best automotive advertising agency in the Washington area and I really enjoy the business. For about seven or eight years, I did everything myself and then broke down and hired a young lady to answer the phone. Today we have twelve people and I run the agency the way I always wanted to work for somebody else. Some of my people have kids and if one of their kids get sick, I understand. They have to take time off and I never say a word. Then I catch the same people in here on Sunday or working until eight or nine at night without me asking.

Having played football helped me in business—absolutely. You're getting me off on one of my speeches, but football is a great teacher. You have to play by the rules and learn to get along with each other. I can't remember being down in the trenches and worrying about what color the guy next to me was. As long as he protected my outside, I didn't care if he was white, black, or green. You live together and die together. Everybody has to come up through the ranks and I've done the same thing here. All of my people, including my own kids, have come up the way I did.

The only way we get the work done is to wear a multitude of hats. Everybody goes wherever the help is needed. When I was playing football we only had thirty-three players and I was trained to play seven positions. If you had a bad season, you might end up with only twenty-four men who could actually play. We were playing the Steelers in 1953 and when I looked up, Harry Gilmer, who was our backup quarterback, was playing in the tackle slot next to me. He must have weighed all of 140 pounds and I said, "You're going to get hurt." He said, "I know."

I'm also very involved with the NFL Alumni. I'm the president of the Washington Redskins' chapter, and a member of the Executive

Committee and the Board of Directors of the National Organization. They just elected me secretary-treasurer. When the NFL Alumni was formed back in 1959 or 1960, there was no funding and the thing just floundered. Then we found Vic Maitland, who had played for the Giants and Steelers. He was working for the Youth of America and thought our organization could help him at the same time he was helping us. I wasn't very active before he came along and because of his inspirational leadership he got me—and a lot of others like myself—involved. We've got people on our board like Jerry Ford, Bob Hope, Lee Iacocca, and Walter Cronkite and the alumni is now the largest organization of former professionals in sports.

Among the things we do is to sponsor golf tournaments all over the country and raise money for various youth groups and charities. Another project the alumni worked on, which got a lot of publicity, was the pension plan for the pre-'59ers. Something that I think is just as important, but doesn't get mentioned very often is the Dire Need Fund. The alumni contributes to men who, for whatever reason, are incapable of earning $12,000 a year. I'm working now to bring it up to $20,000. I think we have about thirty-five or forty men receiving money and I can't tell you who they are because I don't even know.

Another thing, what happens if a guy who helped put this game on its feet, and his luck was very bad after football, died unexpectedly? He didn't have any insurance, didn't have anything, and his wife is left penniless. She's a fifty- or sixty-year-old woman with no home, no money, and there's nothing we can do for her. We do something locally here in Washington, but I'd like to see something done across the country for these people. My other pet project is some kind of training program for players. A program for life after football. You have kids today who sign multimillion dollar contracts when they're twenty-two years old. By the time some of those guys are thirty, they're on drugs and booze, broke and frustrated. Now what do they do? It doesn't happen to everybody, but enough to want to do something about it. We have successful people all over the country who can take a kid into their company. I've had several in my agency to observe the business.

It may sound corny when I say it, but I believe I'm giving back something to the game and the people who were instrumental in my success. I've been very successful and I'm not ashamed of that. But I owe something to the guys who were there alongside of me.

STOP THAT, YOU'LL GET A DISEASE

MICHAEL JARMOLUK

TACKLE

Chicago Bears 1946–47

Boston Yanks 1948

Philadelphia Eagles 1949–55

Massive Mike Jarmoluk, Jr., the 6-5, 240-pound terror tackle who has been the Eagles' defensive leader the past several campaigns, yesterday was elected captain of the 1952 Birdmen . . . Big Mike, a star at Frankford High, Bordentown Military Institute, Temple, and with the Chicago Bears for three seasons before joining the Eagles in '49, was elected unanimously by his teammates.

—Hal Freeman, Philadelphia *Inquirer*

No team in football can offer a tougher defense with a five-man line than the Eagles . . . This group has made the Eagles as tough to run against as a 120-m.p.h. wind . . . Kilroy and Jarmoluk, the former

Templars, are accomplished "red doggers." The 250-pound Kilroy is playing his twelfth year with the Eagles. Some day he may slow up. Jarmoluk, also 250, has only been playing eight years. So nobody thinks about how much longer he'll go at top speed.

—John Bell, Philadelphia *Inquirer*

IF you liked the challenge, if you were able to take the beating and come back, see what you could give back to the other guy—that was what it was all about. You've got to have it inside yourself if you want to play professional football. There was many a Monday morning when I would have black-and-blue marks all over my body and could hardly get out of bed. I didn't wear hip pads. I'd bounce off the ground, and there would be a big strawberry on my hip. Just as it would start to heal, bingo, there I'd go again, bouncing on the same place.

"Bucko" Kilroy and I never wore pads because we wanted to be fast. Don't laugh. I remember one year, the number one draft choice on the Eagles was a halfback out of Missouri. "Bucko" and I both beat him in the hundred-yard dash and he wasn't in camp after two weeks. We both thought, where the hell did they get this number one draft choice who's supposed to be a halfback and he's not as fast as a couple of linemen. He must have had a good press agent.

The game I remember best was when I played for the Bears and we beat the Eagles in 1947. A lot of guys don't believe me when I tell them I played end that day and scored a touchdown, so Jimmy Gallagher of the Eagles gave me a videotape of the game. We were having our poker game at my home one night, and I said, "All right, you SOBs, I've got the proof right here," and made them watch it.

The Eagles were undefeated that year, and Steve Van Buren was their predominant player. We had a pretty good defensive unit and figured if we shut off Van Buren, we could beat them. All week long George Halas was saying, "Jarmoluk, you're going to have to play end because Wilson and Kavanaugh are hurt. Ed Sprinkle is the only one left, so we're going to have to use you." I said, "Are you sure you want me to play end?" He said, "Yeah, but I'm only going to use you for blocking on end runs and off-tackle plays and to keep everybody off Sid Luckman when he's passing." The night before the game, "Bucko" Kilroy, who was playing with the Eagles, got in touch with me as soon as he got into town. I told him, "Bucko, I've got a big surprise. You won't have to worry about me doing too good against you guys tomorrow because I won't be playing my regular position."

During the course of the game, the information came down from Luke Johnsos in the booth, "Throw Mike a short pass over the middle—nobody's paying any attention to him." In the huddle Sid Luckman looked at me, "Go down five yards, cut across five yards, and I'll hit you right in the hands." I said, "You've got the wrong guy. Sprinkle is on the other side." He said, "No, it's you." I said, "Jesus Christ, don't throw it to me, throw it to Sprinkle." He told me to shut up, hit me right in the hands, and I ran thirty-eight yards for a touchdown. I'll tell you, there I was, standing in the end zone with those ivy-covered walls of Wrigley Field and the whole crowd roaring. The hair on the back of my neck stood up, and I didn't know what the hell to do with the football. I wanted to throw it up in the stands, but I was afraid George Halas would charge me twenty bucks for the ball. The referee was standing near me, so I threw it to him and headed back to the huddle. We beat them 49–7, and Bucko wouldn't talk to me after the game.

Bucko was so tough that nobody wanted to room with him, so I ended up with him for seven years. We both went to Temple at the same time; in fact, we knew each other way back in high school. He was at North Catholic while I was at Frankford. A gal lived about two doors away from me that he was running around with, and he'd always stop over to my house around dinnertime. Naturally my mother, being ethnic Polish, would always have *kielbasa* and sauerkraut. I'd always say, "Mom, make a lot of mashed potatoes and sauerkraut—then he won't eat as much *kielbasa.*"

Bucko had a reputation as a dirty player, and I think part of that was professional jealousy. He was a good, hard-hitting football player, and if he had a chance to flail his leg and block you, so you couldn't get to the quarterback, you can't blame him for that. He'd kick a guy in the shins, and that was just part of the game. I had nothing but scars up and down my shins from being flailed and kicked. You had to wear shin guards taped to your legs. Man, if they missed you with their shoulder and fell down, around would come that leg. Ed Sprinkle was another guy considered by some to be a dirty ball player, but I think he was a hell of a good defensive and offensive end. I don't know if Sprinkle has been chosen for the Hall of Fame yet, but someday I feel that he will be in there. That is, if they get back to some of the old guys. They're so busy getting the new guys in there that they're forgetting about the guys who played for nothing.

I was born and raised in Philadelphia. My mother and father were both immigrants, she came from Poland and he came from the Ukraine in Russia. They both worked very hard and couldn't afford to send me to Catholic school, so I went to Frankford. I started playing football in ninth grade and graduated ahead of my class. Since I was only sixteen, all the schools that wanted me to play football for them wanted me to go to prep school for a year. The reason they were going to salt me away was so I would be the same age as the other kids when I got into college. I was bigger than the average guys at that time and played in high school at six-foot-three and 220. By the time I got into college, I was six-five and weighed 250.

Duke, Florida State, Yale—all the schools up and down the East Coast were interested in me, but Temple University was the only one willing to foot the bill for prep school. I ended up at Bordentown Military in New Jersey for a year, and they had quite a program. I really learned how to pay attention and study because if you didn't you'd be walking guard duty.

Early in my third year at Temple, they came around and told us we could finish our education if we joined the Army. I signed up in December and they took me in May. I was a staff sergeant in charge of two machine guns. They wouldn't allow anybody in our outfit to play football, but I'd pick up a copy of *Stars and Stripes* and read about guys I'd played with or against having a good time in places like Paris or Egypt. Oh boy, they were having a ball playing football and I was in a foxhole freezing my feet and ass off during the Battle of the Bulge. I was in the 30th, the Old Hickory Division, and they called us "Roosevelt's SS" because every time we butted heads with Hitler's SS, we would wipe them out. When the Germans broke through the 75th Division, they sent us in and it was a hell of a time.

When we were training in the States, they told us that machine guns would be fired from behind our own troops in a long arc into the enemy. When we got overseas, we found that those same troops wouldn't go to sleep unless the machine guns were set up out in front. We would have our two machine guns set up at an intersection, and some Tiger tanks would come down the road and chase us out of our foxholes. We'd be hiding in the basement of some farmhouse and when we came up, half the house would be gone. I spent two years in the Army and a short time in the hospital after we got back to the States. Because my feet were frozen, I have a problem with numbness in certain areas, and my toenails are a little distorted. Beyond that, nothing that serious.

A lot of us grew up in the war, especially those of us who went in when we were eighteen or nineteen. It made you realize what death really was, and when I got back I was a lot tougher. I played in the Blue-Gray Game in 1945, and we had a lot of Temple guys on the team. We could have made all kinds of bets down in those bars in Montgomery, Alabama, because the South had Y. A. Tittle at quarterback and "Sugar" Kane, a big end from Texas or some place like that. They also had a couple of linemen who were supposed to be big yahoo All-Americans. Here were all these guys playing against a bunch of little kids from Temple University and we beat the South pretty bad.

Most of the guys from my class at Temple are retired now. A lot of them taught high school, and a few were involved with coaching football. During the winter, eight of us get together quite often and shoot the breeze. It's usually what happened with different broads, what happened at the fraternity house, how many kegs of beer we won when we played some other house. You could get hurt worse playing two-handed touch against frat houses than you could on the regular varsity.

We'd hang out at the Extra Dry Bar on Columbia Avenue and they had a good dart board. We would lull the old fogeys at the bar into a game and win free beers. Then there was Pete's Bar at 13th and Montgomery. Pete was a Lithuanian and all the "hunkies" would go in there and he would always buy us a free drink. That's all torn down. Doc Wilder's drugstore is torn down too. He was quite a fan of ours and was always good for a free soda.

The team practiced at the stadium and we used to go over in a double-decker bus. We'd all get up on the second level and start to rock it back and forth. The driver would be scared silly, and he'd stop and say, "You bastards, cut that out or I'm going to chase you all off the bus and you can walk."

But the greatest thing was when I got my Studebaker. Bucko, Earl Baugher, and John Rogers didn't like the bus so they'd ride to practice with me in my car. This was before I went in the Army. The tires finally wore out and I said, "All right boys, I'm going to put it up on blocks because I can't afford new tires." Bucko came up with a set of tires, and pretty soon we were driving to practice again. I don't know where he got those tires, and I don't think I want to know.

I was a nut on sports and got four letters while I was at Temple—football, basketball, wrestling, and track. I would wrestle a guy in the afternoon in New York, catch a train back to Philadelphia, and play basketball that night. Just because you were into sports, however, didn't mean that you didn't go to class. The coaching staff stayed on top of everybody, and they had a program where the teachers would report back to the coaches to let them know where you stood with your grades. If you didn't have passing grades, you didn't play. It was that simple. There were professors at Temple who were real gung-ho about football, and they would have special classes on Saturday for anybody who was falling behind. Today it seems like it's a completely different ballgame in these schools, and I don't know what the hell is going on. I heard that a couple of guys down South got degrees in basket weaving and a couple of other wild subjects. I guess it's all that big money. When I played, I think the tickets to a bowl game were a buck and a half. Look at what they are today. You only have to look at the basketball playoffs to see what's happening. In the NCAA, if you win the first game, you get two hundred grand. Win the second, you get another two hundred grand. If you go all the way, you can take in two million dollars for your school.

I was a phys ed major at Temple and was thinking about a career in teaching. Then I was drafted by Detroit. I refused to report because I wanted to stay in Philadelphia. Detroit traded my rights to the Bears. George Halas's brother was coaching at one of the local colleges, Drexel, and he came over and talked to me. When we were doing our practice teaching in our senior year, they had educators from Delaware, Maryland, and New Jersey talk to us and tell us what we could expect in a teaching career. You would start at $3,200 in those days, and I had an offer from the Bears in my pocket for $3,800 and a $300 bonus. I decided I would go there and play a couple of years and then he told me Halas would trade me to the Eagles.

I went out to Chicago and played there for two years. It wasn't long before I moved right into the first string and we won the World Championship in 1946. We each got $1,900 for winning, a far cry from today. After two years up there, however, I wanted out. They wouldn't let us practice at Wrigley Field when there was snow on the ground, so we would go out to a park near the lake in a school bus and a bulldozer would clear an area for us to practice. That wind would be blowing and the snow would be three feet deep. I went to see George and said, "Chicago isn't for me. I'm going back to Philly and if you don't trade me, I'll just retire." He turned around and traded me to Boston.

The team in Boston at that time was called the Boston Yanks and they traded me for George Conner, their number one draft choice out of Notre Dame. The owner of the team was Ted Collins, Kate Smith's manager, and I told him I would only play for one year and then I wanted to be traded to Philadelphia or he could just drop me. Actually it wasn't a bad deal because I was getting $7,200 and the Bears were only paying me $5,400. I played that one year and the next year Collins didn't believe me so I didn't report. He traded me to the Eagles for Frank Tripuka, another Notre Dame All-American. It was a trivia question for a while, who was the guy from Temple, honorable mention, All-East, who was traded for two Notre Dame All-Americans? That's how I arrived at the Eagles and I played with them until I finished out my career in 1955.

Everybody thought Steve Van Buren was a multimillionaire when he was making $15,000 a year, and we all protected him because he was our meal ticket. Steve was a great runner, and when we played Los Angeles in the championship game in 1949, he had over 200 yards on the ground running in the mud. We went out on the train and I was working for the Ortlieb Brewery at that time, so they gave me ten cases of beer to take along on the trip. It cost me five bucks to get a redcap to put it on the train, and then Greasy Neale wouldn't let us touch it. "Jarmoluk, check that beer and don't pick it up until we come back on the train." So I had to pay for checking and another five bucks to the redcap. I got that beer for free, but it ended up costing me three bucks a case by the time I was finished.

It started raining a couple days before the game and we beat them, 14–0, in ankle-deep mud. Los Angeles had this big defensive tackle who was supposed to be so terrific, and he kept forearming Al Wistert in the mouth. Van Buren saw what was going on and told Tommy Thompson, our quarterback, to run an off-tackle play. Steve took the ball and he was really fast off the start. *Pssssssst!* He hit that guy right in the stomach with his headgear and knocked him flatter than a pancake. That guy was all-pro, and he was so easy to block it was pathetic. If you played for Los Angeles or New York, you became all-pro instantly if you did anything because those teams had great publicity departments that would just keep pumping out stuff about a guy. Maybe that player was buddy-buddy with a writer out on the West Coast or running around with a movie star, who knows.

Steve Van Buren, Alex Wojciechowicz, Tommy Thompson, and Greasy Neale were all great horse players. We would have meetings during the week where we watched films and set up our offense and defense for the next game. We'd get to a very boring situation where they would stop the film and Greasy would start in, "Now here's what we want you men to do . . ." Woji would look over at Steve and say in a loud voice, "Hey, Steve, we'd better get our bets in. It's almost two o'clock and we've got that hot horse." Greasy would look back at him and the meeting wouldn't last much longer. The four of them would all be out in the lobby around the public telephone booth trying to get through to the bookie. Then they'd chase over to the track to make the seventh or eighth race. It was just great for the rest of us.

Another trick we had involved Tommy Thompson, who was a scratch golfer. Greasy loved golf, and he thought he was pretty good. We'd say to Tommy, "Why don't you invite Greasy over to play at the Hershey golf course this afternoon and give him five strokes a side. We had two practices, one in the morning and another in the afternoon. At lunch Greasy would get up and say, "You boys have been doing pretty good, so I'm going to cut this afternoon's practice. We'll see you tomorrow morning." And away they'd go to play golf.

We had some great quarterbacks in the NFL when I was playing. Otto Graham was the tops in our time and he just hated Bucko. I think he tried to kick Otto in the head at one time or something like that. When I was with the Bears, we had Sid Luckman, and of course, before him, it was Sammy Baugh. I played against Baugh during his last few years in the league and he was something else. Bobby Layne was another good one, but he was crazy as a bedbug. He would miss the train and they would fine him a thousand dollars. I think one year they fined him seven times. The team was saving some money there.

Tommy Thompson with the Eagles was phenomenal. There was a guy who didn't have vision in both eyes, and he could thread a needle with that ball. Tommy was a terrific golfer, and then, all of a sudden, he was crippled with arthritis in his hips and was in a wheelchair. It wasn't too long ago that the Eagles chapter of the NFL Alumni brought him up to Philadelphia and took him over to the Shea Eye Institute. They transplanted a cornea, and today he can see with that eye. We paid for his transportation, hospitalization, whatever it cost. We also paid for his wife to come up with him. I'll tell you, he was one hell of a quarterback.

I retired in 1955. I felt I could have played several more years, but my wife was bugging me to get out. She claimed that every summer, while everybody else was enjoying themselves at the seashore, we didn't do anything because she would have to stay home with the kids while I went to training camp. So I quit, and my wife and I got a divorce two years later. I probably should have stayed because I didn't really have anything wrong with me other than a broken toe that somebody stepped on and some torn nerves in a finger when Carleton Massey and I got into a little hassle.

I was running down under a punt, and out of the corner of my eye I saw somebody coming. I had pretty good peripheral vision and I thought the guy would cut in front of me and try to block me. No, he came across with a forearm. I never wore a face mask and he caught me right on the nose, the kind of hit where your eyes start to water, so I grabbed him and hit him, *pow!* The only trouble was, he had a big face mask on, and I hit that instead of him. We were both thrown out of the game.

Forearms, clotheslines, blind-blocking—it was all part of the game. A guy would be running in one direction who didn't see the guy coming from the other direction. It looked to the fans and some of the media like a lousy shot. Not so—it was perfectly legal.

I have never looked back at the ten years I spent playing pro ball and said, "Hey, I was crazy to do that." It was such a phenomenal feeling to just be able to play with those guys. I think it was the greatest experience I ever had. We played hard and we played both ways. The only time that you would be pulled out of a game was when you were hurt or playing lousy. You didn't want to play lousy because the guy who replaced you might be playing good and you'd end up on the bench. We didn't want anybody to take our job because we weren't happy to just be a backup. Today backups get a quarter of a million dollars to sit on the bench.

As I said, I never wore headgear—I mean a face guard. I almost made a *faux pas.* We always had a saying, "See that guy over there? He played football without headgear and that's why he's so damned dumb." I'd never had my nose broken or lost any teeth, or anything like that, and what do you think happened to me during my final game? I slid down a guy's back—one of the Modzelewski brothers, Little Mo, who played for Cleveland. Ed came out of the opposite side of the line and I was playing right tackle on defense. I cut back and caught him by the collar, slid right down his back, and his heel caught me right in the chin. It drove my teeth right through my lower lip.

There I was, supposed to go out at halftime and get my gold belt buckle for my retirement, and I was in the locker room waiting for the doctor to sew me up. I was standing in front of a mirror blowing smoke through the holes in my chin and Freddie Shuback, the trainer, said, "Stop that, you'll get a disease."

We were winning the game and Jim Trimble, the coach, told me I didn't have to go in. Hell, it was the last game of the season and the last game of my career. I said, "Coach, I want to go in there for one reason. I want to see if I'll flinch." While I was getting sewed up, Freddie had put a face guard on my helmet, and I'll tell you, that face mask gave me a false security, a false lack of fear. I went out there and was tearing everybody up because I didn't think they could get to my face. I'd always wondered why Bucko wore one all those years and I found out that afternoon.

When I quit, I was already working for Ortlieb Brewery in Philadelphia. I started with them as a salesman in 1949 because you weren't getting paid that much to play football. They paid me seventy-five dollars a week and all the beer I could drink. Henry Ortlieb even paid me when I was in training camp because I maintained my customers through the mail. I worked for fourteen years with Ortlieb and then went to Packaging Corporation of America, where I've been for twenty-four years.

There are a lot of football players in sales who don't know anything about the thing they're selling. When I started selling boxes, I went to Farleigh Dickinson University and got a degree in packaging engineering. I feel I know what I'm talking about, and I can come into a plant and look at their operation and make suggestions.

The majority of people I call on want to talk about football. Some of them will see something in the paper about me and they'll say, "You've been coming in here for three or four years. Why didn't you tell me you played professional football?" Hell, so many years have gone by, especially if it's a youngster that's doing the buying. He wasn't even born when I was playing. If they ask me, I'll tell them—otherwise they have to find it out from somebody else because my prime objective when I walk in the door is selling my product; not selling myself as an ex-football player.

The crowning glory of my football career came recently when the NFL finally decided to pay us a retirement. It was long overdue because if you played five years in professional football, I think you should get something. It was funny because just before I found out about it I read a horoscope—I call them "horror scopes"—and it indicated that something was going to happen to generate some additional wealth and that my wife and I were going to have to figure out what to do with it. I get sixty dollars a month for every year I played—that's $600. I also did two years of scouting for the Eagles, so if I get credit for that I'll get $8,640 a year. I didn't start to make more than that until I was in my seventh year in the league. It didn't take my wife long to figure out what to do with that extra money. She got a fur coat.

PUT YOUR HATS ON AND GO TO WORK

NICHOLAS SKORICH

GUARD
Pittsburgh Steelers 1946–48

Without question, having Nick Skorich as part of the officiating department has proved invaluable—certainly to the commissioner, myself, the assistant supervisors Nick works with; all of our officials. Because of his extensive background as a player and coach, he has developed a great rapport with the coaches throughout the league. He speaks their language.

—Art McNally

Skorich the amateur gardener didn't step into any Eden when he took over the Browns in 1970. He had a jackhammer at his head. He was only the third coach the Browns had had, and the first two were legends . . . Skorich transmitted his own tenacity to the club. He grew up tough in the river town of Bellaire, Ohio. He worked in the mines, in construction. He painted bridges and pumped gas. He tended bar and swept streets . . . don't take Skorich cheap. His little garden is not the only furrow he plows.

—Edwin Pope, Miami *Herald*

WHEN World War II broke out, I was in the Navy reserve, but I managed to finish my college football and graduate from the University of Cincinnati before I went in the service. I was drafted by the Pittsburgh Steelers, but football didn't seem like the most important thing in the world at that point so I volunteered, went to midshipman's school in Chicago, and became a ninety-day wonder. During the war I was in the Navy Amphibious service on landing craft and managed to get on the beach at D plus six hours during the invasion. We were bringing in tanks and dropping them off on the beach.

Bert Bell was Pittsburgh's coach, and I kept getting letters from him every six months while I was in Europe telling me not to forget about the Steelers. When I was discharged, in 1946, I contacted the Steelers, but by that time Bell had gone to Philadelphia and become commissioner of the league. The Steelers, however, were still interested and offered me $200 to sign and $3,300 to play, which I was very glad to do. I played for them in 1946, '47, and '48, got hurt, and had to give it up.

I stayed in Pittsburgh and coached at an all-boys' high school, Pittsburgh Central Catholic, for four years. From there I went to RPI, Rensselaer Poly up in Troy, for three years as head coach, and then back to the Steelers as line coach. Walt Kiesling was the head coach at that time, and I was there with him for four years. When they changed coaches, I went up to Green Bay for a year with "Scooter" McLean. That was a year prior to Lombardi's arrival there, so the following year I moved to Philadelphia as an assistant coach, offensive coordinator, and was there when we won the World Championship in 1960. I took over as head coach in 1961, spent three years doing that and in 1964 went to the Cleveland Browns as an assistant coach under Blanton Collier. That year we beat Baltimore for the title. I spent eleven years with Cleveland, the last four as head coach.

My time with the Browns was the most enjoyable of my coaching career because I think I had more highs. It is very exciting to be involved with a championship team because that's an experience that not all of us get an opportunity to share. I was very lucky to be there twice, once with Cleveland and another time with Philadelphia.

The most exciting game I coached was the World Championship with Cleveland. We were playing Baltimore, and Don Shula was their coach. The "experts" picked us to lose by seven points and we ended up winning 27–0. That was one of those games where everything starts going the way you planned it, and the things you thought would work did work, and that doesn't happen very often. On the other hand, in 1960 when we beat the Packers when I was with Philadelphia, we won by four points going down to the last few seconds. Bart Starr was still throwing passes when time ran out.

Coaching is a very difficult job and one that you have to love. It's great when you win, but only momentarily, because there's always next week. In most careers your responsibilities are spread out over an entire year. In football it all comes down to how you do on a few Sunday afternoons. Like all responsible jobs, it's lonely at the top. A head coach today doesn't have enough hours in the day. The demands on a coach have increased dramatically. When I was with the Eagles, we had three assistant coaches. Today a team might have as many as twelve, sometimes more. "Buck" Shaw was the Eagle's head coach and he lived in California. He'd get to Philadelphia on the first of July, and we'd spend two weeks setting up our offense and defense and then go to training camp for eight weeks. When the season was over, the middle of December, he'd be on a plane the following day back to Palo Alto. Everybody went home because there was no such thing as a full-time assistant in those days and you had to have another job to get you through the year. When I was playing, I did some substitute teaching and later on, sold insurance. While I was coaching I went to graduate school and got my masters degree. I was working on my doctorate but got too involved with football and fell twelve hours short of finishing.

You're also involved with very strong personalities when you're coaching. For instance, when Art Modell bought the Cleveland Browns he fired Paul Brown, who was a winner. I think Modell wanted a very active part in running the team, which is contrary to what a lot of owners want. Most of them seem to want somebody else to do it for them, but not Modell. It was a clash of personalities on how the team should be run, and of course the owner always wins. I experienced that sort of thing myself.

When I was let go in Cleveland, I was looking for another job in coaching. I was weighing three different offers when just by chance I heard that the league office was interested in somebody with a football background to join the officiating staff. Art McNally, the supervisor, and Jack Reader, the assistant supervisor, were both former referees. The owners around the league were saying, "You don't have anybody in your office that knows anything about football. All you have are ex-referees." Commissioner Rozelle felt there was room for a blending of ideas from both sides of the fence and I could provide the input from the coaching side. My major in college was education, and I thought there was merit to the idea. I also felt that maybe I could do more for the game in the league office than if I continued to coach. Eventually I called Commissioner Rozelle and told him I'd take the job.

A few of my friends and peers who were coaching offered me a chance to come back as an assistant, after I got into the commissioner's office, but I didn't think about it very long. I had made a commitment to the league office, but I have to admit, for the first three years I had the itch. You smell the leather, liniment, and sweat; it makes you want to get out there again.

I grew up in eastern Ohio in Bellaire, a little town on the Ohio River with steel mills, coal mines, that sort of thing. I've been interested in sports since I was a toddler and tried them all—baseball, basketball, football, and track. In a town like that there was nothing much else to do and everybody was involved with sports, one way or another. My mother didn't want me to play football. She wanted me to get into the band, so I learned how to play the drums. When I got to high school, I convinced my uncle to sign my permission slip. I'd practice football every day and tell my mother I was playing in the band. The following year I made the varsity squad and she found out, but it was too late. My father, on the other hand, thought a man had to find his own place. He was a coal miner, and didn't mind anything hard and physical.

I got a scholarship to go to the University of Cincinnati and was captain of the team my senior year. That was before two-platoon football, and I was playing offense and defense. In fact, I played seven or eight sixty-minute games as a senior. When the ball went over to the other team, I went from guard to linebacker. Fifteen guys played most of the game in those days.

I hadn't thought about a career in professional football until I was drafted by the Steelers. I must have had a couple of good games toward the end of the year because drafting was just getting started and I think everybody went by what they read in the newspaper. They tell the story about Greasy Neale going to the draft with a name written down on a matchbook cover. At one point he pulled it out of his pocket and said, "Let's take this guy—I hear he's pretty good."

Prior to World War II, guys who played pro football weren't looked on too highly. They were considered sort of as athletic bums who couldn't get any other kind of work. After the war the game started to gain credibility because the fans were ready. We were just coming out of a war where violence was an important part of life. A rough sport like football drew the fans, and then along came television. Many more people could see what was going on once they started to put it into their living rooms. Also, some of those so-called "stars" were coming out of college and playing the game. People decided that it looked like fun and went out to see a game.

When I started with the Steelers, they hadn't been very successful. "Jock" Sutherland took over as coach, and we became a respectable team that first year I was there. Sutherland was a disciple of Pop Warner. He was probably the one man I hated the most to play for. At the same time he was the coach I respected the most and learned the most from. He was a strong disciplinarian, the Prussian general type, and made you pay the price. In later years, I think Lombardi probably came the closest to him in temperament.

Art Rooney was out there just about every day at practice, especially when we got into Pittsburgh. Training camp was located in Cambridge Springs, which is north of Pittsburgh. It was somewhat of a retirement place that was famous for its mineral springs. A couple of resorts and a few beer joints, very rustic. There wasn't much to do, but Sutherland didn't give you much free time so it didn't matter. Practice would start at two o'clock in the afternoon and supper would be at six. Many afternoons we would still be out there on the practice field at six. After dinner there would be meetings and bed check was at eleven. You didn't dare try to sneak out because you were scared to death you'd be sent home if you were caught. That's one of the things that's changed over the years. Try to keep those guys in their quarters today.

When I showed up at the Steelers' camp, they had 110 players, and back then they kept 33 or 34 during the season. Players were coming and going every day. At that time they found the answers by scrimmage, scrimmage, scrimmage. The first day of practice we were lined up and there were eighteen pairs of guards. They were going to carry four guards on the team. We were going to open against the Cardinals in Pittsburgh and the Wednesday afternoon before that Sunday, Sutherland called everyone together and said,

"Gentlemen, we have a big problem. We have nine players too many, and that issue has to be decided today. Put your hats on and get to work." We scrimmaged for three hours and I always tell the story that I spilled more blood in that scrimmage than I did during the entire Second World War. Fortunately I managed to make it and stayed for three years. In 1947 I injured my hip in the joint area during a pile-up on the sidelines. The injury started to create pain down my leg. During my third year, when it continued to bother me, I got advice from an orthopedic doctor that it would be wise to quit before I did permanent damage.

In my time the players were pretty tough. They weren't as big and strong as the guys today, but in their own way they were just as rough. They were party guys; a good many of them were beer drinkers, but nothing different from any other young guys their age. I think we came back from the war more mature, with a little more perspective, and knew the direction we wanted to go.

All of us played with a lot of determination and enthusiasm, and there was what you might call today, a macho feeling. We thought that it was sissy to wear a face mask. "You afraid to stick your nose out? Afraid to get your nose broken?" So you'd stick your nose out there and get it broken. Then you'd wear a mask because the doctor insisted on it or you couldn't play. Two weeks later you'd sneak it off, go out, and break it again. I never wore one and I broke my nose seven times. Two operations later, I still don't breathe very well.

I played against a lot of very rough characters. The Bears had a great team at that time, and some of those guys could really hit—"Bulldog" Turner, for instance. He played clean or reasonably so, but he was one tough customer. Ed Sprinkle was another one. Then there was Bucko Kilroy, who played with the Eagles; I was never a real admirer of his playing tactics.

If I was going to rate the best players, at that time it would have to be by position. Running back, Jim Brown at Cleveland. Lineman, Ernie Stautner at Pittsburgh, and receiver, Gary Collins. Collins was a great end with Cleveland and caught three touchdown passes when we beat Baltimore for the championship in 1964. Then there was Tommy McDonald, a receiver with Philadelphia. I'm surprised that he hasn't been given more consideration for the Pro Football Hall of Fame. The amazing thing about him that most people don't know is that Tommy had his thumb and part of a finger shot off in a hunting accident when he was a kid. The things that guy did with a football, you'd never know he had a handicap. Van Brocklin, Jurgensen, they were, of course, great football players. Bednarik was one of the all-time greats I worked with. He was a very easy guy to coach because he worked so hard in practice. He didn't think he was ready to play unless he worked at it, which is the philosophy you try to establish in everybody, i.e., You play like you practice.

Most of those guys were hard workers. Jim Brown, contrary to his many problems off the field, was also a great guy to coach. Nobody worked harder on the practice field, and he was the greatest runner I have ever seen. You might have had backs who did other things better—catch, block—but he did all those things well when he had to, and there was nobody finer when he had the football under his arm. He made the most fantastic three-yard run for a touchdown I've ever seen. I was coaching with the Browns and we were playing Dallas at the Cotton Bowl in 1965. We were on the three-yard line. Jim Brown started to sweep and got hit eight yards deep in the backfield. I think the whole Dallas team had a shot at him. At least ten guys hit him, but he still scored.

Obviously the players have changed quite a bit. The people I played with were brought up differently. A child was raised with more discipline. When he was told to do something, he better do it and do it the way he was told. Yours is not to reason why, but to do or die, that kind of thing. Therefore, when a coach said, "This is the way it will be done," he didn't have to tell anybody why you were doing it that way. A guy like Lombardi would say, "Dig them out of there. Let's move the ball." You dug them out of there. Then, with the changes in the country and with the education system reaching more people, the athlete changed along with everybody else.

The athlete today wants to know why he's doing something, but *esprit de corps,* the team concept, is still the principle that makes a good football team. You have to generate that idea in a different kind of player, and it's just a matter of how you get there. Today everybody is a star. Nobody knew what a guard, tackle, or defensive end was in my day. Today some of these guys who play those positions are selling things on television. I played with Bill Dudley, who is a Hall-of-Famer. Nobody knew who Bill Dudley was in his time except that he was a running back for the Pittsburgh Steelers and was pretty good. In the 1940s and the 1950s there weren't any testimonials. Even people like Van Brocklin and Bednarik never got any paid endorsements.

The old school wouldn't have bought all that dancing around you see today. They might hit you on the butt and say nice going—that was about it. That's all you wanted, your teammates to feel that you were doing a good job. You didn't go around and tell the world you were good. But a coach still has to be a good leader so he can sell his ideas to his team, make them see why it has to be done his way and understand that the team is one family. No one player can be more important than another one is a concept that has always been essential to football. Everybody has to play his part.

Players are also much more specialized. Teams started to scientifically develop each man to the maximum for his position. Back when I played, if you had a guy who weighed over 250 pounds, he was considered a slob. Too fat to play because he couldn't keep up with the game. Now they realize that you can take that same man, train him, give him a proper diet, and develop the muscles that will help him play his position. Work with those big linemen and get their legs strong so they can control people at the line of scrimmage or take a linebacker and develop his upper-body strength.

You can do everything with machinery today. There's all sorts of equipment available, and if a guy needs more shoulder or girdle strength, put him on the machines for a couple of months and he'll have it. When I was playing, they frowned on any kind of weight lifting. They wanted you to do a lot of exercising, running and so forth, but stay away from the weights because you'll get muscle-bound and lose your coordination. Another fallacy I heard from the time I was in high school was that football players should never swim because swimming softens your muscles. They've found out that swimming actually gives you long, lean, strong muscles, but that was the kind of attitude you ran into in the dark ages. "How do you want your steak?" Steak and eggs was it. There was no variation with the diet, and then we realized that a player was better off with something he could digest and use for energy out there while he was playing. I hope you talk to some trainers because they'll tell you what a revolution there has been in athletes' diets.

You asked me what the biggest change has been in the game since I played, and I think it has to do with the rules. The changes that have taken place over the years have altered the game drastically. They've tightened up in so many areas and for good reason: to eliminate injury. That has limited considerably what a player can do today compared to what we did. With the players getting bigger, stronger, and faster, if you let them devastate the quarterback like we did, there soon wouldn't be any passers left. In the grasp and control, if somebody gets a hand on the quarterback, blow the whistle. We used to flip them around and try to bury them. The greater emphasis in the last ten or twelve years to protect the players has made it a better game. The League realized that the game isn't as good when the star players are off the field so often.

In my day if there was a fistfight on the field, you would usually be ejected, but the blows during the game usually went unheeded. You pull some of the stuff we did and you would be disqualified today. The guy from Green Bay who picked up Jim McMahon and threw him on the ground in 1986? If we did that, they probably would have called unnecessary roughness. Maybe. Did he get up? If he got up, it wasn't that bad.

Several years ago the defense was starting to dominate the game and the NFL became concerned. The owners sat down and found out that the average number of points scored by both teams was only thirty in a game. That's not enough entertainment and led to changes in the rules to give the offense more leeway. This year, for instance, a new rule change allows a player to block with extended hands anywhere on the field on a running play. You will see this situation quite often where a guy catches a punt and here comes a defender flying at him. A blocker can now put his hands out and push that guy right by the runner. That was always a foul, but now we want to give that man with the ball more room to run. It makes punt returns and kickoffs more exciting and should lead to more scores. That gives the people a reason to jump up and down and yell, which is what it's all about. Points on the board.

The officials have grown with the game just as the players have. It's a faster game, the rules have gotten much more complicated, and their knowledge of the game has to be much deeper than it was in the past. I'm one of four assistant supervisors of officials under Art McNally. We handle all of the officials in the league—hire, fire, train, and assign the crews to the games. It's a complete program and we keep them busy all year. None of them do it for a living—they do it because they love the game. Most of them are former jocks and a lot of them started officiating in college. We have about a dozen ex-players working for us at present. Gary Lane, he's one. He was my third quarterback at Cleveland. We like playing experience, but it's not a requirement. A guy has to have ten years of experience, five of it major college, and have some sort of sports background. Once they apply, we'll watch them for three or four years.

Each supervisor has three crews that he has to stay with for eight weeks. I rotate my time with these three crews, a different one each week. Every game is taped and I spend seven or eight hours on each tape and grade them on everything they did. A lot of questions are asked, and I want answers back on Monday. If we disagree with a call, we want their answer. If we agree with a call, we tell them why. We are always emphasizing the positive. Anything that makes a better official, a better crew. They are always competing with each other because the best men get to work the Super Bowl.

We'll be involved with instant replay again this year. We're going to train additional people for replay, former officials, and if the owners vote to make it permanent, this year is still experimental, we would get into an eighth man in every crew. He would be a senior guy who would travel with the crew each week and sit in the booth. I think it's inevitable because the technology is here whether we like it or not. We're starting a lot earlier because last year we didn't get into it until July and as a result had all sorts of problems for the first few months. There was a lot of adverse publicity and quite simply we made mistakes. By the second half of the year we had ironed a lot of the problems out and our work with replay improved vastly.

The opening game of the season last year, I handled the replay. The Bears were playing Cleveland in Chicago. As luck would have it, on the third play of the game we got a replay problem. The center snapped the ball and McMahon was in the shotgun. The ball went by his shoulder, they were on their own sixteen-yard line and started rolling toward the goal line. Everybody was diving for it and a couple of Cleveland players went for the ball, *zippppp,* they're out of the end zone. The officials on the play thought they had a touchdown, but it might be a safety. Did the player have possession before he went out of the end zone? They came to me and I sat looking at two tapes, and so far it was a safety because I couldn't see the ball. "Stand by," I told them, "I'm still looking." Then they came back with the reverse-angle shot from the end zone, and I could see the Cleveland player clearly got the ball about a yard from the end line, his knee hit, and then he went out. I told the referee, "You've got a touchdown."

Don't you know the following week a few of the wire services had to carry the story that a former Cleveland Browns coach was doing the replay in Chicago and was that really fair? They doubted my integrity and I didn't take that too nicely. I can't root for anybody. I've got twenty-eight teams and I wish them all well.

THE BUS TO YPSILANTI

JOSEPH SCHMIDT

LINEBACKER
Detroit Lions 1953–65

He's always in the way.
—John Henry Johnson

If I were to start a team from scratch and pick out just one player, I'd select Joe Schmidt to form the core of my team.
—Norman Van Brocklin

THERE'S nothing to compare with my twenty years in professional football. The other businesses that I am involved in are boring compared to that. Working as a manufacturer's representative, I may wait six months or a year before I get a purchase order. There never seems to be an end to sales work, and it seems to just go on and on. I'm sort of an impatient individual and I've had to learn to accept the nature of the business, but if I had my way I think I'd rather go door to door and make seventeen sales a day or none at all. At least I'd know where I stand.

JOSEPH SCHMIDT

Playing football, you know there will be a decision in three hours —you're going to win or lose. You do the job or get your ass fired. In the business world, a guy can make a mistake and nobody knows about it for a year. If you're a football player, you can't bullshit anybody about your ability. When a rookie comes to training camp with a reputation as a Heisman Trophy winner or an All-American, all the veterans can't wait to get him on the field. Once you're out on the field, you have to perform up to that standard, or everybody knows in a couple of scrimmages if the rookie is good or just bullshit. You're out on the field alone, exposed, and there's no place to hide.

I don't think there's any industry, big corporate structures included, where you're so exposed and it's so easy to be the hero or goat. When you win, everything's fine, but if you lose, you have to pick yourself up and go on to the next game. If a team loses a game, the fans go home and do something else. You, as a player, feel like there was a death in the family. It's hard to explain to people who aren't involved in sports how bad you really feel because you're a competitor and want to win so badly. The closest comparison I have is that it's like being pinned down with somebody on top of you. You can't really get relief until you win the next ball game.

My ambition was to be a football player ever since I can remember, and I can recall my parents taking me to my first game at Pitt Stadium—I had to be about five or six—we went to watch my brother play. I enjoyed the band, the crowd, and was thrilled to see my brother. I decided right then and there that I wanted to be a part of that type of action.

I grew up in Pittsburgh, on the south side. My father was an immigrant and, by trade, a bricklayer and carpenter. During the Depression he didn't have much work and we were really hard pressed. I had three brothers; one was killed in the war and the other one died in an accident when he was a kid. My father died when I was about eleven, so it was basically just me and my mother at home.

I think my brother John was my role model. He's a good, honest, hard-working guy and was very influential on the way I came out. John's fourteen years older than I am and played his football at Carnegie Tech. At that time—this was the '30s—they had some pretty good teams, and after he graduated he played with the Steelers for a year.

I went to Catholic grade school and then to a junior high that didn't have any sports so I played for a team my brother coached. The team was called the St. Clair VFW and composed of WWII veterans. They were all in their twenties and here I was, a fourteen-year-old youngster playing with them. When I was fifteen we had an opportunity to play in Western State Penitentiary against the prisoners. They let us through the front gate and searched everybody. Then there was another gate and they searched us again. We dressed in a cell block and went out on the "field." No grass, just a dirt area where the prisoners could take a break. On top of that, it wasn't long enough, just seventy yards, and when we got to a certain point they would have to return the ball back to the fifty-yard line. There was a lot of conversation going on and with the prisoners they weren't afraid to talk, that's for sure.

Playing on my brother's team is where I think I got to be tougher because I played against bigger and older players. I enjoyed hearing stories about the Second World War and the things they had gone through. We used to ride to the games on buses, and they would be talking and I was all ears, growing up just listening to them. Having played against grown men, when I got to Brentwood High School I didn't have any trouble making the team. I played in my junior and senior years and then received a scholarship to Pitt. My high school coach had a big influence on me. His name was Al Crevar, and he made me realize I had a chance to get a scholarship. I wasn't much of a student, just did enough to get by, until Al took me under his wing and made me realize I could do a lot of things if I applied myself.

Defense was responsible for my career in football, and I was lucky to come along when the two-platoon system was still being played. When I first got to the University of Pittsburgh, they played the single wing, but then we went to the T-formation. I played fullback, but my primary position was middle linebacker. I enjoyed college football very much and our team wasn't that bad, but we had four different coaches during the four years I played at Pitt. The new coach would always want to try certain new things, and we were always rebuilding, rebuilding, rebuilding. One of the coaches, Len Casanova, had me concentrate on defense, and during my junior and senior year we played what they call the 5-3 defense, with me the middle linebacker. When I got into pro ball, the Lions used the 7-2 with a big middle guard and I became an outside linebacker. In the middle '50s they found out the 7-2 wasn't flexible enough, so they went to a four-man front. The 4-3-4. The Lions went away from the big middle guard and I moved to middle linebacker. Teams at that time were trying to make guys into middle linebackers who hadn't played that position, and it took considerable time to train them to play a new position. For me it was just like coming home because I had played middle linebacker for two years in college. It was right about that time that the fans discovered defense. Before that they just watched where the ball went and I was lucky enough to come along just when things were beginning to evolve.

I had a lot of injuries when I played in college. I broke two ribs when I was a freshman, broke my wrist and hurt my shoulder the next year, and wrenched a knee in my third year. My senior year I had a severe concussion which almost ended relations between Pitt and Notre Dame.

Pitt hadn't beaten them for about twenty years and we weren't supposed to win. We surprised them and ended up winning 21–20, and I was playing pretty good that day. During the first half, this player was inserted into the game at left tackle. On the next play, which just happened to go to the left, he came across and gave me a forearm to the head. No one wore a mask then, and I don't know whether it was the impact of the forearm or my head hitting the ground, maybe a combination of both, but I was totally out cold and didn't come to until the very end of the fourth quarter.

The following Monday I felt pretty good, and after classes I went to practice and started running. I almost passed out, so they took me to the hospital. I had blood in my spinal fluid and was in there for a good week. I don't know if that hit was intentional or not—who the hell knows—but it was just one of those things you think about. The player who hit me was named Joe Bush—I still remember that—and I looked for him for a long time, but I guess he didn't make it to the pros.

I thought I played pretty well at Pitt and started to think about a career in pro football, but all those injuries had made people a little wary of me. Just before I graduated, I went to a practice session of the Pittsburgh Steelers and met Art Rooney. He took a look at me and then said, "Oh, you're the kid who gets hurt all the time."

The Lions drafted me seventh and I came to Detroit in 1953. I was upset about going with the Lions because they had just won a championship the year before and I thought it was going to be tough to make the ball club. Gene Gedman, who had been a big star at Indiana, was the Lions' number one draft choice, and he invited me to drive up from Pittsburgh to the Lions' training camp with him. We reported to the front office in Detroit before we went up to Ypsilanti, and as soon as Nick Kerbawy, the general manager, heard Gedman was in the office he came out. They shook hands and talked for a few minutes, and then Gedman introduced him to me. Kerbawy didn't seem too impressed and told me, "Joe, I'm a little busy right now with Gedman. Michigan Avenue is out in front of the office. Walk down to the corner and you can catch the bus to Ypsilanti." Then he told Gedman, "Let's go out to my country club and have a little lunch." They went off to play golf and I caught the bus to Ypsilanti.

When I got to training camp, it was far different from anything I had ever seen in the way of a football team before. I saw those giants like Les Bingaman, and I didn't know if I should give it a try or take the next train home. Nobody talked to me, not even the other rookies, and the only time you opened your mouth was when a veteran wanted to hear your college song. They'd make you get up on a chair, put your hand on your heart, and let fly with your alma mater.

The Lions were more into—how should I put it—harassing rookies. They wanted to make sure that you could play the game, that was number one, but they also wanted to find out if you could take their abuse. I think when I got through that first year I felt like I was really part of the team. A lot of harassing is silly, but on the other hand I think it built up a spirit which helped make a solid team. Vince Banonis, who played center, walked over to my locker after the sixth game and asked me where I was going after the game. I was so surprised that somebody was actually talking to me that I just stood there. He told me to show up at Jimmy Kelly's bar. When I walked into the bar, Les Bingaman grabbed me and made me sing my school song. That was the first time I felt like I belonged and pro football started to look like it could be fun.

On the field, the Lions were a well-organized, well-drilled and well-coached team. On their own time they were hell-raisers. I came to Detroit thinking those guys were the pinnacle of professional football and I got my eyes opened up in a hurry. I was the kind of kid who kept himself in tip-top shape all the time, practiced hard, and studied the game every chance I got. I wondered how these guys could be drinking beer and running all over the place and still play football?

After I had been there for a while, I woke up to the fact that, "Hey, I guess these guys can do two things at the same time." They were all good athletes and knew what they could and couldn't do, how far they could go with their off-the-field activities. At that time I was single and went out a lot. We had a real fun group, and it was led, of course, by Bobby Layne. After the game on Sunday night there would be a party someplace, and he would be in charge. On Mondays we'd take care of our injuries and then we'd spend the afternoon at the Stadium Bar, which was next to Briggs Stadium. The guy who owned it always had a buffet for us, and we'd sit around playing cards or shuffleboard or just hanging around. There would be all sorts of skid row types in there, and I'd like to have the money that Bobby gave away to them.

Bobby Layne didn't give a shit. He put his priorities before other people's, and if he wanted to go someplace, he went. If, on the other hand, he didn't want to go, he didn't. Money wasn't a big thing to him; he just used it to do things. You hear all the stories about him, and most of it is bullshit, but he would never deny anything because he loved the image. Bobby did like to party, and the nights when he wanted to go out were something because he never got tired of it. He would get upset if anybody started to wilt, so you had to hang in there with him. I know that he would go out the night before a game with teammates and have dinner and a few drinks. I never saw him drunk the night before the game, much less on the field, the entire seven years I played with him.

Bobby was always thinking up things to cause trouble. Les Bingaman had a favorite pair of pants. They were blue denims, and I think they were the only pair he could get into because he wore them all the time. One day when Les was out on the practice field, Layne cut the legs off those pants. Les went into the shower, and when he came out we were all watching him put those pants on. Bingaman went nuts and chased Layne all over the locker room. He was about 150 pounds heavier than Bobby and got tired before he caught him; otherwise the Lions would probably have been looking for a new quarterback.

On the field Layne was all business. He expected everybody to perform up to their maximum, and if you didn't, he wasn't shy about telling you. In the heat of the game he was known to stop everything and demand that certain guys be taken out because they weren't blocking, that sort of thing. But after the game was over, he'd come over and explain to you why he did what he did. It wasn't necessarily an apology; it was more of an explanation of why he did it. You couldn't help but like the guy because he was a hell of a competitor and always gave it everything he had. When they traded him to the Steelers, I thought it was a big mistake, and I really believe we could have won a couple more championships if he had stayed with the Lions.

There are two things that in my mind have changed the game from our time to what it is today. First, the onset of people using the face mask has made the game more vicious. If you go back and look at the old films, you don't see guys hunched down like they do today. They used to keep their heads up to protect their faces. I don't care how tough you are, nobody wants to stick his face in there and get his teeth kicked out or his nose broken, which happened all the time anyway. The hits weren't so severe because we used our shoulders more. Today they use their heads a lot. When they started using the mask, everybody became more aggressive, it was just natural, and they've got their heads down and are really coming.

The second important change was when black kids were able to play. Everybody says the game is faster today. Hell, who do you think made it faster? You have these running backs and cornerbacks; it just seems that white kids can't run as fast. I used to argue with the black guys all the time when I was coaching, and they'd tell me the white kids are just as fast. I'd say, "Bullshit." If that's the case, where are all the white running backs today? Those talented black kids changed football and made it more exciting. Everybody wants to see that guy get his hands on the ball and run eighty yards.

I don't watch football like I used to. I just enjoy the game like any other fan. You can't help but admire the athletes today, the way they run and move, the size of those players, but there are things that bother me today, particularly the drugs and steroids. It seems the use of steroids runs all the way down into high school. A high school athlete who wants a scholarship knows a school won't take him unless he's big and strong. I hear some of my friends who are still involved with pro football talking, and they won't consider somebody for the offensive line unless he's 275. Where the hell is it going to end? What damage are they doing to their organs, kidneys, and such? Why not go with raw talent and cut out this artificial crap? If everybody quit and let their bodies seek their own level, the guys would be bigger anyway because of better training and diet.

As far as drugs in sports are concerned, I'm sorry, it's ridiculous. I'm not saying I was an angel, or any of us were angels, but good judgment tells a guy he has to draw the line somewhere. I'm disappointed that the players themselves aren't doing more to clean this thing up. Football, baseball, basketball—they've got a beautiful thing going. Playing a game that really is a boy's game, getting all kinds of exposure, and money, and they make up these excuses, "We're bored, we have so much travel, we don't have anything to do." That's a piss poor excuse and just because you have time on your hands, you don't have to do cocaine. I think the Players' Association will have to approach it from the point of view that we're professionals, let's act like professionals. Otherwise it will destroy the game because people will become disappointed with the professional athlete. If they keep it up, you're going to end up with a bunch of freaks running around out there, and that's not what football was supposed to be, a freak show.

The pressures on ball players are much different than they were in my time. I played for $5,700 my first year and made $35,000 the year I retired, thirteen years later. Today you're talking about hundreds of thousands, millions of dollars. A player has pressure from an agent, an attorney, whoever, and of course he's got to answer to the coach. He's also got to answer to television because he's being scrutinized much more than we were in the '50s and '60s. If a player does something good, a camera zeroes in on him. If he does something bad, the same thing happens and he has to handle that. The fans are more sophisticated because of television. You talk to these fans today, they know a lot about football and you can't fool them like that. Great coverage, instant replays, and the color analysts, who are usually ex-players—all of that gives the fan much more information than he's ever had before. "The coach was in the two-minute drill, he should have called time-out right away"—that sort of thing.

I was very fortunate to play thirteen years, and most of the time we had good teams. In the '50s we won three championships, and in the '60s we had good teams but always seemed to end up second to Green Bay. "Buddy" Parker was a great coach, very good at analyzing the other team, knowing what to attack. He wasn't a speech-maker by any stretch of the imagination. He would talk a couple of minutes, if that, and the way he would instill enthusiasm in us was to put somebody on waivers or fire somebody. George Wilson was just the opposite, a motivator. He had played on some of the early Bears' teams when Halas was coach, and he could relate to the ball players. Buddy was one personality and George was another, two coaches altogether different, but both were enjoyable to play for.

In the back of my mind was always the idea that I had to get something established because I knew I couldn't play forever. When I retired, I knew that it had ended. There were guys I played with who haven't come that full circle, even today. When you're a football player, they tell you when to get up, what time to eat, when the bus is going to leave. It's all regimented and in a lot of cases, you're not really thinking for yourself or preparing yourself for what comes next. You can do certain things well. Catch the ball, run with the ball, play defense, whatever, and these things came easy to you because of your natural abilities. You've also been trained all along to improve on these abilities. Then, when you're thirty, thirty-one, or thirty-two years old, you're in a totally new atmosphere where those skills don't mean a thing. You have to start over, and it's not easy. Now you have to go out and be with people who weren't involved with football and do completely foreign tasks. Then again, a lot of ex-players are very successful because of that discipline they got from sports. They have set personal goals for themselves, and they just carry those over into another field.

Most players had jobs while they were playing because the money wasn't that great. On the off-season I worked as a substitute teacher one year, and then worked for a trucking company for two off-seasons.

The last few years I played, I went to work for a manufacturer's rep, similar to what I do now, and started learning about the automotive business. When I retired from football, I decided to go into my own business and had no thought of coaching. Then Mr. William Clay Ford, owner of the Detroit Lions, asked me if I'd like to coach. I told him I'd try it, so I became an assistant for a year. That was 1966, and Harry Gilmer was the head coach. I became the linebacker coach. We didn't have a very good football team and when Harry got fired, they offered me the job. I was reluctant to accept the head coaching job after only one season of experience. There I was, thirty-five years old, an ex-player with some so-called experience, and they wanted me to be the head coach. That's like being a newspaper carrier and all of a sudden they want you to become the editor of the player. I had an idea of how things should be done, but I didn't really have any hands-on experience. After many hours of discussion with Mr. Ford, he finally prevailed upon me.

The Lions gave me a five-year contract, and I felt I knew what the team needed to win, the kind of players we should get, and I was very fortunate to get assistants who had experience and were very loyal. Bill McPeak, who played a few years ahead of me at Pitt and had been head coach at Washington, was my offensive coordinator. My offensive line coach was Chuck Knox, who is now the coach at Seattle. Jimmy David, a guy who played with me on the Lions and had been a coach with the 49ers and Rams, John North, Jim Martin, it was a pretty good staff. They knew football and we had a lot of fun.

The first two years we didn't do very well. In the third year we were 9–4–1, and in the fourth year we went to the playoffs. The team started to deteriorate because of loss of defensive personnel and in my last year we were 8–5–1. I really enjoyed coaching and think it helped me mature as a person because the experience taught me how to analyze people and be more objective. The pressure was immense and you're walking a tightrope all the time. You're handling a whole multitude of personalities and then I had the extra problem of coaching guys I had played with. I think they respected me because they knew I would be fair. Looking back on it now, I only wish I had more knowledge about football when I took over, that I was better schooled in the intricacies of the game. We might have won a few more.

REF, HE'S HOLDING

DALE DODRILL

GUARD

Pittsburgh Steelers 1951–59

An underweight—for his position—overachiever.
—Dan Rooney

Dodrill, Captain of the Steelers, really is a marvel. Coach Paul Brown of Cleveland goes nuts every time he sees Dale out there. Brown screams, "He's too small to play that middle guard—run over him!" And then Dale stacks up someone coming his way.
—Pat Livingston, Philadelphia *Press*

WE were playing the Eagles in the midseason of my rookie year. Philadelphia fumbled near the end of the game, and somebody from our team picked up the ball and started to run with it. *Wham!* Before I knew it, I got an elbow in the face. Face masks weren't used then, and as a result of that well-placed elbow my nose started bleeding profusely. It didn't stop, so I went to see the team doctor after the game.

He said, "You just have a nose hemorrhage. I'll pack it with cotton and that'll do it." Monday was our day off, and Tuesday morning it was still bleeding and hurt like hell. I went to see the trainer and told him, "I don't care what the doctor says, I've got something wrong." He sent me up to a specialist at the Pittsburgh Medical Building, and that doc said, "When did this happen?" I told him, "Sunday." He couldn't believe it. "We're going to get you in the hospital and operate as soon as possible. You've got a broken upper jaw." They operated that afternoon; I didn't have time to call my parents before I went to the hospital. Some sportswriters came up to my room and took a picture of me in the hospital bed, all bandaged up, and they ran it in the local papers in Colorado where my parents lived. My mother was scared to death! She called up to find out what had happened and to be sure that I was in one piece.

The next morning my roommate came to see me. Hank Minarik was another rookie, and we were staying together on the fourth floor of a rooming house. Hank's clothes smelled like charcoal and he had on a pair of old football socks and slippers. I said, "My gosh, what's wrong with you?" He said, "Our apartment house burned down last night. You know that fire hydrant in front of the house where we got all the tickets? They hooked up the hose and there wasn't any water." I asked him how he got out. "The firemen still don't believe me. There was smoke coming under the door, so I climbed out on the roof and jumped over to that big old tree in the corner of the yard." The firemen told Hank that it was impossible for him to jump over to that tree, but I guess he was inspired because otherwise he was going to get scorched. He asked me if I wanted to room with him again, and I said, "Sure, but when you do find a place, buy a piece of rope." When he showed me our new room, there were two big ropes coiled up in the corner.

I was raised on a farm near Stockton, Kansas, which is in the central part of the state. My grandfather came over from Germany, settled first in Virginia, and then homesteaded in Kansas. My father worked that same farm until 1936, when we moved out to Colorado. I had four brothers and one sister, and those were the dustbowl years. There were four or five years when you couldn't grow anything and so much soil was drifting in the air that my father used to walk around in the middle of the day with a lantern. He tied ropes from the house to the barn so we could get back and forth without getting lost.

We moved to Loveland, Colorado, and I went to school and played football at Loveland High School. Our team won the state championship one year, finished second another, and I was playing tackle and guard. That was during the war, and in those days when you graduated from high school, you were in a uniform the next day. I went in the Army and ended up with the 30th Infantry Division, thirty miles from Berlin. That was when they had the Americans stop at the Elbe River and let the Russians catch up. I don't think that was very smart on our part and have to agree with Patton, who said, "Let's go all the way."

My unit has reunions every year, and this year was the first one that I've gone to. I'm not one to dwell too much on the past. Those guys just went in a big room and relived the war for three days, and I couldn't do that. It was good seeing some of those fellows, and quite a few of them looked different from when I saw them last. I remembered them with shrapnel wounds and scars on their faces. Plastic surgery can do wonderful things. I lost one brother at Bataan and almost made enemies of the other two when I tried to convince them to take advantage of the GI Bill. It seemed the right thing to do, get an education, and that opportunity was one of the few good things to come out of the war.

Anybody who was in the war came back with a great deal more maturity then he had when he left. A lot more mental and physical toughness. Some coaches didn't like the guys who had been in the war because they could never really discipline them. They couldn't get them to do things the way they wanted them done. Then those same players would go out and win championship after championship. After those guys retired and the new generation of college guys came along, who hadn't been in the war, coaches could mold them any way they wanted. The only problem was they couldn't win quite so often with those guys.

While I was in Germany, I got an infection in my jawbones. The dentist had to pull one quarter of my teeth at a time for the infection to heal properly so I had to wait a year before I could start college. While I was waiting for my jaws to heal, I worked in a lumber camp in a park above Fort Collins. That fall I went to school at Colorado A & M, which is now Colorado State University. One of the reasons I chose Colorado was because you could play varsity ball when you were a freshman. I played four years of football, and we never did win the conference, but I think we ended up in second place three years in a row. There were four of us on that team who went into pro ball. Thurman "Fum" McGraw, Jack Christensen, and Jim David went with the Lions and the Steelers drafted me, either fourth or sixth. I never did figure out how the Steelers scouted me because there were never any pro scouts around that I knew of.

It's probably hard for people to believe it today, but there wasn't much interest in professional football except in a few specific areas. In those days a lot of people weren't exposed to the game. The Steelers used to train at St. Bonaventure University in Olean, New York, which is south of Buffalo. I had an old Army buddy who lived in Buffalo, and the first year we played an exhibition game in Buffalo I went to see him. We hadn't seen each other since the end of the war, and he wanted to celebrate by having a drink. I said, "I can't. I've got a football game tomorrow." He said, "Oh, come on, for old time's sake. We've got to have a beer." I kept telling him, "No, I can't. I've got a football game tomorrow." He finally said, "You keep mentioning this football. What's football? What do you mean by pro football?"

The Steelers' training camp was terrible. Throughout the league it was said that when guys got cut or traded, they would pray that they wouldn't go to Pittsburgh. Everybody also said if you could last through a Pittsburgh camp you'd make the team. The Steelers were the only club that went two scrimmages a day until the first league game. They also didn't have the best facilities. In fact, some of them were just plain bad. The locker room at Forbes Field had a dirt floor, and the groundskeepers would take a tour about twice a day around the field and shoot the rats that were living in the garbage under the stands.

About my sixth year with Pittsburgh, I got a letter that we were going to train that year at California State Teachers College. I thought to myself, "Boy, this is going to be great. Get out to California, lots of sun, sit on the beach." Then I found out differently. California State Teachers College is in the Monongahela Valley, south of east of Pittsburgh. I never did find out where that school got its name.

The food at training camp was never the best; that was before they had dietitians, and everything was served family-style. There were long rows of tables, and if they started the food at the other end of the room, you never did get a bowl with much of anything in it. Some of those guys could really eat, especially the ones who shouldn't have.

I don't know what it's like now, but there were only thirty-three players on a team, and some of those men had played together for a while and didn't want anybody breaking up their group. Those players really watched out for each other. They like to say that players help each other today, but it's my experience that a guy isn't going to help you any more than he has to, and if he does help you, it may be in the wrong way. It was tough to break into a team and it would take two going on three years before they figured you weren't a rookie.

My first year with the Steelers, we played the Bears, and I learned what a rookie was in a hurry. We were playing in Chicago, and at that time the Steelers were still using the single wing. I played the middle man in the line and this guy on the Bears was a real veteran. He was an artist. Every time I would give him a forward thrust, he would grab my arms and wrap them up. Then he'd fall over and pull me down with him. Sideways, backward, it didn't make any difference which way he went because I'd go with him. I was getting mad and I told the ref, "That guy is holding. He's holding me every play. Watch him." The ref said, "I'll watch him." The ball was snapped, and sure enough there went the flag. The ref called me for holding. That was my first lesson—keep you mouth shut and don't try to get those old-timers into trouble.

We never had too much to cheer about at Pittsburgh while I was there. Teams didn't like to play us because defensively we'd beat them up a little bit, but they didn't worry about us offensively. We might have ended up second in our division a couple of times, but we never did scare anybody. We had a receiver who would on occasion drop a pass when he was running in the open. I asked him why he did that, and he said, "You make a touchdown and people forget about it. Drop the ball and people talk about it for a long time." If we didn't have at least one or two good fights during a scrimmage, we didn't have a good practice. The guys would get into fights when they went out at night and end up breaking a wrist or spraining something. The next day during practice they'd go into the pile and come out claiming they got hurt, holding that hand or knee they'd hurt the night before.

When we played the Eagles, it would usually get a little rough and dirty. Pittsburgh and Philadelphia were in the same state, so it became a real intense rivalry. They always used to accuse each other of hurting a ball player in the game before, and there would be talk about how next time it's your turn. That's how it went, back and forth.

We had some good players on the Steelers, but they always seemed to be at the end of their careers or just passing through on their way up. Teddy Marchibroda came through there. Earl Morrall, Jack Kemp, Lenny Dawson, Johnny Unitas—I can't remember them all. Bobby Layne was there for a while, and he was a real competitor. Bobby would get it done one way or another. We had both of the Modzelewski brothers, Dick and Ed. Big Mo and Little Mo. Big

Mo developed a back problem in training camp, and it carried on so long that he couldn't practice. The Eagles traded him to Cleveland for Marion Motley. Big Mo went to the Browns, and they got him some sort of medication. That straightened out his back and he had some great years with Cleveland. Motley, on the other hand, came to Pittsburgh at the end of his career, and I can still remember the first time I saw him at practice. It hurt to see him run the knees he had.

Little Mo wanted to go to Cleveland and play with his brother, so the Eagles obliged him. We had Billy Ray Smith with us for two years and he was sent off to Baltimore, where he became a great one. Jimmy Orr also went to Baltimore. Those were the kinds of things that kept happening, and I think it was the reason we never had a really great ball club.

You asked me how it was playing for Pittsburgh in those years, and that's the only reason I'm relating this to you. The kinds of teams we had in those days can be best explained by the fact that for three or four years I was getting the award given out by the Monday Morning Quarterback Club for the most valuable player on the Steelers. Now this is a real successful club when they have to give a linebacker all of these awards and you don't have anybody who can win ball games for you getting any. I'm not putting myself down; I know I was a good ball player, but normally a quarterback, running back, or receiver would be getting those awards if you have a successful ball club, people who can get points on the board.

It really didn't make any difference to me who was coaching. As far as playing, you had to go out there and play, and pro ball was enjoyable because, unlike high school and college, you had one assignment. If a guy does this, you do that. It's the players who make the great coaches, and during a season a coach may win one or two games with coaching. Look at Otto Graham. He wasn't always on target; nobody is. He'd throw the ball behind Lavelli or Speedie, and a defensive guy would have perfect coverage on them. You'd see those receivers reach back with their left hand and just roll the

Pat Summerall puts his foot right into the ball. Yes, the same Pat Summerall who shares the booth with John Madden and sells hardware. Though he is one of the most popular sportscasters working today, many younger fans don't realize that Summerall spent ten years playing for the Chicago Cardinals and New York Giants. He sees a lot of comparisons to what he did as a player at his job today: "I look at every telecast as a championship game. One slip is like missing a field goal. I didn't get paid to miss then, and I don't get paid to miss now."

The impassioned shouts of "De-fense! De-fense!" that have become such an integral part of football games started in New York. Jim Katcavage, Dick Modzelewski, Roosevelt Grier, and Andy Robustelli were members of what may be the most famous defense in history. A great leader on and off the field, Robustelli was one of the finest pass rushers the game has ever seen. When asked to describe Robustelli, Allie Sherman said, "Watch Andy on the field and you're studying a real master. Terrific speed of mind, hands, and feet make him the best."

Although George Ratterman was a starting quarterback for five years before he got to Cleveland, he is usually remembered as Otto Graham's backup. A fun-loving gentleman, he was one of the few players to revolt against Paul Brown's vaunted system. After listening to guard Joe Skibinski tell him what plays Brown wanted called, he told him, "I don't like the play. Go ask Brown for another one." Skibinski immediately started toward the bench, and Ratterman was fortunate that he and a couple of his teammates were able to catch him before he got there. "Otherwise the next signal Brown sent me might have been a 6:02 bus ticket for Fort Thomas, Kentucky."

In a business where flash and hype are the norm, Dan Rooney keeps a low profile. His father, Art Rooney, Sr., sports' most beloved man, founded the Steelers in 1933, spending $2,500 for the franchise, a far cry from the football empire his son runs today. While understanding that "we have to run the Steelers like a business," Dan also respects the personal touch his father brought to the team. "It would be a shame if we didn't remain a mom-and-pop shop. I spend a lot of my time with league business, and the league has become very, very profitable. It's unfortunate because you lose some of the human element and our product is human."

A member of the Philadelphia Eagles dreaded "Suicide Seven," "Big" Mike Jarmoluk spent ten years in the NFL and probably didn't get this much altitude very often. Very popular with his fellow Eagles, Jarmoluk was defensive captain in '53, '54, and '55—the last years the players voted. Very active today with the Eagles Alumni Association, he belies the fact that they didn't have any big men playing back in those days.

Before the "Steel Curtain," "Orange Crush," and "Purple People Eaters," there was the "Suicide Seven." This group of Philadelphia Eagle buccaneers made life miserable for offenses throughout the National Football League. Two of them, Bucko Kilroy and Wayne Robinson, played with such enthusiasm that they were featured in a *Life* magazine article, "Savagery on Sunday." This resulted in a lawsuit that Kilroy and Robinson won. Kilroy explains, "Some players are just heavy hitters. Other players will say, 'You don't have to hit so hard,' but, instinctively, you do. It was self-preservation out there, and in the 1940s and 1950s the heavy hitters wore the black hats and became the villains."

The Philadelphia Eagles team of 1947: Bosh Pritchard is #30, and Bucko Kilroy is in the front row, third from the left. Note the great face masks.

Ed Sprinkle played so rough that *Collier's* magazine called him the "meanest man in football." Equally destructive on defense and offense, Chicago Bears' line coach "Hunk" Anderson said, "Sprink blocks like a fat lady on an escalator."

The three years he spent with the Pittsburgh Steelers were only the beginning of Nick Skorich's career in pro football. He went on to coach at Rensselaer Poly, Pittsburgh, Green Bay, and Cleveland before joining the league office as an assistant supervisor of officials.

Dale Dodrill played guard for nine years with the Pittsburgh Steelers. "I played the game when it was automatic and everything was fun." In 1960 Dodrill joined the coaching staff of the then brand-new Denver Broncos and was surprised that he lasted five years. "If you spend your life with the kind of discipline we grew up with, it amazes me that a modern coach can put a team on the field."

Doak Walker carries the ball against the Cleveland Browns in the 1954 championship game. One of the most popular men to play pro football, Walker was the ultimate All-American. He was so popular during his college career that the Cotton Bowl ("The House That Doak Built") had to be expanded, and a racehorse was named O.K. Doak. When he retired after six years with the Lions, he stated, "I wanted to get out while I still had all my teeth and both knees."
(PHOTO: NFL PHOTOS)

ball in. They were comparable to the receivers Bradshaw had when he won all those Super Bowls. Those are the types of players who create champion teams.

John Michelosen was the coach when I got to the Steelers and was the last man to coach the single wing in pro football. Next they brought in Joe Bach, one of the original Four Horsemen, and I forget how long he lasted and then we had Walt Kiesling. He'd been with Rooney for years and had played with teams like the Duluth Eskimos and Pottsville Maroons in the real early days. Kiesling lasted three years, and when Buddy Parker got there he was going to change everything around. Any time a new coach takes over, he has things he wants to do and certain kinds of players he wants. There's nothing wrong with that, but I wanted Parker to release me because I could use that I wasn't going to work into his plans for the future. He told me, "Art Rooney has an investment in you, so you have to stay here. You can sit on the bench for the rest of the season." I said, "I think Art Rooney's got his investment out of me a couple of times over." Then I went to see Art and told him I didn't think Buddy was being fair. "Well," Art said, "I'm sorry, Dale, but Buddy is running the show." That was the year of the expansion, and I was sure if they did trade me it would have been to one of the expansion teams. The handwriting was on the wall because every team had to put up so many players, and after nine years in the league I didn't want to go through that so I quit.

While I was playing I had worked in a bank in Omaha for a few summers and became interested in the insurance business. It was very difficult to get a summer job if you were playing football because an employer knew you were going to leave when the season started. Companies in those days wanted somebody who would be around forever. Now it's just the opposite, and if they can get a player to work for a company, they're overjoyed because it's great public relations for the time he's there. I started selling insurance in the off-season because it was something I could do on my own time, and after I retired I told my wife to pack up. "We're going back to

Colorado." My wife said, "What are you going to do there?" I said, "I don't know, probably the same thing I'm doing here, but I don't want to spend more than two more days in Pittsburgh." When I got back out here, I worked for the same insurance company and formed my own agency in 1963.

When they founded the American Football League in 1960, the Denver Broncos' management heard I was in Denver and offered me a coaching job. Frank Filchock was the head coach—he coached the offense, and I coached the defense. I told my wife, Jan, just last week that those first years in the AFL were just like the kind of football that you saw during the recent strike. The caliber of players was different, sure, but there wasn't that much difference between them and the regular players. They were guys who had been cut by the NFL or passed up in training camp and it was an exciting brand of football. You never knew what was going to happen and there were lots of big plays. I think it was fun to watch.

I quit coaching for the same reason I quit playing—when it became harder than work. You have to get some enjoyment out of your work, and when it gets to be too much work it's not worth doing. I played the game when it was automatic and everything was fun. Sure it was a lot of sweat and you had to keep in shape, but it was very enjoyable. I played nine years and was very surprised that I lasted five years in coaching. I just didn't have the temperament to be a good coach, especially in dealing with modern-day youth. My old college coach, Bob Davis, was the kind of coach I could relate to. He was a tough disciplinarian, but he was also fair. The whole squad respected him, and that was reflected in the kind of team we had. I see these players today sitting on their helmets during a game, and I know what would have happened if we'd done that. You have to keep yourself in the game, and that attitude is the difference between getting hurt and not getting hurt. That kind of discipline is from another world altogether, and if you've spent your life with that kind of philosophy and gone through a war on top of it, it's no wonder that so many guys from my time are so confused by the attitudes of the current players. I'd talk to a player for five minutes and then he'd tell me, "Now it's my turn, I get to talk to you for five minutes."

I've always enjoyed every type of work that I've done. Even if some of them weren't that enjoyable, each one served a purpose. In everything I did, I tried to achieve a certain degree of skill and success, and that included football. I think about my war experiences, and sometimes I relate them to pro football as far as the people who take part in it. During the war they had a saying that the man survives the war but he can't survive the peace. A lot of guys came out of the war; they're alive, but they're so emotionally destroyed that they couldn't return to peacetime life. I've known a lot of pro football players who survived the game but can't survive the peace. They can't survive on the other side of the tracks because they don't know what it's like. They can't handle life after football because they went through high school, college, and the pros and never really thought about anything else except football. You talk to them today, and all they want to do is relive the past like those guys in my Army unit. I see football as another step in my life, nothing more. My first salary was $4,500 a year, and in those days you even had to buy your own football shoes. Then, after the season was over, you had to pay your own way home. You made a living—that's what it amounted to.

PART

II

TRIGGERMEN

THE YANKEES OF PROFES-SIONAL FOOTBALL

OTTO GRAHAM

QUARTERBACK

Cleveland Browns 1946–55

It was an end of an era that could never again be duplicated because, though we tried, we never found another Otto Graham.

—Paul Brown

IF I had to choose my most memorable game, it would be when we won the championship in 1950, the Cleveland Browns' first year in the National Football League. The commissioner, Bert Bell, scheduled us against the Eagles for the first game of the season. They had been the champions for two years in a row, and we knocked them off in Philadelphia by a score of something like 35–10. We just killed them. Later on during the season, we lost to the New York Giants and then ended up beating them by a couple of points in the playoff game. We beat the Rams in the championship game, winning it in the last twenty seconds with a field goal by Lou Groza. That year had to be the high point of my career because now we were playing with the big boys.

I don't think back in those days we thought too much about the future. You thought about which team you were going to play next week and how you were going to beat them. That's about as far as you went. Today's players are thinking about their pensions, the union, and selling sneakers. We didn't have agents, never even heard of them. I'm not against the players having agents because a kid can't go in today, not with the kind of money they're making, and negotiate for himself.

However, I do not agree with a kid hiring an agent who is going to take 20 or 25 percent of his earnings for life. I think a player could easily find somebody who went to the school he graduated from, a successful businessman, and let him negotiate his contract. A guy like that would be thrilled to be involved, and he wouldn't be in it for the money. Oh, don't get me wrong, there are some good agents, no question about that, but there are also a lot of them who just take advantage of young athletes.

Football is not a game today, not like it was when we played. It's a business. That's a problem because it all comes down to dollars, especially at the college level. In some schools it's basketball, but in most it's football receipts that finance the entire athletic program. If you win, people watch and that brings in the money. If you lose, the stands are empty and that means trouble. I'm not saying that those guys who have to win every week are wrong and I'm right; I'm just saying that with my philosophy about sports, I don't want any part of it today.

When I quit playing football in 1955, it was for a combination of things. I feel that I could have played for at least another five years, but when you're thirty-four years old, the bumps and bruises don't heal quite as fast. Also, the regimentation of training camp started to get to me. I knew I had to go through it—there was no question about that—but that didn't mean I had to like it. And every year it would get tougher. You would be away from your family for six weeks while the kids were growing up, and that was hard for me. Also, I don't care who it is—Paul Brown, Lombardi, or Tom Landry, whoever—they lay down the rules and treat you like little kids, and you end up resenting it. I resented it more and more as time went by because I knew I wasn't going to go out and break training rules, stay out late and miss curfew, that sort of thing. Later on, when I went into coaching, I realized why you have to do it. The rules are made for the lowest so-called animal on the totem pole, not the top people. I found myself saying and doing exactly the same things that I momentarily hated Paul Brown's guts for.

There also was the feeling, every Sunday morning, of so much responsibility on my shoulders, and I really got to hate that. Getting up and not being able to eat, my stomach growling, and so forth. You need that desire to really want to play, or you're just not going to be very good. Finally—and I felt this was very important for any future I might have in business—I thought it would be best to quite when I was on top, to quit a winner. I always recall Joe Lewis, a great champion, who for reasons we all know ended up having to fight when he was old and out of shape. When you see an athlete having to do that, you start to forget the good years.

I was born in Waukegan, Illinois, Jack Benny's hometown. My mother and father were both musicians. She played the organ and taught the piano; my father taught practically every instrument ever made. He was a high school music teacher, and he had played baseball when he was going to college. I played the piano and violin, and then later switched to the French horn, which I continued to play when I was going to college. My major in college was education and my minor was music. I think music helped me in sports because music means rhythm and rhythm means timing.

I played both football and basketball in high school and went to Northwestern University on a basketball scholarship—just tuition, no Cadillacs. I didn't play football in my freshman year but went out for spring football. Lynn "Pappy" Waldorf was the coach, and I had a real good spring that year. The next fall I played and went on and did well for the next three years. I also played baseball, which was nice because it got me out of spring football from then on. I signed up with the Naval Air Corps V-5 program while I was at Northwestern in 1942 and was called to active duty in January of 1944. I was handed my degree—never had to take final exams—and ended up at Pensacola for the final phase of my training. The war ended before I finished up. The Navy gave us the option of staying in or going home, and I opted to go home. What the hell, the war was over and I just wanted to go home and get married.

When I graduated from Northwestern, I really had no idea what I wanted to do. Then, when I got out of the service, I started playing sports for a living because it looked liked a good way to make some quick money; then I thought I would go into something else. I played one year of professional basketball for the Rochester Royals, who later on became the Cincinnati Royals. From there they went to Kansas City and are now in Sacramento, California, the Sacramento Kings. Red Holzman, who coached the Knicks, and Chuck Connors, the TV Rifleman, were on that team with me. A couple of others were Tom Rich and Bob Davies, who I saw recently at a Hall of Fame golf outing in Florida. Football, basketball, baseball, and hockey Hall of Fame players are invited, and the money goes for research for people who have been paralyzed, like Nick Buoniconti's son.

To tell the truth, I wasn't very happy about the basketball situation because you were traveling all the time. You'd be home five or six days every month, if you were lucky, and the rest of the time you were on the road. At least when you play football, you fly out to the game, play, and come back.

Paul Brown had signed me while I was in the Navy and the next year, 1946, was the first season for the All-American Football Conference. We were all new at it with the Browns. It was Paul Brown's first year as a pro head coach, the first year he'd ever coached the T-formation, and on top of that most of the players were rookies. I had been a single-wing tailback all through school and was now starting at quarterback, a new position for me. We played our first four years in the old All-America Conference, and I think we were one of the main reasons that league folded. The Browns dominated the league right from the beginning, and you have to have good competition or the fans will stop coming to the games. After the league folded, the 49ers, Colts, and our team joined the NFL.

The reason we had such a good team was because we had a great coach in Paul Brown. He was the type of guy who would have been an admiral or general if he went into the service or the president of a company in the business world. Everything was first class with him, and he expected the same from everybody in the organization. We always traveled first class, and you were expected to wear a tie and coat—none of that old pro football image of pot bellies and big cigars. There were, of course, guys on the team who smoked and drank, but none of them did it front of Paul Brown. He always told us that he wanted the Cleveland Browns to be the New York Yankees of professional football.

Every year he would get up in front of us at training camp and dictate to us the rules. Nothing was left to chance, he was so organized. How to do calisthenics, how to run, how to put one foot in front of the other—it was amazing. He also had what he called the "Tuesday Rule." He felt sex was bad for a guy before a game, so he would lecture the married guys that they should abstain after Tuesday. It used to irritate me and we kid him about it today that he would only talk to the married guys, not the ones who were single. I think only .0000001 percent of the players—if that—ever observed the rule.

Paul also had great assistants, which you need if you're going to win. Weeb Eubank (everybody knows him, of course), Fritz Heisler, Bill Edwards—they were all good coaches. Blanton Collier was our backfield coach for many years, and he had a lot of theories on how you should run the ball, the steps you take, and so forth. He finally became so disgusted with us that he said he was going to teach us the way we played instead of the way he thought it should be done.

They were all good coaches, good teachers, and, good people. I think that is very important because you can be very talented, have all the talent in the world, but if you're also an SOB, you're not going to do as well. The Browns had a good organization from the top to the bottom, and sure we had our ups and downs like any other team, but they were mostly ups because the players we had on our teams were great football players.

Marion Motley was one of the best. An all-around player, he could run, catch the ball, and, most important, was a terrific blocker. I couldn't very well throw the ball lying flat on my back, and I was lucky to have tremendous protection. You also have to have the receivers who can get open, and we had them too. Dante Lavelli, Mac Speedie, Horace Gillom, "Dub" Jones, Ray Renfro—I could go on forever. It takes all the different parts to have a good team, and we were lucky enough to have all those parts at the same time.

As a quarterback, you have to take what the defense gives you. Today, more than ever, you can't dictate to them because the defense can do all sorts of crazy things. Safety blitzes, camouflaged pass defenses—it's a big guessing game out there. A lot of today's receivers actually change their patterns and run something different than the play called in the huddle. A quarterback will throw the ball and miss a receiver by twenty yards. The fans think, "My God, that was a terrible throw. What a bum." We didn't have too much of that when I was playing, but Lavelli, who was one of my great receivers, would occasionally change one on me. Maybe he was supposed to go down to the corner, but it looked open at the post. He'd go there instead, and more than once we'd get a touchdown.

We played hard in my time, no question about that. There were a lot of tough guys, and I got to know a lot of them. The 49ers had a linebacker, Hardy Brown, and he was the kind who would never tackle you. He'd use a forearm to the head or try to knock your head off with his shoulder. They said he had an "educated" shoulder. Ed Sprinkle was a big end who played for the Bears, and he wasn't about to ease off if you had your back turned. I never really had any problems with anybody who came to play hard; it was the guys who would give you the cheap shots. There weren't too many like that, but hey, there are cheap-shot artists in every profession.

I wrote an article for *Sports Illustrated* in 1954 about violence in football. I thought the league didn't always crack down on dirty players like they should have because they wanted to protect the game. I wrote the article and it happened to come out just after my chin was split open by a 49ers player. The guy who wrote the article with me quoted me as saying he did it on purpose. Now, I didn't actually say that, but I know for a fact that I was at least two yards out of bounds when he put an elbow in my face and knocked me out.

After the article came out, Bert Bell was asked about it and he said, "Everybody's temper will flare, but I never heard of a player who maliciously did harm to another." Bull! I remember one game where a guy on the Rams took off his helmet and started slugging guys with it. Nobody can tell me that he wasn't trying to hurt somebody. Oh, there were some things they did that I think were just plain dirty football. If a receiver is cutting across the middle and a defensive back sticks out his arm and "clotheslines" him, I think that's dirty. When a guy picks up a quarterback or runner and instead of tackling him, drives him into the ground as hard as he can with a shoulder, that's dirty. I don't think pro football needs that, and over the years they've gotten rid of a lot of those things.

I must say, however, that the dirty players were in the minority. I played in every ball game for ten years, and there was only one game I shouldn't have played in. We had played three games in eight days, and I had hurt my knee somewhere along the line. The trainer taped the knee, and it felt better so I decided to play anyway. Throughout the entire game nobody on the 49ers tried to hurt me once. in fact, the few times they did get to me it seemed like they eased me down to the ground.

After the game I went over to the 49ers locker room and talked to Norm Standlee and Frankie Albert, whom I knew pretty well, and they told me that before the game Buck Shaw, the 49ers coach, had told them, "The first guy who goes out there and purposely tries to hurt Graham is off the team." I don't think there are enough Buck Shaws around in football, or in any professional sport for that matter.

After we won the championship in 1954, I wanted to retire. We beat the Lions, 56–10, and we really wanted to win that one because they had beaten us two years in a row. I actually did retire after that game, but Paul Brown asked me to come back, and when we beat the Rams the next year for the championship, I felt it was time to get out for good.

When I retired from the Browns, I was asked to coach the College All-Stars by Wilfred Smith, sports editor of the Chicago *Tribune.* I told him I'd never coached anything in my life. We decided that I would be an assistant coach in 1957 before becoming head coach the next year. "Curly" Lambeau was the head coach, and he was an easygoing guy, not as well organized as Paul Brown. After that year there was no question in my mind. After working under Paul Brown, I knew I could coach. We beat the Lions in 1958 and everybody thought I was a genius. I knew it wasn't true, but I didn't argue.

At that time I was already in the insurance business and doing a little bit of radio and television work. I stayed in Cleveland for four years and then got the chance to come to the Coast Guard Academy. George Steinbrenner was the guy responsible for me getting a shot at the job. He lived in Bay Village, a suburb of Cleveland, and was a neighbor of mine. The admiral in charge of the Coast Guard in Cleveland had been assigned to the Coast Guard Academy as superintendent. After he had been there awhile, he wanted to get a new football coach so he called up George because he knew a lot of people in the sports world. George told him he should call me. The admiral said, "Oh, he's not going to want to come down here." George said, "Oh, hell, go ahead and ask him." My first reaction, quite honestly, was "Where the hell is the Coast Guard Academy?"

My wife and I went up to New London by train and spent three days looking around. Bev spent her time driving around the area looking at homes with the admiral's wife and I don't think she was too impressed. I spent three days talking to the officers, coaches, and cadets. I liked it very much, and even though I had said I'd never go into coaching, this was a whole different situation. There's none of this win-at-all-cost pressure, which I never did believe in, even when I was playing. I believe in doing your best, that's very important, but if you end up on the short side of the score because the other team makes a great play, or is just better than you, the world doesn't come to an end. Of course, the average fan doesn't believe that, but I couldn't care less about that because over the years I learned to despise so many of them. Every team has many loyal fans, but the majority (in my opinion) of them are fair-weather fans, and it really bothers me when you have the kind of people in the stands who just like to boo. I'd like to see those same people have somebody looking over their shoulder at work, whatever they do, and every time they make a mistake, boo like crazy in their ear.

I felt the Coast Guard Academy could be the best of both worlds. I could coach football, in addition to being the athletic director, and still enjoy life. The cadets are high-class kids, and they come to the Academy to become Coast Guard officers, not to play football. We feel the athletics are a very important part of their education because it teaches leadership and so forth. You never give up until the last whistle or gun, whatever. Even if you're thirty points behind, it's pouring down rain, and you're dead-tired, you don't give up. Later on in your career, that same guy is now at sea and some poor soul is out there on a rubber raft. Sure, it would be easy to say, "Aw, hell, there's no chance in a million of finding that guy. Let's go back and get some coffee and climb into a warm bunk. Forget about him." No, you stay out there, and I have talked to people who have been lucky enough to find somebody in just that type of situation.

There are lots of things you learn in football or basketball, any kind of sports. I realized I would enjoy teaching these high-class kids, and I would never get rich, but I would make a decent salary. We got back on the train to go home, and I can recall very vividly, Bev turned to me and said, "Thank God we'll never have to see that place again." I turned to her and said, "Bev, I liked it," and she almost died. We did, of course, come back, and it was a nice life for all of us.

At one point I stopped coaching and became just the athletic director. I didn't miss looking at films and that sort of thing, but I really missed the close association with the kids. You're not as close to them as you are when you're on the football field coaching them. The true character of any young boy or girl, as far as that's concerned, comes out on the athletic field. You find out what they're made of. Over the years I went to bat for some of my football players who got into trouble for whatever reasons, and really fought for them. They kept a few guys, and later on those same guys became very fine officers so I knew it was all worthwhile.

In 1963 I coached my sixth All-Star game. We played against the Packers and Lombardi, and we beat them. We also had an undefeated, untied season at the Academy for the first time in its history, and again I looked like a genius. Everybody there thought I was the greatest coach in the world, and again I knew that wasn't true, but I still wasn't about to argue with them.

Edward Bennett Williams, the president of the Washington Redskins, contacted me toward the end of 1965 and wanted to know if I would like to coach the team. It just so happened that we had a new admiral coming in. You get a new one every two or three years, and this guy could care less about athletics. I started talking salary with Williams, and I put my demands way up high, and he kept saying yes, yes, yes. It got to the point where I didn't think I could turn it down because of what it would mean financially to my family.

The Redskins weren't doing very good at that time. I went down there, and my first year we put together a .500 season, which was the best they had done in ten years. It wasn't too long before I realized that pro ball was a lot different than coaching Coast Guard cadets or All-Stars. When I had my undefeated, untied season at the Academy, I don't think I saw one reporter. Our first exhibition game with the Baltimore Colts, we didn't look very good and lost the game. There must have been forty of those guys around me raising hell and asking me questions. My philosophy about playing football is that, first of all, it's got to be fun. If it's not fun, the hell with it. Fun for me as a coach, fun for the players, fun for the reporters, and fun for the fans. I told those guys, "I'd rather have a season where I lost a couple of ball games, 35–28 or 30–28, than win all our games by a score of 3–0." I thought it should be pretty obvious to those guys what I was getting at. I didn't want to be involved with dull football and would rather have a lot of scoring. The next day the headlines read: GRAHAM SAYS HE WOULD RATHER LOSE. I realized very quickly that the press and I were not going to get along, and we didn't. I make no bones about it, and you can quote me, but over the years I have had no use for the press in general. I'm not talking about specific people who are good reporters, but the majority. I have had too many instances where they will put only half of what you say in their piece or twist it around so it reads differently than you meant it. Often it comes out as a downright lie. I think the majority of the press are negative writers, and if they don't have something negative to say about you, they won't write anything.

I had a five-year contract with Washington, and I lasted three years. Sonny Jurgensen was my quarterback, and he could throw the ball as well as anybody who ever played the game, but the next year we had all kinds of problems with injuries and we went downhill. The third year was the same thing, and we ended up 5–9. That was the first year that Lombardi wasn't coaching the Packers. He was the general manager, and I can recall walking around together before we played the Packers and talking. I'll never forget his words to me. "Otto, if you want to survive in pro football as a head coach, you have to be a son-of-a-bitch 100 percent of the time." I could never have coached like he did—it's not my personality to be an SOB—

but I found out later that Lombardi was also a great actor. Mike McCormack was one of my assistant coaches at Washington, and he had coached under Lombardi after I left. He told me that Vince would raise hell out on the field, and when he got back in the confines of the coaches' quarters he'd say, "How did I do out there?" Oh, he got mad at times, but how much was act and how much was real, who knows. He was a very, very good coach.

I know now that if I had been an assistant coach in pro football for a couple of years I'd have done a lot better, but I was trying to coach them like I coached cadets or All-Stars. I guess the best way to describe the differences would be this way. We would have a meeting scheduled for nine o'clock in the morning. Lombardi time, Paul Brown time, Don Shula time, nine o'clock is nine o'clock. If you're late, you're fined. They don't care if you're five seconds late or ten minutes late, you're late. I'm the kind of guy, if I was sitting there and busy doing something, not ready to start the meeting, if a guy walks in five seconds late, why take five hundred bucks out of his pocket? Guys like Paul Brown and Vince Lombardi knew what they were doing. They knew the very next meeting the same guy would be thirty seconds late. Then, the next time, they'd be two minutes late, and maybe a couple of other guys wouldn't show up on time. You can never allow that to start. There can be no forgiveness whatsoever, and you have to be a tough SOB, just like Lombardi said. If a player's wife is going to have a baby, he should arrange for somebody else to take his wife to the hospital. If you have a blowout on the way to the stadium, get there somehow and make sure you leave early enough so you can get there no matter what happens. That's what I mean by being an SOB. My assistant coaches told me those guys would take advantage of me. I said, "No, they won't do that." My assistants were right.

That year Lombardi let it be known that he wanted to get back into coaching, and Williams went out and got him. I can't blame him for that. My God, if you can get Lombardi over Graham, I'd take Lombardi too. I stayed in Washington for one year as the highest-paid gardener in town. I was still getting paid by the Redskins and I didn't have anything to do, so I worked in the yard and had a good time.

It was the only time in my life that I was fired, and later on I realized it was a blessing. But at the moment I didn't feel that way. You name an emotion, and I felt it. Irritated, mad, upset, angry, ready to shoot somebody. It wasn't long afterward that something happened that convinced me it was the best thing that ever happened to me. Don Shula was coaching the Baltimore Colts, and even though they had been doing well, they had lost a couple of ball games. He told me he had been invited to play golf on Saturday afternoon with Spiro Agnew, who was, at that time, Vice President. Bob Hope was also going to be included in the foursome. Now I don't care if you're a Republican or Democrat, how many times do you get to play golf with those guys? By Saturday the die is cast as far as the game on Sunday goes. The plays are in, the strategy is in, there's no more preparation possible—what more can you do? Don said that if he went out to Burning Tree Country Club with the Vice President and Bob Hope, there's no way that could be kept quiet. The press, the fans, all the negative thinkers would say that Shula should be home working on his game plan. He's goofing off, and that's why he's losing. He just couldn't take the chance, and I thought to myself: "If you can't take a few hours out to enjoy yourself, I'm happy to be out of it." From that point on, I never looked back.

I went back to the Coast Guard Academy as athletic director. I coached again for two years, when our coach up and retired very quickly. We interviewed a dozen coaches and finally picked a guy from Notre Dame. Two days before we were going to announce he was the new coach, he called and told us he didn't want to leave Notre Dame. Rather than go through the whole thing again, interviewing and so forth, I took over for a while. But trying to be coach and athletic director at the same time was too time-consuming, so I said the hell with that noise and went out and got that same guy to come as coach. I remained as athletic director until I retired in 1985.

I fool around with odds and ends but no nine-to-five job. After I left the Academy, I worked for the Warner Lambert Company for two years, but that's ended. I had cancer ten years ago, cancer of the rectum, and to put it bluntly, the reamed me out, and I had to have a colostomy. Warner Lambert makes a great product called Early Detector, which picks up early symptoms of colon cancer by detecting hidden blood in the stool, and I was the spokesman for that product. I am disappointed that the sales declined all over the country, even among competitive products. Early Detector had over 50 percent of all sales nationwide, but the amount of business didn't warrant me traveling all over the country as its spokesman. It's too bad, but the honest truth is that the general public is not overly concerned about cancer. I guess we need a person of President Reagan's stature to be afflicted once a year to make people aware of the problem.

My message was—and still is—if you're forty years old or older, the chances of having colon cancer really increase. It's the number two killer after lung cancer, and roughly 53,000 people are going to die this year from the disease. I tell people, "Get a checkup every year because cancer doesn't discriminate." Everybody thinks it's going to happen to the guy next door. Me, I was a big shot and it couldn't happen to me. Former athlete, champion quarterback, Hall-of-Famer, I didn't smoke or drink, but I found out differently.

It may sound corny, but I think I'm a better person because of the experience. If anybody had said years ago that I'd be talking like this, I'd have told him he was nuts. When you're playing football and you can throw touchdown passes, that's great. People pat you on the back, tell you how great you are. Sure, I like that stuff as well as the next guy, but these days, when I'm out on the golf course, and somebody walks up and says, "You saved my father's life. He saw your commercial on TV and went to the doctor for a physical and found out in time," that makes me feel pretty good. I get a lot more personal satisfaction out of that than I got throwing those touchdowns. I know I'm a better person today than I was when I was playing. Not that I was a bad person, but I used to go to all the various charity affairs because I thought I had to. Now I go because I want to.

After my operation, a fellow from the Ostomy Association came in and explained everything to me, and that really helped. Doctors are notorious for cutting people open, fixing things, but they really don't know the first thing about taking care of it because they haven't had to deal with that part of it. I tell people to join the Association and not to worry about the cancer coming back. I kid around a lot and try to get people not to dwell on the negative side. That's the best solution for some people. I tell them if I had to go back to the old days—bowel movements and everything—I wouldn't do it. No more filling stations with dirty toilet seats, no hemorrhoids, and the best part of it, when you guys have to go, you have to go to the bathroom. I can sit here and just keep on telling you what a great football player you think I am. I get them laughing and talking, and they realize that the world's not coming to an end.

It wasn't until after I recovered from my illness that I realized how important my football experience was in my recovery. In the NFL, you face a crisis every weekend and I assure you that nothing is more important in the world at that moment to each player in that game. You have to face peaks and valleys and learn to survive and live with them. You learn to bounce back and try even harder, regardless of the odds. It's too bad everyone in the world can't play a little football. You learn it makes no difference whether you are black, white, brown, red, Protestant, Catholic, Jew, whatever. You learn to give and take; respect other people and ideas even though you might no agree with them. There is no doubt in my mind the world would be a better place to live.

THE SORCERER'S APPRENTICE

EDWARD LEBARON

QUARTERBACK

Washington Redskins 1952–53
Calgary Stampeders 1954
Washington Redskins 1955–59
Dallas Cowboys 1960–63

Eddie is one of the greatest T-formation quarterbacks in America—one of the four finest passers I've coached in sixty years.

—Amos Alonzo Stagg

I wish I had a hundred more men who could take charge just like that little fellow, and who had his poise and cool judgment.

—Marine Colonel Herman Nickerson

EDWARD LEBARON

WHEN I was playing college ball, we were going to play Northwestern, and in those days you went by train. Three of us decided to go down to the dining car to get something to eat, and when we got there an elderly lady wanted to know who all of these large gentlemen were. One of the guys explained that we were the College of Pacific football team. At that time I was sixteen years old and not a very large specimen. I was the youngest college football player in the country. Most of the other guys had been in the service, and a few of them were in their late twenties. The lady looked at one of our big linemen and said, "How nice that you can take your son along on the trip."

They had all sorts of nicknames for me—"Supermouse," "The Sorcerer's Apprentice"—but the one that stuck was the "Little General." When I first started playing professional football, nobody said much about my size, but as time went by and the players started getting bigger, they started to make more of a thing about it. I never felt any physical fear of any kind and was never intimidated by the larger players. My game was based on a lot of faking and moving around, and I basically stayed out of their way. Frankie Albert was one of my heroes, and I patterned myself after him when I started to play. He was a great ball handler who came out of Stanford and was the 49ers quarterback when I was playing college football.

From the time I was old enough to participate, I was involved in sports of one kind or another. I must have gotten my first football when I was four or five years old and was either throwing it or kicking it all over the place from that time on. My father didn't get to go to college, but he did attend San Rafael Military School, which was right across the bay from San Francisco. It was one of the top prep schools at that time, and he was a football, baseball, and basketball player. I also had an uncle, Jack Simms, who played at St. Mary's during the 1930s. They had a real good team, and he was a great punter and threw the ball well. It was a big thrill for me to go to games and see him play. Between my father and uncle, I guess it was natural for me to become interested in playing football.

IRON MEN

My father was always in the farming business, and until I was eight we lived in Sonoma County, north of San Francisco. We had dairy cows and a sheep ranch. The dairy was a couple of hundred acres and the sheep ranch probably around three thousand, so it was a pretty good-sized place. This was during the midst of the Depression, and things weren't too good in the farming business so we moved to Oakdale, a city in the San Joaquin Valley. My father got into the business of buying and developing ranches. As I grew up on a farm, the hours were long, but I never minded the work and it was a great place to be when you were a kid.

I went to Oakdale High School when I was twelve and played football, basketball, and was on the track team. Track was the big sport in the part of the world, and I ran the low hurdles, sprint relay team, and threw the shot put. Yes, the shot put. Because of the war we only had two coaches, so we didn't have a baseball team until I was a senior, but I got to play a couple of years in college. The football team was using the single wing and I was the first-string tailback for my last two and a half years. I did all the passing, kicking, and most of the running.

The colleges didn't exactly come looking for me because we were a small school. However, nine guys on that team ended up playing college football. I was going to go Stanford without a scholarship, but then the assistant coach at College of the Pacific, Larry Siemering, talked me into going there. My freshman year, Amos Alonzo Stagg was the coach. I probably think more about the fact that he was my coach now than I did then. I was sixteen years old and just happy to be there. To me, he was a nice little old man who obviously had a great reputation. Stagg was an amazing guy. He wasn't highly organized, but he was very sharp and innovative for a guy in his eighties.

At some point during the year, I ripped my uniform pants during a scrimmage and went to see Stagg. He told me to leave the pants in his office. The next day he gave me my pants back and they were stitched up very neatly. He said, "Our budget doesn't allow us to buy any new equipment, but I think Mrs. Stagg did a good job repairing them, don't you?"

Stagg retired after my first year and Siemering took over as head coach. He had played with the Boston Redskins and before that had been a great player at the University of San Francisco. He also had a winning record as a high school and junior college coach. Larry was a great coach and, along with Tom Landry, one of the finest coaches I've ever been around. He replaced the single wing that we had used the year before with the T-formation, and that really helped my game. He also believed in faking and we spent a lot of time working on the mechanics. I used to get a couple backs and a center to come out with me, and I'd practice faking until they didn't want to do it anymore. When I was in my room, I used to stand in front of a mirror and work on my technique. A lot of people have said that I invented the "double spin" while I was at Pacific, but if I did anything, I just perfected it. I was also credited with establishing the "belly series," which was the forerunner to the wishbone. During one game with San Jose State, I faked the ball to the fullback and then threw a pass that would have tied the score. The referee was as faked out as everybody else because he whistled the ball dead. When he found out that the fullback didn't have the ball, he took both the down and the completion away from us. Don't ask me why.

We had a pretty good team while I was at Pacific and were ranked number ten in the nation my senior year. I think we lost two games during my last three years. While I was playing college ball, I wasn't thinking at all about the pros. You didn't have to think about keeping your marks up because that's the reason you were going to school, not to play football. I was majoring in business and economics, and I've been told that in my senior year the football team as a whole had the highest grade-point average of any group in the school. David Gerber, who was head of MGM Television, Ken Johnson, who was vice president of Capitol Cities, and Bruce Orvis, who was a very successful farmer and rancher in California, were a few of the guys who played on that team.

I graduated from Pacific in 1950 and played in the All-Star game that year. We had one of the great All-Star teams of all time because a lot of those players had been in the service and were not only big and strong, but were extremely tough. Leon Hart, Leo Nomellini, and Clayton Tonnemaker were on that team. Not everybody was big. Doak Walker, Charlie Justice, and myself were in the backfield, and we called ourselves "the Abnormal Midgets." Philadelphia had some great players at that time too—Tommy Thompson, Bednarik, Kilroy, guys like that—and it was a real thrill to beat them.

The 49ers drafted me when they were in the old All-America Football Conference. That league could draft you when you were a senior, so I went up to the 49ers camp and looked around. That's when pro football started to look interesting, but I still wasn't serious about it. Then the Redskins drafted me and I decided to take a shot at it.

While I was in college I had joined the Marine reserves, and right before the All-Star game they called me up. I managed to play two exhibition games with the Redskins before I went to Quantico, Virginia, to officers' training school, which was a seven-month deal. While I was there, I got to play football and we were rated the number one service team that year. From there I went to Korea and was there for about nine months.

A while back they had a television show about the Korean War, and it was interesting to see the hills and valleys I was familiar with. I was a rifle platoon leader in the 7th Regiment of the First Marine Division and received the Purple Heart, Bronze Star, and a letter of commendation. It was a truly United Nations effort, and we were tied in with Belgians, English, Turks, Koreans—you name them. We would push the North Koreans back, and then the peace talks would start up and we'd sit there and watch them build up the lines again. Then we'd have to go knock them down again. It was a very frustrating war. When I got back, the Marines wanted me to teach in the basic school and play football for them. I did teach for a while and gave some serious thought about staying in, but I figured if I was going to play football, it might as well be with the pros.

The Marines didn't discharge me until August, so I got to the Redskins' training camp a little late. After marching around Korea, I had a hard time getting back in shape and it took me awhile to get my legs and arm back. We played six exhibition games that year and kind of barnstormed around the country. Training camp was in Occidental, California, and we took the train across the country to Chicago, stopping along the way to play. Kansas City, St. Louis, in those days you went anyplace you could find someone willing to put on a game.

One of the difficult things about playing with the Redskins that year was the fact that I was going to replace Sammy Baugh. There was nobody like Sam. Some people compared me to him as a passer, and I think that was the silliest thing I've ever heard. I considered myself a pretty good passer, but Baugh was one of the greats. He threw long and hard, long and soft, short and hard, short and soft. He threw off the hip and he threw off his ear and he threw off balance. Sam could throw everything but a knuckleball. He played three quarters of the first game and a quarter of the second. From then on, I was the first-string quarterback. Sam gave me everything but his throwing arm, and whenever he could, he would sit next to me on the bench and give me suggestions. The best advice he gave me was when he told me, "Son, you've got to do things your way. If you try to do them my way, we're licked."

Dick Todd was the coach when I got there, but he was fired during the preseason and Curly Lambeau took over. Curly was an old-timer who helped start the Green Bay Packers back in the 1920s and then was involved with Chicago, I think, before he came to the Redskins. I got along fine with him at first, but after a while he and I didn't see eye to eye. He was really a defensive coach, and at some point he turned the offense over to somebody else. In the two years Curly was with the Redskins, he probably didn't know more than ten offensive plays. In 1953 if we'd won the last game of the year, we'd have tied or been second in our division, so we didn't have a bad ball club. "Choo Choo" Justice was on that team. He broke his arm and came back later in the year. "Bones" Taylor was a great wide receiver. Leon Heath, Harry Gilmer, Hall Haynes—it's hard for me to remember them all.

At the end of that season there were three of us who had a parting of the way with the Redskins. It was evident that Curly wasn't the kind of guy we wanted to play football for, so Gene Brito, Don Campora, and myself went up to play in Canada. In effect, George Marshall gave us a year's leave of absence. The rules were a little different in those days. Larry Siemering, my old college coach, was the coach at Calgary, and that's the reason I went up there. It was interesting and I really enjoyed playing up there, but Canadian ball was different. We played twice a week and one of the big factors was the weather. We played under some conditions that were pretty grim and I never could get used to that. Calgary was one of the better teams until it got cold and wet; then we weren't so good. If we had stayed up there and played together, we would have been pretty good, but Marshall fired Curly in the preseason of the next year and wanted us to come back to Washington.

I liked Marshall. Everybody thought he was a little irascible, opinionated, and just about everything else you can think of, but I always got along well with him. He liked people he could argue with, and I did it without getting him mad. He could yell and scream with the best of them. In the days when I was going to law school, he would have me over for lunch about once a month. He had a little lunchroom in his office and an excellent cook. There would always be a senator or some general, or somebody else interesting, and Marshall was a great conversationalist.

Joe Kuharich took Curly's place. He may have never been considered a great coach, but Joe was a super guy. He was a coach I would have loved to win more games for because he really treated his players well. In 1954 the Redskins had only won two or three games, but in 1955 Brito and I came back from Canada and Joe went out and got some good players like Johnny Carson, J. D. Kimmel, and Mike Davlin, and we ended up with a pretty good defense. We were 8–4 and finished second to Cleveland. That was the first year the Redskins beat the Browns, and that was very satisfying. I threw two touchdown passes and ran for one, and that game probably stands out as much as any game I played in.

The only bad injury I had during the entire time I played was a bad knee, but I did that stepping in a hole during training camp so I don't really count that as an injury. I was pretty lucky and only missed two or three games in all the years I played. There were a lot of very tough guys playing in those days, but I think if you have athletic ability and quickness, you could avoid a lot of them. Doug Atkins, Gino Marchetti, Chuck Bednarik, they were tough and great. There were guys with picturesque names like "Wild Man" Willey and "Bucko" Kilroy. Hardy Brown, who played for the 49ers, he was scary. There were a lot more elbows being used then, and Ed Sprinkle was famous for his clothesline, although he certainly wasn't alone.

The rules allowed more rough play, and they didn't protect the quarterback as much as they do now. As I'm sure you know, until 1955 or '56 we didn't have face masks and they also changed the rules so you couldn't get up and keep running. Guys were dropping knees and knocking and hitting after you were down. They'd look innocent and say, "Well, he can get up and run, so I have to make sure he stays down." There were a lot of rule changes during that period of time because a lot of people were getting hurt, especially quarterbacks. People like to mention how Big Daddy Lipscomb would always help me up. What they didn't know was that he was squeezing my passing arm as hard as he could. You found it was smart to get up from the pile in a hurry.

I played twelve years and that is quite a while. Once you get past the fourth or fifth year, especially if you're playing first string after your first or second year, you know a lot more about the game and can avoid situations that a younger player might find himself in and end up getting hurt. You also have to be just plain lucky not to get hurt, and you also have to be lucky that some great young player doesn't come along and take your job. Every year we had all kinds of quarterbacks show up in training camp when I was with the Redskins, and I'd hear, "This is it. This is the year that we're going to replace you, LeBaron," but it didn't happen.

My last year with the Redskins was 1959, and after seven years I thought it was time to get out. It wasn't such a big thing to retire for me because the money wasn't like it is today. Also, it was getting to the point where I thought I should be starting to practice law. I had been going to law school at George Washington University while I was playing for the Redskins and finished up right before I retired.

I went down to Texas to practice law. I'd always been interested in the oil and gas business and had a job in Midland. Just as I was getting ready to take the Texas bar exam, Tex Schramm called me and wanted to know if I'd like to play for the Dallas Cowboys. I had no idea that the Cowboys were even in existence, but it seemed like a great chance to play some more, and I had a great deal of respect for Tom Landry. Tom wanted me because I had always done well against the Giants when he was there, and he thought it would be helpful to have a veteran quarterback to help Don Meredith come into the league.

Dallas was the only expansion team that didn't have a draft their first year. They had to make do with expansion players from the other teams in the league, and it was a lot of guys who were at the end of their careers, guys who were hurt, and kids right out of school. That first year was interesting. We practiced at an old baseball stadium, and the conditions were just terrible. We had rats in the dressing room, and the drains were plugged in the showers. We put tape over the holes in the building, but when we dressed down there in November, those northers blew through the holes and it was colder than the devil, a far cry from the present Cowboy facilities. Something like two hundred players came through training camp, and it was like a Greyhound bus station. I was throwing passes to guys I had never seen before and never saw again.

We should have won two or three games that first year, but ended up 0–11–1. It was fun, though, and there was never any question that Tom Landry was going to have a great football team before he was finished. We didn't have the talent at first; none of the expansion teams did. If you go back and look at the rosters for those first few years, not too many of the players are household names. But it wasn't very long before you could tell that the Cowboys were going to be good. Each year things got a little better, and when guys like Bob Lilly and Chuck Howley came along, and Don Meredith started to show his potential, you knew Dallas was going to be a winner.

There was never any friction between Don and myself because it was obvious that he was the quarterback of the future. We became more friends than competitors, and that was a lot of fun because he had his own style. It was exciting, working with somebody I got along with so well. The last year I was there he was starting to come along real well, and I've always thought he was a really good quarterback who's terribly underrated. If you look at the record, he took the Cowboys to several championships and also played with a lot of pain along the way.

When the '63 season ended, it was obvious that Don would take over, so I thought it was finally time to bow out. I suppose I could have stayed with the Cowboys for a few more years, but I just didn't want to spend those years on the bench. Today with the salaries these guys are making, I'd probably have done it, but that's really not true either. I was making good money for the time, and I just had no desire to stand around and watch other people play football.

When I quit, I was an old football player and a young lawyer. I went to Nevada and ran a cement plant operation that Clint Murchison of the Cowboys owned for a year and a half. Then I went to practice law with a firm in Reno. From Reno I went with the Laxalt firm, and we opened up an office in Las Vegas to handle the Howard

Hughes account. No, I never got to meet him. You'd talk to people up in that suite where he was, and there would be voices in the background. You thought it was him, but that was the extent of it. I was out there for thirteen years and left in 1977 to go with the Atlanta Falcons as their general manager.

A position like that is the same in all sports. You have big ups and you also have big downs. Everything is based on winning, and how you do financially is kind of secondary to how you do in the standings. It's a lot different than any other kind of business, where you're only trying to make a profit. You're also in the public eye all the time, and everybody is watching how you do. They know a lot more about you than the average businessman. It was a very interesting experience, and some parts of it were very enjoyable. Other parts were very frustrating.

About two years ago I left the Falcons and I'm now a partner in the law firm of Powell, Goldstein, Frazer, and Murphy, a large law firm in Atlanta. We also have offices in Washington, and I spend time between the two places. During the recent strike, I was retained by the management council of the National Football League in connection with the negotiations, and then, when they broke down, with the strike. I was involved with the replacement players and the teams that played through. Ultimately I think they'll be able to work this thing out because both sides really do want a bargaining agreement.

I was the players' rep for most of the years I played. The Players Association came into being in 1956, and we never felt that we wanted to be a union. I think we made some progress during that time, but it became a different type of organization after people like Garvey got involved. It isn't a group trying to help the sport anymore; now it's strictly an adversarial situation. The last thing I was involved with was the initial beginnings of the pension plan, and we thought that was a big step forward.

There wasn't the money involved when we were playing, and most of us felt that playing professional football was a nice way to set aside a little money until you found out what you wanted to do. You have a lot of players today who want to play football for a few years and then never have to work again. That's bad thinking. They should see it for what it is, a great game that you can play for a few years while you get ready to do what you're going to do for the next thirty or forty years of your life.

GEORGE, YOUR FRIENDS ARE CALLING YOU

GEORGE RATTERMAN

QUARTERBACK

Buffalo Bills 1947–49

Montreal Allouettes 1950

New York Yanks 1950–51

Cleveland Browns 1952–56

The greatest all-around athlete in the history of Notre Dame.

—Frank Leahy

SOMETIMES I worry about myself. To this day, I'll be watching a game, and if some guy really gets nailed I'll say to my wife, "Hey, come watch this guy get hit." I participated in the sport for ten years, as a professional, in high school, and in college before that, and you get so you appreciate the hard hits. Somebody gets blasted, and you find football players laughing and carrying on.

If you're a smaller guy, like I was, you sort of take pride in the fact that you could go out there with those big people who were trying to hurt you and still get up. Artie Donovan told me one time, "The thing that made me maddest about you was chasing you around in the backfield and you'd be laughing at us." I always tried to laugh at them and not try and intimidate guys like Donovan. You didn't want to tease them, do things like point fingers in their face. If you're a boxer, there's two ways you can win. You can outbox the other guy or you can knock him out. Same thing in football. You can out-finesse the other players or beat up on them, intimidate them, put them out of the game—that's one way of winning a football game, and there's nothing dirty about it. If you're going to play the game, you have to be able to stand up under physical combat. Your good quarterbacks stay in there and throw the ball, even if they know they're going to get knocked down. Then they get up and throw it again. "Bucko" Kilroy, Ed Meadows, Hardy Brown, Ed Sprinkle; they were going to win by intimidation. A guy like Doak Walker or "Crazylegs" Hirsch—they weren't going to hurt anybody, so they went around them.

Ed Sprinkle always played right end on defense and, being a right-handed passer, I didn't see him coming a lot of times. We were playing the Bears in a preseason game, and at one point they took Sprinkle out of the game. I was relieved about that, but then they put in some kid who was determined that he was going to be meaner than Sprinkle. I wasn't paying too much attention to him, and after the play was over he kicked me. I was out for two weeks because Ed Sprinkle's replacement kicked me in the rear.

Bucko took a swing at me one day, and I wasn't even playing. You feel pretty safe if you're a second-string quarterback standing on the sidelines. A play came our way, and when Bucko came running by he looked up at the last minute. He must have seen a face that wasn't familiar, figured I must be on the other side, and swung an elbow at me. Fortunately I ducked and the elbow sailed over my head. Bucko probably deserved his reputation, but it was hard for me to understand a guy like that. He had a big family, and I couldn't imagine him with all those little kids at home going out and acting like that on Sundays.

I don't know what they do today, but in my time it was fairly common for everybody on a team to throw in a buck, and whoever got the opposing quarterback out of the game, he would get the $32 jackpot. When I was playing for New York, the Rams had beaten us in Yankee Stadium, and I walked over to the Rams' locker room to say hello to Bill Smyth, an old friend from Cincinnati. I walked in and heard somebody saying behind a row of lockers, "What are we going to do with the Ratterman money?" I asked Bill what they were talking about, and he explained that I had lasted the whole game. They ended up giving $25 to a lineman who had suffered a fine during the afternoon, possibly trying for me, and put the rest into the pot for next Sunday's game.

In those days players were more susceptible to what you might call short-term injuries. You could knock a guy out of the game, but he would be playing the next week. A lot of backs didn't have face masks, so you could break a guy's nose, things like that. You didn't have the pads. They developed the armor they wear today, the face masks and huge shoulder pads, to avoid the minor injuries, and now they put a guy out for the year. Finally they developed artificial turf and now you can lose somebody for three years.

I grew up in Cincinnati, where you played baseball because at that time Cincinnati was strictly a baseball town. Everybody followed the Reds, and the American Legion team that won the championship in Cincinnati automatically went on to win the national championship. I played baseball in high school and college, but I wasn't good enough to go beyond that. At one point I played two years of semi-pro ball, and that's when I first started to notice that the pitchers were getting better and I wasn't.

My father played a lot of sports when he was young, and he encouraged us to get involved with athletics. I had two brothers and one sister, and he always provided us, depending on the season, with the tennis racket or whatever piece of equipment we needed.

The only thing he didn't want me doing was playing golf. My high school athletic director told me that years later I'd never thought about it, but sometimes I'd ask him if I could use his clubs, and he would always find a way to say no. "Why don't you go play some tennis instead?" Tennis was fine because you were active, and after you played you came home. At that time we belonged to a country club, and he didn't want me hanging around and meeting the wrong kind of people.

My oldest brother, Fred, was an excellent athlete. My other brother, Pat, was also older than I, but he only played a little basketball. Fred went to the University of Michigan and never played a game of football for them because he hurt his knee. In those days when you got a knee injury, that was that. When Fred got hurt, Pat said that was the only time he ever saw my father cry.

I had my first experience with professional football when I was just a youngster. Bill Hewitt was a great end who played for the Bears at one time. He didn't wear a helmet until the league passed a rule that he had to. My brother knew him because Hewitt played at Michigan. The Bears were in Cincinnati to play a preseason game, and they were staying in the Metropole Hotel. After the game we went to Hewitt's room, and he asked me if I would like the "game ball." This was about 1934, and in those days you didn't have three dozen footballs to use during a game. You had the "game ball." When my brother and I were leaving, we heard a voice down at the end of the hall. It was George Halas yelling, "Bill, someone told me you had the 'game ball.' Do you know where it is?" My brother grabbed me and we started down the hall and I dropped the damn ball. Fred recovered the fumble, and, with me in one hand and the ball in the other, we went down the fire escape with Halas yelling at us that we were stealing the "game ball."

In high school I threw the football long and often, if not always with dead-eye aim. We played one team that had us considerably outmanned, but we almost won the game by my heaving the ball sixty-two times. We played everything in high school—single wing, double wing, the Notre Dame box, and some T-formations. They called me a quarterback no matter where I lined up. In my senior year we were good enough to win the city championship, and I've still got a series of letters that my father wrote to Earl Blaik at Army. He told him that first of all, I would win a national championship for them in football. That would be sort of automatic. Then I would be the greatest general that the Army had ever seen. The gist of his letters was that the government was being remiss if they didn't insist that I go to West Point. I think he sent some similar letters to Annapolis, where he said I'd be a great admiral instead of a general.

When I was a senior in high school, I enlisted in the Navy V-12 program. You could list three schools that you wanted to attend, and I put down Notre Dame as my first choice. My father and mother took me to see Ed McKeever, who at that time was the head coach at Notre Dame, and he described it later: "This guy brings his kid over to my house, and the kid looked like he had consumption." At that time I weighed 149 pounds and was a little over six feet. I wasn't too husky. McKeever continued, "The kid never said a word all evening. The father did all the talking, telling me how his kid would be the savior for Notre Dame football." At that time they had just won the national championship, and Bertelli and Lujack were the quarterbacks.

McKeever must have thought I could do something because I did end up going to Notre Dame in 1944. The Navy had us standing watches in the middle of the night, and they marched us around a lot, but we were mainly college students. You couldn't play college athletics your first semester if you were in the Navy; however, they would let you practice. I managed to break my collarbone, so it really didn't matter.

I played football, basketball, baseball, and tennis at Notre Dame. They seem to want players to stick to one sport today, which I think can be a mistake. You pick up different competitive skills from playing basketball, or some other sport, that you don't get from football. It's also a lot more interesting. Today the football coach wants his players lifting weights in the off-season, and it's questionable how healthful it is for these kids. You see these guys with necks bigger than their heads who weight over three hundred pounds. What's going to happen when those guys get to be fifty and aren't getting any exercise?

I started to think about a career in professional football when they booted me out of Notre Dame for missing curfew. At that time Notre Dame was a pretty strict school, and people ranked it right up there with West Point and the Naval Academy as far as the rules went. It was springtime, my third year, and I wanted to get married, so I said the heck with it. I had an offer to play professional football with the Buffalo Bills of the old All-America Conference.

I had actually contacted the 49ers first. Buck Shaw, who was a Notre Dame guy, was the coach out there, and Frankie Albert was their quarterback. Albert was in the construction business and wanted to move to Los Angeles. Shaw thought he might need a quarterback, so he came to Cincinnati to see me. He offered me $5,000, which was sort of standard for those days, and after some negotiating I got him up to $7,000. When I had lunch with him the next day, he upped it to $7,500. I thought if things were moving this quickly I should contact some other teams. Clem Crowe, another Notre Dame alumnus, was an assistant coach at Buffalo, and I contacted him. Pretty soon the 49ers and Bills were bidding against each other. I finally got both teams up to $11,000.

I think I had a reputation in the professional football world as being pretty good at negotiating contracts. In those days you didn't do that. Paul Brown or whoever would say, "You're getting $8,000." That was it, and if you didn't sign you had better find another way to make a living. The other players seemed to admire the fact that I was willing to stand up to the general manager and get a good contract. One piece of advice my father gave to me—he was a lawyer and a CPA—was to always wear a hat when I was dickering with a businessman. I used that advice when I was talking to Ted Collins, owner of the New York Yanks, and even went so far as to buy a fancy briefcase which contained nothing more than the morning newspaper.

I was with my father at Toots Shor's restaurant in New York one evening, and several prominent sportswriters, including Red Smith, were sitting at the next table. My father had cancer at the time, and I went over to their table and asked them if they'd come over and say hello to him. My dad got a big kick out of that, and Red Smith was kind enough to pay me what I still consider a glowing compliment. He told me, "You may not be the best passer in the National Football League, but you do have the best reputation for talking contract."

Playing in Buffalo was fine because it was just a bigger version of South Bend. A shot-and-a-beer town. There is a very large Polish population, and most of them are Catholic. Anybody from Notre Dame is the greatest person in the world. The only thing I didn't like was the weather. My wife and I stayed there during the off-season one year, and they actually had to put ropes along the sidewalks in downtown Buffalo for people to hold on to. Otherwise the wind would blow you right out into the street.

At that time we played in War Memorial Stadium. The city is going to tear it down this year, so last summer they had a dedication ceremony in reverse. A bunch of old football and baseball players from different eras were invited back, and we had a real nice time. War Memorial wasn't a bad field to play on because all football fields were the same in those days. You saw one, you saw them all. My first year, 1947, we were 8–4–2. We came in second in the Eastern Division, and the next year we got into the playoffs and Cleveland killed us.

During the off-season I had been attending law school, and I decided that I would skip the 1949 season and go to school full-time for a year. I made arrangements with Frank Leahy at Notre Dame so I could work on the coaching staff while I was going to school, and I signed a contract with the New York Yanks for 1950. Buffalo lost their first game in 1949 and made me an offer I couldn't resist. I said, "I'll play for you, but it's got to be a one-year contract. I've already signed with the Yanks for next year." That year we were 5–5–2, and Buffalo went out of business when the league folded.

After I got to New York, I had a dispute with the Yanks and ended up going to Canada and playing for the Montreal Allouettes. In those days if you were an American and went up to play Canadian football, you were a big hero. It was like a Canadian hockey player coming down here. You're going to win the championship for them. Unfortunately, our team was 3–9 and instead of a big hero, I was the big goat. I was sort of happy to get out of Montreal after that season because we didn't have a good line and I wasn't a running quarterback. I was getting tired of getting knocked over backward. The Yanks sued me, claiming that I was under contract with them, and I settled that by coming back after the Canadian season and playing the final six games with New York.

The first year, in New York, I think we had one of the finest group of football players I've ever seen on one team. Buddy Young, Zollie Toth, George Taliaferro, they were all good backs. Sherman Howard, Spec Sanders, we had good material all over the place. John Yonaker came to New York from Cleveland, and he said that in his opinion the Browns didn't have the material we had in New York. And they were the champions.

We were leading the league, 6–1, and then Duke Iverson, a great linebacker, got hurt. We only had thirty guys in those days, and they had to play Lou Kusserow, who had been a fullback at Columbia, at linebacker. He had never played linebacker in his life and probably never should have. We lost four straight games and were out of it, but we still had a great team.

When I came back in 1951, the Yanks were an entirely different organization. A lot of the players had left, and there was talk about moving the team to Dallas. I went to see Ted Collins, and he assured me that it was just a rumor. I said, "Then, you won't mind writing in my contract that if the teams moves, I'll become a free agent." It amazed me, but he put it in, and when they moved to Dallas the next year, I was technically free to go where I wanted.

Frankly I more or less arranged my trade to Cleveland because I was fascinated by Paul Brown. I had played against his teams, very unsuccessfully, and had heard so much about him that I wanted to find out what made him tick. Cleveland was way ahead of everybody else because Paul Brown was a great coach and he had very good assistants. Blanton Collier coached the defense, and every winter he could take the films home with him to Kentucky and go through them, play by play. He'd grade every player on technique, blocking, all of that, and nobody was doing anything like that in professional football at that time.

I played behind Otto Graham for four years and only threw six passes my first year. If we were way ahead or way behind, I would go in, but very few times in close ball games. As far as Paul Brown was concerned, your first year with him was your rookie year. Forget everything you learned any place else. We were playing San Francisco at home, and Otto was having one of his mediocre afternoons. Late in the third quarter, the 49ers intercepted a pass and the fans started chanting, "We want Ratterman!" Since I was the only reserve quarterback, I knew they had no other choice. Brown beckoned to me and I took off my hood, reached for my shiny unmarked helmet, and went down to find out how I was going to win the game. "George, your friends are calling you," Brown said, pausing for dramatic effect. "Maybe you'd better go up there in the stands and sit with them awhile."

Otto Graham was one of the great quarterbacks. He was very competitive and always on the winning side. Other people would have better statistics, could throw the ball farther or harder, but Otto's team had the most points at the end of the game. He reminded me of Joe DiMaggio. Ted Williams could hit the ball better, but the Red Sox never won the championship. DiMaggio was very quietly doing his thing and the Yankees won every year. One of Otto's other talents was his ability to put his foot in his mouth. He would invariably say something to somebody that he shouldn't. He'd be talking to a group of people and would make some ethnic comment, and it would turn out that somebody in the group was Greek or Polish, or whatever.

In addition to calling all the plays from the sidelines, Paul Brown always gave us the first six plays of the game. He was always afraid that the locker room might be bugged, so even in our own stadium he wouldn't say anything. He'd get up there and write on the board, "The first play is," and would then make a motion. The first time I saw it, I asked somebody, "What's he doing?" They said, "He wants a screen pass." Then he'd hold up two fingers and wigwag another motion. That meant we were running off-tackle. Anything he wrote on the blackboard, he would erase immediately. Mike McCormack told me, "Any outsider who wandered in during our pregame briefing would think Brown was coaching the State School for the Deaf."

I guess if Brown was doing that sort of thing himself, he figured the other teams were doing it too. When I was with Buffalo, we played a championship game against the Browns. We were working out in Cleveland Stadium the day before the game, and for some reason they picked that day to paint the stadium. We noticed that when we started practicing, the painters would put down their brushes and take out pads and pencils. They were writing down everything we were doing.

Unfortunately for me, Otto retired after the 1955 season and I had to play. In the fourth game I was hurt on a quarterback sneak. Lou Groza was pushed by somebody and hit my knee from the side. I found out it's not supposed to bend sideways. The doctors said that surgery wouldn't guarantee anything, and since I was thirty years old I decided to move on to something else.

In the off-season I had been working in the investment business. When I was in New York I worked for a firm on Wall Street and when I moved to Cincinnati I went with the same company because that's where their main office was located. Eventually I started my own company, which didn't go well, and then worked for a wealthy family in Cincinnati as their investment adviser. At the time I was living across the river in Kentucky, and I got involved in a reform political movement. First thing I knew, I was elected sheriff of Campbell County. It was very exciting, but somebody stole my gun and I lost by badge, so I decided I wasn't cut out to be a sheriff. I had broken off my connections with the investment community in Cincinnati, so when I had an opportunity to work with a firm out here in Denver, we moved. That was 1967.

Today I'm primarily a teacher. I teach real estate, insurance, and securities for a proprietary school, Real Estate Prep, and also do similar teaching for the University of Colorado on a part-time basis. I've been doing that for eleven years and really enjoy the work. A lot of the people I teach are adults who are getting their real estate license for a second career. Out of twenty students there is usually going to be some guy who, at about the third lecture, says, "Are you the George Ratterman who use to play football?" I say, "Yeah," and he goes out at the next break and tells everybody that I used to play professional football. They, of course, all say, "Bullshit." Everybody expects a football player to be somebody who weighs 280 and snarls instead of talking to you. Some of the time I use correct English, and they really don't expect that.

PART

III

HITTERS

THE MEANEST MAN IN FOOTBALL

EDWARD SPRINKLE

END

Chicago Bears 1944–55

Ed Sprinkle of the Chicago Bears has a peculiar talent for winding up in gridiron brawls. He gets that way apparently living up to the club motto: "Do unto others before others do unto you."

—Bill Fay, *Collier's*

Sprink's got to go in high—with his arms up—so he can slap at the ball or tackle around the shoulders. He's got to push and shove and claw his way past those blockers, and if somebody gets an unintentional whack in the nose now and then—well, that's football.

—George Halas

I grew up on a farm near Tuscola, Texas, south of Abilene. I never knew there was a Depression going on because we were pretty well self-contained. Everything we needed we grew on the farm, and there was enough money to buy a few staples and our clothes.

Tuscola High School was very small, and we didn't have enough players for regular football, but during my senior year they organized a six-man football league. We played touch-tackle, and it was fast. There was a center, two ends, and three backs, and everybody was eligible for a pass. We didn't have many reserves. In fact, I was one of two boys in my graduating class. I was offered an academic scholarship to Hardin-Simmons University in Abilene, Texas.

"Bulldog" Turner had made All-American at Hardin-Simmons the previous year, and when I was a freshman, he came back as an adviser to help with spring training. I knew, of course, that Bulldog was playing pro ball for the Bears, but I never planned a career around it. I was majoring in mathematics because I always had a good head for figures and wanted to get into some kind of engineering. Back then the media coverage wasn't anything near what it is today, and professional football was far removed from the state of Texas. All your teams at that time were in the east, and we didn't hear that much about it.

Bulldog liked my speed and thought I was aggressive enough, but told me I should forget about being a running back. To tell the truth, he told me I was too awkward to be a back and should play somewhere on the line. I took his advice and played center and tackle for the next two years. The first year I played at Hardin-Simmons, we played single wing, and then they brought in a new coach, Warren Woodsen, who had been very successful over the years. With Bulldog's help he installed the T-formation, and it was very effective. It was a very basic type of T-formation, but we had a great running game. In my junior year we had the nation's leading ground gainer, a guy by the name of "Little Doc" Mobley.

After three years at Hardin-Simmons, I got an appointment to Annapolis and played one year of football there. Then I dropped out of the Academy and joined the Naval Air Corps Reserve in what they called the V-5 Program. You were able to go to college at the same time you were getting your naval pilot training. I wanted to become a fighter pilot, but I guess the Navy was overstocked and they canceled the program during the summer of 1944. I went back to Texas and was trying to figure out what to do next when Bulldog called and asked if I wanted to drive up to the Bears' training camp with him. He thought I might be able to make the team, so I figured I didn't have anything to lose. It was just one of those things that happens.

I think I was very lucky to come into the league when I did because a lot of the regular players weren't back from the service yet. The Bears had a team that had won three championships in a row, and there wouldn't have been openings for more than two or three guys if the war hadn't come along. By the time they got back, I was pretty well established, and I guess they knew I was a football player. I think, without a doubt, the person who helped me the most with my career was Bulldog. If it hadn't been for him, I don't think I would have ever had the opportunity to play professional ball because I was pretty small and he really went to bat for me in training camp that first year. If I had come up to camp on my own and tried out at tackle, they would have probably cut me right away because I only weighed 190 at the time. The press likes to write about the time I broke Bulldog's nose, but it was something I didn't even know about at the time. We had played Green Bay and were having a beer afterward at the Cottage Restaurant. He walked in with a broken nose, and I said, "What happened to you? Who did that?" He said, "If I told you, you wouldn't believe me. You did!" I guess I had run by him while he was on the ground and swung my elbow and hit him right in the nose.

"Hunk" Anderson was coaching the Bears at that time, since Halas was in the Navy. When Hunk asked how much I weighed, I told him, "About 188." He said, "Things are tough, but they aren't that tough. We can't use 188-pound tackles. You play guard." I didn't mind because I was just glad to make the team, so I played guard until Halas came back from the Navy in 1946 and took over again as coach. He told Anderson, "The big boys are coming back. We better move this kid out to end before he gets killed." I played ten years as a defensive end and also played some offense in the beginning. I didn't have the greatest nimble fingers, but I did manage to catch a few passes.

Halas was a very tough task master, and I was never happy with he money he paid me, but we got along all right because I think he respected me as a football player, and I respected him as a businessman, coach, and tactician. I think the game of football, even today, has to have a certain amount of what guys like Halas brought to the game. You take Vince Lombardi, Don Shula, Paul Brown, or Mike Ditka—they're showing the same capabilities; it's a highly regimented game, and you can't just let everybody go helter-skelter in their own direction and be successful.

I was always proud to wear number seven when I played for the Bears. When Halas first started the team, he owned it, coached it, and also played end. That was in the 1920s, and he wore that number for seven seasons. You had to be tough to wear number seven and play for the Bears.

There were a few guys who didn't have the right attitude and they didn't last long, especially back in those days when there were so few teams. I know Halas didn't keep them around, and once you were released, there was no place else to go. Halas would call up Art Rooney and say, "Don't take him, he doesn't want to play," or "Take this guy, he's one hell of a hitter." Those owners were great buddies, and they would deal back and forth that way. If you crossed one of them, you might as well forget about a career in professional football.

As far as my reputation as a player, I figured I had a job to do, and I wasn't the biggest guy in the world to do it, so I had to try other means. *Collier's* magazine had an article about me called "The Meanest Man in Football." Bill Fay, who worked for the old *Sun Times* or *Herald American,* I forget which, wrote the article, and it probably did more harm than good at the time. I never really played dirty football in my life, but I'd knock the hell out of a guy if I had a chance. It was just part of the game of football to me. If a halfback ran by, you clotheslined him. If I had an opportunity to hit someone, I hit them. When I was playing, I had the reputation with my teammates and George Halas as being the roughest player the Bears ever had. I don't think that means that I was a dirty player. I always thought that article was a bum rap.

They used to write about the fact that Charlie Trippi and I were having a feud, but that wasn't how it was at all. We were big rivals at that time, the Bears and the Cardinals—they were the Chicago Cardinals then—and it was my object to stop Trippi. It was my *duty* to stop him. Naturally you're going to get some tempers flaring up in a situation like that, but the media would make a big issue out of it every time we'd play each other. They'd act like it was going to be war out there. I've played in several golf tournaments with Charlie, and we get along just fine. I never had any hatred for anybody I played against. I'd beat the hell out of a guy all afternoon and then go out and have a drink with him.

When players were going both ways, they would usually excell in one or the other. I liked to play both ways, I really did, because I enjoyed blocking, especially hitting those linebackers, but I guess I was better on defense. On defense there were all sorts of things you could do to keep a guy from catching a pass. The easiest was tripping and that's pretty easy to figure out. You sort of put your foot out and let the other guy fall over it. Then there's chucking, where you put your hands out like you're going to push the receiver, but you grab onto his shirt and hold on for a couple of seconds. This throws off his timing. The hardest was spinning. You grabbed a guy's shirt as he was running by and yanked. If you were strong enough and timed it right, he'd spin himself right out of the play.

Everybody that's played the game realizes that the quarterback is the guy who can beat you. In those days you had guys like Baugh, Waterfield, and Graham, and there was no way you were going to beat those teams if you gave those quarterbacks time to throw the ball. Sid Luckman was the reason the Bears had been so successful. He was the first T-formation quarterback with the Chicago Bears, and Sid was blessed with wonderful talent himself and good receivers. The Bears had talent galore. Sid would throw that ball out there and his receivers would find a way to catch it.

I think my forte was quickness. I couldn't go through or over those big linemen, so I'd go around them to get at the passer. I'm left-handed, and that definitely helped me on my pass rush. Since I played right defensive end and my strong side was my left side, I could come in there and reach over blockers and get the quarterback. My left arm was always toward the passer. They call them sacks now and keep records and make a big deal out of it. We called it tackling the quarterback, and it was your job. If you could knock the quarterback out of the game, that's what you'd try to do.

When we played the Browns, I used to belt Groza, and it got so he didn't like to block me. He'd switch blocking assignments and have Abe Gibron come out and block on me. I weighed 210 and Gibron was 270, something like that, so there's a guy I would have to go around. The Browns were always tough to play because they were just so good.

The Eagles had Steve Van Buren and you really knew it if you got in front of him. He was one of the first of the big running backs and was as big as I was. A lot of those quarterbacks and runners were big stars, and I don't think they thought they should be hit as hard as I liked to hit them.

The 49ers had a hell of a team, and when we went out there to play them we had some really great games. Hugh McElhenny was their big star at that time, and during one game I hit him probably as hard as he'd ever been hit in his life. He really got mad, and it seemed to me that he wasn't used to being treated that way.

There were a lot of great football players around when I was playing, and they're the ones who are responsible for the game we have today. You can go way back into the 1920s, and there were some damn good players in those days, but the pro game wasn't organized enough at that time. Hell, you'd have fifteen or twenty guys on a team and they might practice two or three nights a week. They didn't even play a schedule a lot of times, they just played whenever they could arrange a game. College ball was much more sophisticated in a lot of ways, and they had all the press coverage. When Halas brought in the T-formation, it really began to turn into the modern game and people started to notice professional football.

I don't envy the guys today—by that I mean all the pressure they have to play with that we didn't have to worry about—but I do envy the opportunities that they're getting. When we had championship teams, a guy might get a little press coverage, but it didn't really amount to much and endorsements were unheard of. Look at the Bears after they won the Super Bowl—they were doing everything. Not only did they win, they were very charismatic, and you need that if you're doing to sell anything. I've heard it said that William "The Refrigerator" Perry made about $4 million that one year, and that's a great deal of money for a lineman. All of the Bear players were going out on personal appearances, and they were getting $20,000 for doing the same thing we were lucky to get $25 for. Show up, talk a little bit, and then open it up for discussion. You can get $20,000 for that?

The players today are big and fast, I have to grant them that, and they're probably better athletes than we were, but we were just as tough and played just as hard. Television, money, a lot of things like that have changed the concept of the game, and being mean like a few of us were isn't part of the game today.

I was a very physical player, and it got to a point where, if I played hard on Sunday, it would be Wednesday or Thursday before I felt like I could really run at 100 percent. I guess you could say I was getting old and it was getting harder to play like I wanted to—everything had taken its toll. Plus the fact that the times were starting to change. Just after I retired, they started to go to the four-man line and you really had four tackles up there. You didn't have an end like I was, you had somebody like Doug Atkins, who took my place on the Bears. He was six-eight, 270 pounds, tremendous, and that's another thing that helped me make up my mind to quit. If I played today, I'm sure I could have beefed myself up a lot from where I was in those days with the weight programs and other things they use, but I probably would have had to play weak-side linebacker.

My last year was 1955, and I had already gone into the tile-and-carpet business while I was playing. I stayed with that for twenty years, but new construction got a little slow in the 1970s and I'd had enough. I was always chasing my money, so I decided I didn't want to bother with it anymore. I'm now working as a rental fleet manager for Motor Vacations in Elgin. We sell recreational vehicles, and the business is interesting and getting bigger all the time. My job has a certain amount of public relations work that goes along with it, and that helps sales and rentals. Somebody will come in who remembers who I am and we'll get to talking about the Bears and every little thing helps. Most of them it's the ones who are my age, and that's good for business because they're the people who can retire and buy one of these motor homes.

I never had the opportunity to get into coaching. At one point I mentioned it kind of offhand to Halas and he said, "Well, yeah, why don't you come on down," but never offered me any money. "Come on down and do it for free" is what he meant. It was probably just as well because I thought I owed it to my family, after twelve years, to get out of the game. Coaching, you're away more than when you were playing. You have to go out scouting and interviewing, and if you were on Halas's staff, he would have meetings at ten or eleven at night, every night. My wife would have probably wound up leaving me.

I couldn't stand to sit in the stands for the first few years because I wanted to go down there on the field, but I finally got away from it far enough to just enjoy it as a game. Then it got to the point in the 1970s where the Bears were such a decadent ballclub, from the front office on down, that we didn't even want to go to the stadium. I had season tickets, but it was so discouraging that I got rid of them and watched the Bears on TV. At least then if they were bad, you could turn them off. Now they're exciting again and they've got a good coach. Their defense is quick, and there's no question in my mind that Jim McMahon is the best quarterback around if he's healthy and keeps his head on straight. When they won the Super Bowl, I saw him do things that were unbelievable. Shades of Otto Graham or Bobby Layne or Terry Bradshaw—he could do it all. I think the Bears are back, and they've got a lot of fans all over the country.

I don't really have any one game that I could pinpoint as my ultimate game, but the championship game we played against the Giants in 1946 meant as much to me as any game I was ever in. I got into the Giants' backfield and hooked my arm around Frank Filchock's chin. He threw short, and Dante Magnani intercepted it and ran it back for the deciding touchdown. Steve Owen, the Giants' coach, said later that I was one of the dominant factors in the game, and that made me feel pretty good.

The fans would get on me when we went out of town, but that's typical and it never got to me, one way or the other. I think that's one of the things that makes pro football so popular—the fans need somebody to vent their feelings on. The Chicago fans always liked me, and for a number of years they would introduce the former players at halftime when the Bears were at home. I always got a great ovation when they introduced me.

They had a day for me the last game I played before I retired, "Ed Sprinkle Day." There was a nice halftime ceremony and the Bear fans gave me a nice new Olds 98. We beat Detroit, and it was just a fitting climax to what I thought was a great career. It was a long way from that farm in Texas. I would never have believed it if somebody had told me when I was a kid that I would someday play football and get paid for it.

LOVE YOUR GOD, RESPECT YOUR ELDERS, AND FEAR NO SON-OF-A-BITCH THAT WALKS

FRANCIS J. KILROY

TACKLE

Phil.–Pitt. Steagles 1943

Philadelphia Eagles 1944–56

The Philadelphia Eagles are known around the league as ornery critters, and the orneriest of them all is Guard Frank Kilroy. His advice to men playing alongside him: "Use your feet, not your hands—you'll only bust your hands."

—Life

At the trial they called different witnesses for and against Kilroy and at one point Cloyce Box was on the stand. The Judge asked him to define an "ornery critter" and Cloyce said, "In my part of the country it's a domesticated animal that ain't been domesticated yet." Even the judge started to laugh.

—Doak Walker

MY real name is Francis, and people didn't start to call me "Bucko" until sometime in the 1950s. Before that, I was Frank Kilroy in the league. There was an old public relations guy, Al Ennis, who worked for the National Football League, and he started saying, "Frank, you're a fine bucco of a fellow." They changed the spelling and the name stuck. The league office doesn't like it, and they always call me Frank. They don't think Bucko sounds right, especially when I have a lovely name like Francis.

Half of the personnel people in the league started out working with me, and if you get around the business end of professional football you'll hear about "Buckoisms." For instance: "In our day the coaches tested the players; today the players test the coach." I'll never forget when I saw it starting to change and the guy who brought it to my attention was Rip Engle, the Penn State coach. It must have been around 1960 when he said, "I can't believe it. For the first time in my life I've been questioned by a player. I guess we're dealing with a new breed."

I've been in this game four decades, going of my fifth. When I went with the Eagles, I will never forget telling my teammate Vic Sears, "Oh, I'll play pro ball for a couple years just to prove I can do it. Then I'll quit and do something else." You figure the average football player is in the league for four years, so I've seen ten different generations of players and I think I've grown with them. I like the players today, but there's a big difference between the type of individual they are and what we were. In the days you're talking about, you had to be a complete ball player. Most of the people today are specialists and could never play our game because they wouldn't have the endurance to be able to cover on special teams. You watch these players, and after four or five plays they're tired. In fact coaches try to keep the defense off the field because once they rush the passer a few times, the big guys are exhausted. For these players who weigh 280, 290, 310 to play our kind of game, they'd have to get down to around 230.

They have the same frames that we had in the 1950s and, to be perfectly frank, one of the reasons they're so big today is steroids. That's been going on for over twenty years, but people have just begun speaking out in the last four years. They're illegal in pro football and college, but it's a big problem since kids are using them in high school because they're afraid they won't get a scholarship. We test at the beginning of the year and then again at the end of the year. If there's a reason—and we have to have real cause—we can test them again. In the past two years these colleges have tested and banned these players from postseason bowl games. They didn't have to test for anything when I was playing because all we did was drink beer. We couldn't afford anything else.

There wouldn't be any game today if those players hadn't been willing to play for almost nothing. Maybe a few players like Sammy Baugh were getting paid good money, but just about everybody else had to have another job to survive. I was always in the automobile business, first selling Hudsons and then a Lincoln/Mercury dealership. The customers knew me from football, and that sure did help to sell a lot of cars. That's another Buckoism: "Any athlete who has any kind of recognition should be in sales."

I grew up in the northeast section of Philadelphia, and my father was a restaurateur and politician. They go pretty good together. He was a World War I hero and had won all kinds of medals, including the Distinguished Service Cross, for wiping out a couple of machine-gun nests, that sort of thing. He was gassed seven times, and that's what finally killed him. He had holes in his lungs and died when he was only fifty-six.

We owned several bars around Shibe Park; they were all called Kilroy's, and one of them had the longest bar in Philadelphia at that time, seventy-two feet. When the baseball games let out, everybody would go in and have a beer. They call them sports bars now; in those days they were called saloons.

My family has always been involved with athletics, and two of my grand uncles, Matt and Mike Kilroy, were big league baseball players. Both of them were pitchers, and when Matt was playing for the Orioles he pitched three no-hit, no-run games during the 1886 season. Matt also has the strikeout record, the old one, for one season, 504. I was primarily a baseball player when I was a kid. My father and uncle were very close to John Shibe, the owner of the Philadelphia Athletics, and Connie Mack, the manager. They all wanted me to sign with the Athletics, but by that time I was playing pro football. I actually didn't play much football until I started to go to Northeast Catholic High School, the biggest Catholic high school in the world at that time. We had 5,600 boys, and two of the years that I was there we were not only undefeated, we were unscored upon one year. It was all single wing, and I played guard and tackle. I actually started out as a fullback, but I got big all of a sudden, so that ended that.

When I got out of high school, I went out to Notre Dame. I was there for practice in September of 1939, but then my father got sick. Being the eldest son, I had to come back to Philadelphia. The only school I could get into was Temple because school had already started. Going to college at that time was tough. After the 1936 season, the schools had come in with something much like the section 48 of two years ago. Before that, some of the schools were letting people play who were not actually going to school. They were called tramp athletes or ringers, and they'd transfer from one school to another and they did a lot of other things that weren't exactly on the up-and-up. That all ended and you had to have a C average and no flunks, or you didn't play, period. You had to also pass an entrance exam to get into college, and I know a lot of people who didn't pass, and some of them were real good athletes.

Then the war came along and it got even tougher. If you were in the V-5, V-7, or V-12 programs and your grades weren't good, you'd be a PFC or Seaman Second Class real fast and off you'd go to war. All of that made you really bite the nail. They graduated us as fast as possible. I had my degree in twenty-eight months, so I only played two years of college football. We had some pretty good football players on that team, and my last year we were 8–2, something like that. Just about the whole team ended up playing for one pro team or another. A guy by the name of George Sutch played for the Cardinals. Al Drulis also went with the Cardinals, and his brother, Chuck, was with the Bears. Chuck also coached seven or eight years with Green Bay. Andy Tomasic was one of our backs, and he ended up with Pittsburgh.

I wasn't interested in professional football until I got into college and started talking to some of the other players the team who were thinking about a career with the pros. It seemed to me a way to continue playing football after college, so I went with the Eagles. You couldn't stay in school unless you were in the service, so I had joined the Navy while I was going to Temple, and after I graduated they stationed me in New York. I was doing mostly convoy duty in the North Atlantic and the Mediterranean, first on cargo ships and then on transports. You name it, I was on it. Scary. Believe it or not, they'd ship me back to New York for the football season, and when it was over, I'd go to sea again. The government was doing that with baseball and football players because they said they were keeping the games going for the morale of the civilian population (laughs). I used to come into Philadelphia on Friday night and practice two days with the team and then play on Sunday. By the way, we practiced at night, which was really a job.

My first season, 1943, we were called the Steagles because Philadelphia and Pittsburgh merged for that season. I played for the

Eagles a total of fourteen years and I started out playing both ways, and then they settled me in after the war on offense. I still played defense as a backup player and started playing defense around 1950.

The Eagles in those days were like the Raiders are today. We were tough and we intimidated teams. When people accused us of playing dirty football, our answer was "That's how losers talk." The kind of offense that we had added to our toughness. Our backs were taught to cut back against the grain, and that put the blockers on the other side of the tacklers so we blindsided most of the players we were playing against. They didn't see us coming and we demolished them.

After the war it was a rougher game. The attitude of the 1940s was so much different than it is today. We were part of the American tradition in the old-fashioned meaning. We were raised to love your God, respect your elders, and fear no son-of-a-bitch that walks. That's why we won World War II. In the 1940s, right into the middle 1950s, you couldn't be an athlete and not have been in the service. Those guys who came out of World War II were different kinds of people. I knew them and played with them and they were fearless. After all, most of them didn't have easy duty. They were in the infantry, something like that. A lot of our players didn't come back, and you can check the list of pro football players who died during the war. A lot came back wounded and lame and were never able to play again.

I've talked to a lot of people about it and coming out of World War II, having seen the frustrations and violence of the war, it had to affect the players and the game they played. When was the last time you saw a dead body? I guess that's what I'm trying to say. Most of us never saw one before we got in that war, and then we saw so much, so much of that stink and rot, that when we came back to play football, we play like terrors. We were tough. Everybody used to say, "What outfit was he in?" That was what you asked a guy, not what school he went to. You'd see somebody really getting into something on the field. "What outfit was he in?" "He was a

Marine." "Ohhhhhhh." "Guadalcanal." "Ohhhhhhh." You'd just shake your head.

A lot of things were legal when we played that aren't legal now. The forearm was legal and a strong man can break a two-by-four with a forearm. Our hands could never be out away from our body; they had to always be in close, so that's why we used the elbows. The elbow can be a devastating weapon. Holding will cause a lot of penalties and a lot of fights. If a guy was holding you, the only way you got his attention was to throw an elbow. Up until this March, clipping from behind was legal within a certain area, but that's finally been changed. I'm one of the people who really fought for this change.

Our team that won the World Championship in 1948 and 1949 was made up of people out of the war—Tommy Thompson, Jarmoluk, Walter Burns, Van Buren, Pihos, and all the rest. That was a great football team, and we played and lived together, which established a real close feeling. I was with Dallas when we won championships, and I was here at New England when we won championships. In fact I was coaching when the Eagles won the championship in 1960, but none of those experiences came close to the feeling of being part of the 1948 and 1949 Eagle team. We felt as if we had been through so much together and really thought and played as a team. Both of those games were shutouts, and the 1948 game against the Cardinals was played in a blizzard. The weather was terrible, and the game was scoreless until the fourth quarter. Then I recovered a fumble when Chicago's quarterback, Ray Mallouf, got hit. A couple of plays later, Van Buren ran it in for a score. The next year we played the Rams in a downpour and beat them 14–0.

We used to have a saying, "Don't get hurt because you'll have to play anyway." I didn't really have any bad injuries until the first game of the 1955 season. We were playing the Giants, and when I made a tackle I got caught in the pile, and one of my own players fell on my knee. The Giants were supposedly after me because I had put Arny Galiffa out of a game three years before. Nobody on the

Giants hurt me, but somebody said, "He was the guy," and it started a lot of controversy. I didn't play until the last game of the 1955 season and the knee seemed all right. The next year I twisted my knee again in the last preseason game against the Colts, and it started to swell up. As a result, I was done for the season and retired at the end of that year. The last guy I played against, believe it or not, was Gino Marchetti. "Everybody who plays this game thinks he will play forever." That's another Buckoism. I thought I had a lifetime job in the league and would play until I was at least sixty years old. One thing I try to do in personnel is impress all these players coming in that playing professional football is not a lifetime job. It's a shock when it ends, but you've got to go on from there.

The year I was hurt, *Life* magazine ran an article called "Savagery on Sunday." It was all about violence in the NFL and why I was the worst of the worst. They labeled me "Bad News" Kilroy and the general idea was that I was a villain, the dirtiest player in the league—if not the dirtiest that had ever played. They said I shouldn't be allowed in pro football and that the Giants had caught up with me because of Galiffa and hurt my knee. It was all a bunch of garbage, so I sued them. There were two of us involved: Wayne Robinson, who also played for the Eagles, and myself. We had witnesses for us, they had witnesses against us, and the trial lasted eighteen days. The league had the records of how many times I had been penalized for unnecessary roughness, things like that, and how many times I had been thrown out of a game. The penalties against me were minimal, and I was only thrown out of two games. There were one or two instances, which you are going to have in any contact sport, and those were thrown out of proportion. The Ray Bray case was one of those and got a lot of publicity. In a preseason game with the Bears, Bray was wearing a face mask and I wasn't. After he hit me, he came down on me with that mask and split my nose open. I was on the ground and couldn't do much, so I kicked him in the balls. Bert Bell fined me $250 and my wife gave him hell. She told him that he had cost her a new coat, so Bert said if I behaved myself and didn't get thrown out of any more games he'd give me the money back. I didn't get into any real trouble the rest of the season, and after the last game Bert gave me a check and made me endorse it over to my wife. The joke was that Bert made a mistake and the check was for $500. When she called Bert and told him about it, he said, "Boy, am I lucky. If Bucko had gotten his hands on that money, I would have never seen the other $250."

Robinson and I got the verdict, and we were both awarded $25,000, which was a lot more than I was making playing football at that time. I talked to Bert Bell and a couple of coaches years ago about the case and the reputation that some guys got as rough or dirty football players, and they all said the same thing, "Some guys are just heavy hitters." Any fight fan knows what I'm talking about. Some fighters are pushers, and some really throw a punch. They're the heavy hitters. The same thing in football. Hardy Brown, for instance, was a heavy hitter. Chuck Bednarik was a heavy hitter. Ed Sprinkle was a heavy hitter. Myself, I was a heavy hitter. Of course, the other players will say, "You don't have to do that. You don't have to hit so hard," but instinctively you do. It's been said that you should have eyes in your ears if you want to play football, and these players I've mentioned had great peripheral vision and reacted to anything that happened around them. If somebody got near you, you just reacted automatically. Those players were also good football players. Hardy Brown, in spite of all you hear, was pretty good and he had a snap. He hit you right; he really hurt you. The same with Sprinkle, he had that snap. Bednarik, everybody says he was such a great linebacker, but he was also one of the best centers that ever played football. It was self-preservation out there, and in the 1940s and 1950s the heavy hitters wore the black hats and became the villains.

Another thing, they weren't using public relations in those days like we think of it today. The P.R. of those days was based on exploitation and promotion, especially things of a violent nature. They were trying to sell tickets because the game wasn't anywhere near as popular as it is today. Today public relations is mostly in the business of covering up stuff.

You might have been a villain in the other towns but not in your own stadium—there you were a hero. I never heard any boos in Philadelphia. Now in Chicago, oh boy, you didn't want to get too close to the stands because they'd throw pop bottles at you. Pittsburgh, Cleveland—I could tell you about them all, but that was just part of the game. I never let them get to me, and most of the time it just made me play harder.

The last three years I played I was also coaching the defensive line, so after I quit I stayed with the Eagles and coached for six more years. I enjoyed coaching, I guess, but the Eagles began to send me out to sign players, so I started to get into the personnel business. At the same time I was working part-time for Bert Bell in the league office, viewing films and running the projectors, and I became more interested in the business end of the game. I became the Eagles' player personnel director and was one of the five original scouts in the league, the entire league. Today each team has at least five. At that time the Rams were ahead of everybody else because they had hired a full-time scout, Eddie Kotal, who had been an assistant coach at Green Bay, to scout for them. I'm talking about the 1949, 1950 team, and you know who the general manager was? Tex Schramm of the Cowboys. The publicity man? Pete Rozelle. Those people had a head start and were great, but we gave them a little competition. When I first started scouting for the Eagles, I drafted ten guys who made the team, and four years later, in 1960, we beat Lombardi's Green Bay Packers for the World Championship. After that we learned a lot and got better.

There were very few ex-coaches scouting at that time, and everybody else was being hypothetical. They were all dreaming about what a football player should be, and most of them were drafting out of *Street & Smith's*. That's the truth. I used the players who were on the field at the time as a barometer. During that period of time, the late 1940s and 1950s, there were more superstars in pro football than at any other time. There are those individuals who determine the outcome of the game and a lot of people don't like to hear this, but for that period of time, checking the records and rating the players, we had two hundred of those players in the league. We've never hit that number again; in fact, we've never gone over a hundred and seventy since. I used those great players as a barometer, and we started to gather the numbers—speed, size, basic skills, strength, mental attitude, all that stuff.

I used to go out and time people and measure them, and some of the other scouts used to ridicule me. When we started giving them IQ tests, they really started in on me. We were the first to do any of that, and the other scouts would say, "Aw, why the hell are you doing that? Just look at the guy." A lot of players got drafted based on their looks in those days. We also didn't get into personalities. A lot of guys I played with, as I'm sure you've found out, didn't like me. I didn't like a lot of them either, but that didn't make them bad football players. It wasn't a popularity contest we were running, and we used to say: If you want a popularity contest, you should go to Atlantic City and get in the Miss America contest.

It took us quite a while to accumulate all of that data because when I was with the Eagles I only had Jimmy Gallagher helping me. He was in the office, and I was on the road doing all the scouting. I'd send him back all the information, and he'd keep the records on each guy. That material we gathered helped me when I went with the Redskins, Cowboys, and finally up here to New England.

I went to Washington as personnel director with Bill McPeak, head coach–general manager, in 1962 and worked there until 1965. I had some phenomenal drafts down there (Charles Taylor, Paul Krause, etc.), which I'm still very proud of. Anybody can come up with the first-round choices, but take a look at a guy like Chris Hanburger. He was something like an eighteenth draft choice and ended up playing in seven or eight all-pro games. Buddy Hauss was another one. He was around a ninth-round choice and ended up an all-pro. At the end of the 1965 season, Washington fired Bill

McPeak so I went to Dallas and was there until 1971. That was a grand life with the Cowboys. They work hard when they have to work, and the easiest way to describe them would be to say that they're the most comprehensive team in football. Everything is thought of in advance, and all the bases are covered. They called me the "super" scout while I was at Dallas and somebody once asked me the difference between a scout and a "super" scout. I told him, "Money."

When I came to New England, I had to start from scratch. They didn't have any scouts—nothing. We have been very successful here because Billy Sullivan was the owner and Chuck Fairbanks was the coach at that time, and Chuck gave me a free hand. We put some pretty good teams together, and the players we drafted in those years, '73, '74, '75, and '76, were the who's-who in the National League for quite a while. When Chuck Fairbanks left, I became general manager and later vice president of personnel, and I'm also a director of National Football scouting. What I'm primarily doing now is looking at top picks and signing draft choices.

I still enjoy football very much and think it's a great game. It's a much better game than our game was because the NFL has been very flexible over the years. They've made the adjustments, and the rules, the playing conditions, everything has changed for the better. The game we played was more of a drudgery, but it was the best available at the time. It was just the hand dealt to us.

Today they talk about the locker room mentality. That mentality has changed from the days when I played, and you can see it in the problems we're involved with today. Drugs, steroids—we're going to have to deal with them just like we've dealt with problems in the past. Look at this strike we just had. Sports people didn't think about such things in my day because we played for the love of the game, not the Yankee dollar. It's a good thing we did because we weren't getting any.

P A R T

IV

GLORY BOYS

FROM THE OUTHOUSE TO THE PENTHOUSE

GEORGE SUMMERALL

END / KICKER

Detroit Lions 1952

Chicago Cardinals 1953–57

New York Giants 1958–61

If I ever got cancer, I'd want Pat Summerall to be the one to tell me.

—Beano Cook, ABC sportscaster

He has an amazing talent, the best memory of anyone I know. At meetings and talking to coaches and players, he doesn't take notes. I do. Then on the air he can quote what was said better than I can, and I'm the guy who took the notes.

—John Madden

IRON MEN

He's the greatest. As a colleague, there is just none better. No one is more easygoing and pleasant. Even when the pressure is at its greatest, no one is more understanding and more malleable.

—Terry O'Neil, CBS executive producer

FROM the reactions I get going through airports and hotel lobbies and in restaurants, most people don't think of me as a guy who played professional football. They see me as an announcer on CBS Sports and the spokesman for True-Value Hardware. All they have to do is look at my nose and the way I walk to realize I must have done something besides talk into a television camera. My nose was broken eleven times. Tony Trabert and I do tennis tournaments together on CBS and after I got to know him he said, "Pat, you're in the television business. Don't you think you ought to have something done about your nose?" I said, "I already have."

When I was in college, we were going to play Texas. Arkansas hadn't beat Texas for a long time and there was a plastic surgeon whose office was in Little Rock. I was already having trouble with my nose and he said, "If you beat Texas this week, call me when you get through with football and I'll fix your nose for free." I kicked a field goal with ten seconds to go and we beat Texas, 16–14. He called me the next week and said, "Remember what I said." I played ten more years of football and when I retired I called him and he did the operation. I always thought that was a very honorable thing to do.

The older I get, the more those old injuries seem to bother me. I've got a bad knee that's been operated on three times, once about six months ago. While I was playing with the Cardinals, my arm was broken when somebody cut my legs out from under me. I tried to block the fall and somebody else hit me in the arm when I was falling. A few years back my wrist started to bother me and I figured it had something to do with that old injury. I went to see the doctor who operated on Ken Venturi's wrists. At one point Ken was having some nerve problems and he recommended this fellow in Akron, Ohio. The doctor did a series of X rays, not just the wrist but all over. When he saw them, he said, "My God, are all you guys like this?"

I grew up in Lake City, Florida, a little country town seventy miles west of Jacksonville. My parents were divorced and I grew up with my father. I was born with a club foot. My right foot was completely backward; the heel was around front and the toes pointed in the opposite direction. A doctor in Lake City, Dr. Harry Bates, broke my leg and turned the foot around. My entire leg was in a cast for what seemed forever to a kid. In time I began to walk correctly, but Dr. Bates told me, "You'll never be able to run and play with the rest of the children." The most ironic thing about the whole experience is that my right foot was my kicking foot.

My father worked in a bank until it went under during the Depression. He spent a few years in an ice plant, went back to the bank when it reopened, and worked his way up from custodian to cashier. He had an eighth-grade education and thought I was wasting my time playing high school athletics. I think he saw me play one basketball game and one football game the whole time I was in high school. He felt I should be working instead of playing.

My first interest in athletics was probably like a lot of other kids, throwing a ball against the house and seeing if I could catch it. I was always a fan and read every word in the sports section. As far as organized sports, I guess I started playing football in the seventh grade. Lake City was a small school, there were ninety boys in my senior class, and if you wore long pants you were almost obligated to play every sport they had. Especially if you were bigger than just about anybody else, or at least taller, like I was. I played football, basketball, baseball, ran track, and was the Florida tennis champion when I was sixteen. A man named Jim Melton was our football and basketball coach during my junior and senior years and I think he was one of the most influential people in my life. I was a rather passive, reticent individual and Jim helped me go from a guy who was afraid to shoot the basketball to a leader on the team.

I was all-state or all-conference, whatever those deals were, in football and basketball my last two years in high school. When I graduated I can't remember how many opportunities I had for scholarships. My dad wanted me to go to West Point, but when I went up there for a visit it looked a little too much like a prison. The first thing they said to me was, "Yes, we'd like to have you, but we don't think you can pass the entrance exam." They wanted to send me to some military institute in Kentucky to prepare for the exam and I didn't like the sound of that at all.

The gentleman who had been my high school football coach in my sophomore year, Hobart Hooser, had left Lake City and was the line coach at the University of Arkansas. He was good friends with my family and when Hobart came back to Lake City to recruit me, they felt I would be in good hands if I was wherever he was. I ended up at Arkansas with the stipulation in my scholarship that I would play both basketball and football. I did that for a couple of years, but it was too time-consuming and it wasn't long before I realized any future I had in sports was not going to be in basketball.

We had a lot of football talent at Arkansas, but I don't think the coaching was the best. Eleven guys from my senior team ended up playing in the pros. Fred Williams played with the Bears. Dave "Hog" Hanner was with the Packers for a long time and we had the Carpenter brothers, Louis and Preston. I forgot who else was drafted. Our best year we were 7–3, but I don't think we ever got the maximum out of the talent that was available.

In my sophomore year one of the coaches announced that they were unhappy with the player who was kicking off. He asked anybody who wanted to try for the job to come out thirty minutes before practice. I showed up, happened to do pretty well, and that was how I got started place-kicking. While I was at Arkansas field goals weren't an important part of the game. If I recall correctly, when I was a senior I led the nation with four field goals. The guy I beat out was Vic Janowitz, who was at Ohio State. You didn't really work at kicking; it was just sort of an afterthought. You had a tough time getting somebody to hold the ball for you in practice, much less trying to get somebody to run it down each time you kicked. There weren't that many good holders around because I think a lot of players thought it was a demeaning job. It was also dangerous. The holder was squatting on all fours and had a real good chance of getting belted before he could get up. It wasn't until I got into the pros that people started to realize the importance of the kicking game. I suppose that was because of the significance of Lou Groza and the way Paul Brown used him. Everybody started to pay attention to field goals when the Browns started to win games with them.

I graduated from Arkansas in 1951 and signed a baseball contract with the Cardinals. They sent me to a Class C team in Oklahoma. During that summer, I realized that my future wasn't going to be in baseball either. I found out I couldn't hit a curveball, and worse than that, the opposing pitchers found out too. That same year the Detroit Lions drafted me to play pro football and then traded me to the Chicago Cardinals. When the guy from the Cardinals came down to Fayetteville, Arkansas, to sign me, I was playing a pinball machine in a place called Hog's Heaven. He probably thought, "This rube is going to be a soft touch." He gave me the line—I guess it was pretty standard at the time—that for equity and happiness on the team they had arrived at an average salary. The figure they came up with was $5,500. Later on I found out that was an out-and-out lie because Charley Trippi, the Cardinals' star quarterback, was obviously making a lot more than $5,500.

I called my father and told him that the Cardinals wanted to pay me $5,500 to play professional football. He said, "I thought you were going to have to go to work for a living." I told him, "Dad, they also want to give me $250 if I'll sign." He said, "Son, if somebody is willing to pay you that kind of money to play anything, take it." That was the extent of my negotiations. No agents, no lawyers, no anything. I used the $250 bonus to pay a beer bill I had at the University of Arkansas, but I didn't tell the Cardinals that.

I can still remember my introduction to pro football. It was a Monday, the team's day off, and I walked into the locker room at Cominskey Park. There sat Plato Andros in the whirlpool. He had been an All-American guard at Oklahoma and was a very thick heavy-chested guy. Plato filled up the entire whirlpool and had a cigar in his mouth, was reading the daily racing form, and sitting on the edge of the whirlpool was a pint of whiskey. Almost everybody who went into pro football was a pretty good beer drinker in college, but when practice started you didn't drink beer, you didn't do anything. You abided by the training rules and there was no question whatsoever because it was something you had been brought up with since you first started playing in high school. If you were an athlete, you didn't smoke, drink, or stay out late, and the guys who did were considered disgraces. We had two guys at Arkansas—both went into the pros—and when the coaches found out they drank some beer during the season they were suspended. Right off the team. It was quite a shock for me when I walked into that locker room and saw Plato doing everything you weren't supposed to do. Welcome to pro football.

The Cardinals' head coach at that time was Joe Stydahar. He was the only man I have ever known who could smoke a cigar, chew tobacco, and drink whiskey at the same time. He had been a great player with the Bears and had a very violent temper. Joe was also a tremendous physical speciman. He was one of those guys who look bigger than they are. He must have weighed about 265 and his head was as big as a toilet. We didn't have much of a team and Stydahar would go berserk when we lost. At the top, we had some pretty good talent—Ollie Matson, Johnny Olszewski, Charley Trippi—but once you got past those names, we didn't have much. To be very honest about it, we were pretty bad.

In 1953 we were 0–10–1 (we had managed to tie the Steelers) and were going to play our last game, which was traditionally against the Bears. We drew them at Wrigley Field and the week before the game Stydahar said, "I've always thought you guys were a bunch of gutless losers and I'm going to tell you something. If you don't beat the Bears on Sunday, nonc of you get paid." There was an open revolution and we had a team meeting. A couple of the guys said we should talk to the Bidwells, the owners at the time, but nobody had the guts to go to them. We beat the Bears, 24–17.

The next year was almost as bad, I think we won two games, and that was Stydahar's swan song. He used to pay us on Tuesday. He would come down to the locker room and have each of our checks in a little brown envelope. There would always be some kind of editorial comment about your performance on the envelope. "You're not worth shit," something like that. This one particular Tuesday he was about half an hour late and when he came in the locker room it was obvious he had a late night. Blurry eyes, stuff dripping out of his mouth. He had everybody's paychecks wrapped up with a rubber band and threw them across the locker room. He growled, "Fight for them, you bastards," turned around, and walked out.

After Stydahar left the Cardinals, one of his assistants, Ray Richards, took over and he was just the opposite. Ray was a real gentleman and we had a couple of good years. The coaching was better and we got some better players, but I wasn't enjoying pro football. The Cardinal organization was always trying to save pennies and by the time the season ended we were sometimes down to twenty-five players. At one point we almost didn't have enough footballs to practice with. It just wasn't much fun, losing every weekend, and if I hadn't been traded to the Giants I was going to retire.

During the off-season I had been going back to Lake City and teaching school. My undergraduate degree was in physical education and I also have a master's degree in Russian history. When I was an undergraduate, I had a history professor, Dorsey Jones, who taught history like it was a novel. His classes were so interesting I even enjoyed the tests. He was teaching Russian history at the graduate level and I went back to Arkansas while I was playing. That's how I ended up with that degree. The fellow who was the principal of the school I was teaching at had been a long-time friend of mine and I got involved in some farming ventures with him. We were basically doing truck farming, raising watermelons and tomatoes. I wasn't getting rich, but it was a comfortable living.

"Pop" Ivy was named head coach of the Cardinals in 1958. I called him up and asked him where I was going to fit into his plans. As I said, I wasn't having a very good time in Chicago and was thinking seriously of not playing anymore and getting involved full-time in the farming business. I had gotten married and had one child. My wife, Kathy, didn't like living up north because of the cold weather, so I wanted to hear what Ivy had to say. He told me, "Pat, you're one of our key guys and I want you to come back because we're going to do this and that." It was all very encouraging, so I decided I would play another year. A short time later I went down to the post office in Lake City to pick something up and bought the afternoon paper. There was a story in the sports section that said I had been traded to the Giants. Some "key guy"!

I called Jim Lee Howell, the Giants' head coach, and asked him what he wanted me to do in New York. He said, "We need somebody who can do more than kick." Ben Agajanian was the Giants' kicker and he had a garbage disposal business in Los Angeles. He was busy with that during the week and wanted to fly in on the weekends to play. Katcavage and Robustelli were the Giants defensive ends and if one of them went down Jim Lee thought I could fill in for them. They also had only one tight end, Bob Schnelker, and he thought I could also cover that spot. When you only had thirty-three players, a team didn't have the luxury of somebody who just kicked field goals.

Going to the Giants was like going from the outhouse to the penthouse. There was a whole new attitude on the team that I hadn't run into before. Those guys expected to win and they almost considered it a personal insult if they didn't. I had never played in that kind of atmosphere before and it helped me become a better kicker, especially under pressure. I just didn't want a loss to be my fault.

That first training camp I felt like a rookie because the veterans were all suspicious of me. Charlie Conerly was the quarterback and it was a big deal to have him hold for the kicker. At first he wouldn't hold for me because I was trying to take Agajanian's job. For a while I had the backup holder, but I guess that Charlie decided I knew what I was doing. He finally started holding for me and that really helped. At Chicago I never had the same holder two years in a row.

Tom Landry was the defensive coordinator and kicking coach at New York and he really made a difference. Tom is a great coach and he worked with Ray Wietecha, the center, Charlie, and myself. Ray was a terrific center and I never remember having to kick a ball when I was with the Giants where I could see the laces. That helped my accuracy. In 1958 I was 12 for 23. The year before with the Cardinals I was 6 for 17. In 1959 I was number one in the league with 20 for 29.

What was probably my most embarrassing moment in broadcasting involved Tom Landry. We are forever changing the way we produce and show football games and one year they had me down on the field introducing each member of the teams like they do in college football. The Cardinals were playing the Cowboys and I got through the Cardinals fine, including Wally Lemm, who was the coach at that time. Then I started on the Cowboys and when I got to Tom Landry I couldn't remember his name. I had known him for thirty years, played against him, had him as a coach, and there we were, on national television, plus a full house at the Cotton Bowl. I stumbled around and finally said, ". . . and the coach of the Dallas Cowboys." Tom realized I was having a problem and handled it very gracefully.

My first year with the Giants was probably the high point of my career. We needed to win all of our last five games to get into a playoff with Cleveland to see who would play the Colts. Every field goal seemed to be crucial and I think four of those games were decided in the last two minutes. We played Cleveland in Yankee Stadium and there was almost a blizzard. I had been having trouble with my knee and hadn't even worked out. Don Chandler, the Giants' punter, had been practicing field goals all week. Before the game I told Jim Lee that I could play. The score was tied 10–10 with about four minutes to play, and I missed a field goal from the forty. When I went back to the bench, I was thinking that I had blown it and the rest of the guys, especially the defense, said, "Don't worry about it. We're going to get the ball back." They did get the ball back and we had third down on the fifty-yard line. Howell told me to attempt a field goal and I couldn't believe it. That would be the longest kick I had made for the Giants. The field was bad and most of the guys on the bench couldn't believe it either. They wanted Charlie to throw the ball.

I knew as soon as I kicked it that it was going to be far enough and they credited me with a fifty-yard field goal. You couldn't see the yard markers because of the snow and some people say it was longer. But like a lot of things, as time goes by, the snow gets deeper and the kick gets longer. Everybody was yelling and running around and I felt somebody tugging on my arm. It turned out to be Vince Lombardi, who was coaching the Giants' offense. He looked at me and said in that voice of his, "Summerall, nobody can kick a football that damned far."

Those years with the Giants were good years and I hated to quit. I was thirty-one when I retired and I'm sure I could have played another five or six years because they kept raising the roster limits. By that time, however, I had two kids and Kathy was really starting to make noises about not wanting to live up north. I had been working for CBS as an announcer during the last two years I played and really enjoyed the work. I was doing a five-minute radio program that Herman Hickman had originated. Phil Rizzuto took his place, then Frank Gifford, and when Frank got into a sponsor conflict, I got the job. If you were with the Giants or Yankees in those days, you really had a foot in the door as far as broadcasting was concerned. New York was more the center of the communications world than it is now and playing in New York, being on a winning team, made a big difference.

During 1961 we played a preseason game in New York and had four days off. Charlie Conerly was my roommate and the phone rang. The guy wanted to talk to Charlie, who was in the shower, and when I told him he wasn't available, he told me to remind Charlie that he was supposed to be at CBS radio that afternoon for an audition. I almost hung up when I heard the guy say, "Wait a minute." I put the phone back to my ear and he asked me if I'd like to come to the audition too. Alex Webster, Kyle Rote, Conerly, and myself went and I ended up winning the audition. That's how I got started with CBS.

In the spring of 1962 Kyle Rote called me one morning and told me he thought the job of analyst for the Giants' games was going to be available. Johnny Lujack was doing it, but he was a big Chevrolet dealer out in Iowa someplace. Ford had just become a heavy sponsor of the NFL, so Lujack had to bow out. I called Bill MacPhail at CBS and he told me, "You are still an active player and we can't talk to you." I then called Wellington Mara and he told me, "I don't think you can make enough money in the broadcasting business, but I'm not going to stand in your way if that's what you want to do." He is a very decent man and he told me that the Giants would prepare an announcement that I was retiring. I went back to MacPhail and told him, "I'm retired. I want the job as analyst." He called Wellington, just to make sure, and I've been with CBS Sports ever since.

Next year will be twenty-seven years and I couldn't do it that long if I didn't enjoy the work. Over the years I've done everything that CBS has to offer. Dog shows, horse shows, I was an analyst with the NBA for a couple of years, but now it's pretty much tennis, golf, and football. I enjoy tennis, but we don't do that much of it. Golf is the most difficult because you don't know what's coming. The game really doesn't have a pace and you have to be more inventive. How many times can you say, "He's a hundred and sixty yards away and using a eight iron. He's going to try to bring it right to left." It's hard to come up with something new. Physically, broadcasting football is the most demanding, but it is also the most enjoyable. I really missed the game when I retired, but I was lucky. There's only a handful of people who have been able to stay close to the game and I didn't lose the friendships or contacts. Because of the nature of my business, there never was a letdown.

You know when you get in the booth that it's going to be three and a half hours of pushing just as hard as you can because you have to maintain your level of enthusiasm. If it's a good game, that's relatively easy. But if it's not, you just have to keep pushing yourself. Thank goodness I've been able to work with guys like Tom Brookshier and John Madden. They both have a very high level of enthusiasm and that helps a lot. A lot of people don't realize broadcasting is hard work, just like anything else. John Madden works as hard as anybody I've seen in any business.

One of the strange things about the broadcasting business is that it's like a plateau. You stay at the same level for what seems like forever and all of a sudden you feel yourself getting better. You hit another plateau and then all of a sudden you can feel yourself getting better again. Improvement comes in spurts. I think most of the fans understand the game, so I try to tell them what's happening, not how it's done. I worked with Ray Scott in my early years and he taught me a great deal. It's a visual medium and you don't have to tell the viewers what they're looking at. My job is to amplify and clarify.

I don't think anybody can say that I'm biased toward the Giants. I wouldn't be honest if I said I didn't have some kind of feelings or interest in how they do, but it's not a conscious thing. At one time Frank Gifford was so conscious of not being pro-Giant he got accused of being anti-Giant.

I don't see that much difference in the kind of people who play football today from when I played. Once you get past the money, and whatever else goes with it, they're the same kind of guys. I remember talking to Byron Nelson about golf. Everybody talks about the players today and how great they are. I asked Byron what he thought was the biggest change from his era and he said, "The lawn mowers." What he meant by that was the improvement in the equipment and it's the same in football. When I was in college, the pads might have weighed fifteen pounds. But by the time you started to sweat, they probably weighed thirty pounds. With the materials they use today, you don't have anything like that. Look at the artificial turf. From a kicker's point of view, the stuff's great. It's as if the ball is always on the tee. We had to worry about the length of the grass. Was it wet, dry, or frozen—all of that.

Since I retired, I have tried the soccer style of kicking and if somebody told me I had to play today, that's the way I would do it. Not so much because I think it's a better technique, but because kicking straight ahead taxes your body; particularly the large muscle in your upper leg. In my time you might kick fifty times in practice. Today these guys go out and kick five hundred times. It's a sweeping motion, like swinging a golf club, and feels a lot more natural.

One thing that has changed—there aren't as many characters in pro football as there used to be. Cliff Livingston played for the Giants and he was one of those characters. One year he thought he was a race car driver, another year he didn't drink, and the next year he came to training camp thinking he was Robin Hood with all kinds of bows and arrows. Don Joyce, who played with me at Chicago and then went to the Colts, was another one. He was the guy who ripped Les Richter's helmet off and whacked him in the face with it. I always remember that his wife's name was Joyce Joyce.

Hardy Brown played with me at Chicago. Hardy had a reputation as a wild man even before he came to the Cardinals and I can remember putting five dollars in the pot when we played the 49ers. The guy who put Hardy out of the game would get the pot. We were playing the Giants and Hardy used to play linebacker, right next to me. New York started a sweep and Hardy hit Jack Stroud so hard that when I saw Stroud later he had pieces of Hardy's jersey imbedded in his jaw. We were playing the Giants in another game in Yankee Stadium and Hardy had hit a couple of the Giants the year before. It was a pretty close game with lots of time left and Hardy came up to me and said, "Why don't you try an on-side kick?" I said, "I can't do that without the coaches telling me to do it." He kept after me, but I kicked it away. There were at least eight Giants coming right at me, led by Robustelli, and they went *swoooooooosh,* right by me. I looked back and they were chasing Hardy out in right field behind the benches. I realized then why Hardy wanted an on-side kick.

We had a play when I was with the Giants called the "bootsie." The quarterback would take the ball, kneel down, and the other ten guys would jump on the offending player. Jim Lee Howell was a guy who wanted us to get somebody if he thought they were playing too rough. Bill Pellington was a linebacker with the Colts and he was a real mean bastard. He has hit one of our guys upside the head which Jim Lee thought was unnecessary. We were playing in the Polo Grounds and Conerly called the "bootsie" against Pellington. Gifford was split wide as a flanker and, for whatever reason, Charlie called the play off at the line of scrimmage. Gifford didn't hear Conerly, so he came off the line of scrimmage, jumped up, and kicked Pellington right in the numbers. Pellington went nuts and started slamming Gifford around like a rag doll. When they finally got it stopped, Gifford wandered back to the huddle and said, "What the hell happened?" It was a wonder that he wasn't killed.

From what I've seen, the players were closer in those days. When I was in New York, we had twenty-one families living in a hotel on the Grand Concourse in the Bronx. We used to walk to practice together, eat together, go out together, and over the years you find that you keep pretty close contact with the men you were playing with. The people who were important to you then are still important to you today. Every year we have a golf tournament, the team that was in the overtime game with the Colts in 1958, and some of us went back and reenacted the game in Central Park on the twenty-fifth anniversary. We played eight-man touch football. Gino Marchetti, Steve Myhra, John Unitas, Raymond Berry, Frank Gifford, Charlie Conerly, myself—I can't remember who else was there. But I do remember that we couldn't cover Raymond Berry in that 1958 game and when we played them in Central Park, twenty-five years later, we still couldn't cover him. They beat us again.

SHORN RAM ELROY HIRSCH

END

Chicago Rockets 1946–48

Los Angeles Rams 1949–57

Hirsch ran like a demented duck. His crazy legs were gyrating in six different directions all at the same time during a sixty-one-yard touchdown run that solidified the win.

—Francis Powers, Chicago *Daily News*

Only an end like Hirsch could have scored on the Bears when they were out for meat after three straight losses. Come to think of it, Hirsch is the only end in football that could have done it.

—George Halas

WE were playing the Bears in Chicago. That was always a tough ball game because it usually decided the Western Division title. We had a play where I would fake a block and then sneak along the line of scrimmage. Everybody would think that Davis had the ball, and when they went over to stop him, I'd go into the vacated area, stop, and Waterfield would throw it to me for an easy touchdown. We called it against the Bears with about two minutes to go in the half. I was going along, just like I was supposed to, and as I turned back to look for the ball the lights went out. I wasn't knocked out, but I was a little woozy, and when I looked up there was Ed Sprinkle looking down at me. He'd sensed the play and came over and gave me that forearm of his. He got fifteen yards for unnecessary roughness.

The end of that same year, the Cardinals were playing the Bears and that was also a tremendous rivalry. Charlie Trippi was playing quarterback for the Cardinals, and he had a very slow temper. But once it went, it really went. Sprinkle was giving him a very bad time, and every time Trippi turned to hand off the ball, Sprinkle hit him. It was getting to Charlie, and when Sprinkle came in for about the umpteenth time, Trippi whirled around, timed it perfectly, and just popped him right in the jaw. That was before face masks, and Trippi managed to get in a couple more before Ed went down. It was just like you see in the movies. Sprinkle stood straight up, looking surprised, and went down like a board.

Then we went to the Pro Bowl, which is held in January. Sprinkle and I were ends on the West squad, and Trippi was the quarterback for the East. The first day of practice, Sprinkle came up to me. He's really kind of a shy guy. Just talking to Ed, you'd never know he was such a rough player, and the fact is that he was not a dirty player, just tough. He kicked the dirt with his foot and said, "I suppose you're kind of sore at me for what I did to you in Chicago." I said, "No, Ed, let it go." What am I going to say with him standing right there? Then he said, "I got this thing all figured out. You owe me one, and I owe Trippi one, so during the game on Sunday, why don't you hit Trippi and we'll all be even." That was the first I realized Ed had a sense of humor.

I was adopted at a very early age and grew up in Wausau, Wisconsin, 150 miles north of Madison. My foster father worked his whole life at the Wausau Iron Works. I could always run fast as a kid—just a

God-given talent, I guess—and I found out eventually that I could catch a football. I could get a bead on the ball while I was running full speed with my head turned toward it. Then, I'd look back upside-down, adjust the direction of my feet, and follow the ball in. You don't learn it—it's a gift. Al Toon and Jerry Rice have it too.

I used to run back and forth from my house to school and try to step on each crack in the sidewalk, thinking it would make me more shifty. There was a park in town, and I'd go at top speed, heading straight for a tree, then shift the football as I dodged right or left just in time to miss it. I never pivoted, just dodged. It's hard to fake out a tree, and sometimes I'd plow right into one. Maybe that's what's been wrong with me all these years.

Actually baseball was my favorite sport as a kid, and I didn't play any real football until I was a sophomore in high school. That year I weighed all of 122 pounds and played a total of four minutes. By my senior year I was up to 165 pounds and had become the first-string halfback. My high school coach, Win Brockmeyer, was a wonderful guy, and, along with Hamp Pool, who coached the Rams, was the most important influence on my football career. He taught me, among other things, that football is an eleven-man game. Trust, courtesy, the importance of cooperation and loyalty—values that have helped me in my life outside of football. My son is named after Win.

When I got out of high school, my father didn't have money for college and Wisconsin didn't have scholarships. Coach Brockmeyer got together a group of Wausau people who paid my tuition, and I got a job as a night receptionist at a radio station to pay my room and board.

At that time freshmen weren't allowed to play. You got to go to all the workouts and get banged up in the practices and then warmed the bench on Saturday. Another one of those cases of non-athletic people making decisions for athletes. In my sophomore year I made All-American, and our team was 8–1–1 and ranked third in the country. It was that year, 1942, that I picked up my nickname.

Wisconsin played Great Lakes at Soldiers Field in Chicago. At one point I took an end run down the sidelines for about sixty yards. My left foot always pointed out farther than my right. When it goes behind my body, when I'm running, I have to swing it around when I bring it forward. The harder I run, the more I wobbled. That's why I couldn't be a hundred-yard dash man. Francis Powers, who used to write for the old Chicago *Daily News,* was at the game, and he said that I "ran like a demented duck" and that "my crazy legs were going in six different directions." The name "Crazylegs" just stuck.

When I started at Wisconsin, I was pretty young. I turned eighteen my freshman year, and when war was declared a bunch of us went down and joined the Marine Corps. We qualified for the V-12 program, and they called us up in the spring of 1943. Officers' training school was filled, so the Marines sent us to the University of Michigan for training. We were required to wear uniforms, and we studied map reading and mathematics, that sort of thing. Since we were eligible for athletics, I was able to letter in four sports while I was at Michigan: football, baseball, basketball, and track. We were a coach's dream team because we had to be in our rooms by seven o'clock at night.

The only reason I went out for basketball was so I could make the trip with the team back to Madison to see my girlfriend. That same year Michigan's best pitcher flunked out of school, and since I had a pretty good arm, I pitched and we won the Big Ten Championship. One week I was in a track meet and beat Buddy Young in the long jump—we called it the broad jump in those days, but we don't dare call it that anymore—and then I literally had to run over to the baseball field, where I pitched a one-hit shutout against Ohio State. Another time I got in my jumps and then drove 130 miles to Bloomington, Indiana, to pitch in the second game of a doubleheader. During the ninth inning, they came over and told me that my jump had held up for third place and we won the meet.

After three semesters at Michigan, we went to boot camp at Parris

Island, then to Quantico for officers' training. When the war ended, I was at Camp Pendleton, training to go overseas. I got out in May of 1946 and made the biggest athletic mistake of my life. I signed to play pro ball with the Chicago Rockets.

Right after the war ended, I was shipped to El Toro and played on the Marines football team. We played interservice games and people charged a bond to get in. We had a real good team, and our coach, Dick Hanley, became the head coach of the Rockets. I was drafted by both the Rams of the National Football League and the Rockets, who were in the All America Conference. Hanley kind of suggested I sign with the Rockets or I might be sent to China with the occupational forces.

My first contract was $6,000, and I received $1,000 for signing. I really held them up. With all that money in my pocket, I figured it was time to get married. My wife's father was a tough, loving, Old World-type minister, and Ruth was his only daughter. When I told him that I wanted to marry her, he asked me what I was going to do with myself. I announced that I had just signed to play pro football with the Chicago Rockets, and so help me his very next question was "But what are you going to do for a living?"

My first year with the Rockets, we were 5–6–3. They fired Hanley and hired Jim Crowley, one of the Four Horsemen, and we won one and lost thirteen. He was let go, and in 1948 they brought in Ed McKeever. At least we were consistent—we won one and lost thirteen. Playing for the Rockets was some experience. We never had more than two or three thousand people in the stands, and with that wind coming off Lake Michigan, it was so cold there were times we wished we weren't there either. We wore big parkas with drawstrings pulled tight around our faces. You couldn't tell who we were. It didn't make any difference because "Sleepy" Crowley didn't know one of us from the other anyhow. He'd grab a tackle and send him into the backfield.

We had a game against the Brooklyn Dodgers, and we flew into LaGuardia. The plane wasn't very luxurious, to say the least, but we got there and spent the night at the Martinique Hotel. It rained that night and all day, and there were 1,200 people in the stands watching us play in the mud. When the game was over, we went back to the airport and found out that all flights were grounded. Rather than spending any more money on hotel rooms, we had to sleep on the plane. The team went broke three times, and we'd just about play anywhere if we could make some money.

While I was playing with the Rockets, I got a torn-up knee, a bad back, a pinched never in my shoulder, and a fractured skull. That fracture almost ended my career at an early age. We played the Browns in 1948, and at first nobody knew how bad it actually was. They sent me for some X rays and nothing showed up. The next day at practice I was yawning a lot, so they sent me to see a specialist. When I got home that afternoon, the phone was ringing. The doctor asked me what I was doing. I said, "Nothing." He said, "Good. Go right to bed and don't do anything. You've got a skull fracture, and we're going to put you in the hospital." I had a crack right over my right ear, and I was in the hospital for a month. When I got out my coordination was gone, and I couldn't throw or catch a football. During the next year I kept working out, and little by little things improved. In the meantime the Rockets missed a few payments on my contract and the Rams offered me a job.

Clark Shaughnessy was the Rams' coach at that time, and he had a special helmet made out of plastic with extra padding around my right ear. It weighed about a third as much as a leather helmet and made me feel a lot more secure out there. The first year I was with the Rams they had a lot of good backs, and Shaughnessy thought I was brittle. "Red" Hickey, one of the assistant coaches, felt I would make an end, but Shaughnessy didn't think so. That year I didn't do much and was used mostly as a decoy on pass plays. The next year Joe Stydahar replaced Shaughnessy, and he decided that Hickey had a good idea. I wasn't sure it was such a good idea at first. Every time I'd come across the line, either the tackle would trip me up or the backs would spin me off balance. I felt like a fool because I didn't know two bits' of end play, and about fifty thousand fans found that out in a hurry. It started getting better, however, and I managed to catch forty-two passes that year and scored touchdowns.

I was the first of the flankers, and on most pass plays I would be split outside on the line of scrimmage, four to ten yards from our right tackle. I could take a little rest on the bench and nobody would miss me. Bob Boyd was on the other side and Tom Fears was in tight. With Waterfield and Van Brocklin, we had a hell of a team.

Moving from the backfield to end helped a lot because a back pays for other people's mistakes. If a guy doesn't block, you get hit. Somebody hands you the ball, and you have to fight your way through half a dozen big defensive linemen weighing between 220 and 260 pounds. Then if you do get through that wall, all you have to worry about are two or three of those big linebackers. I remember that one time "Vitamin" Smith, who weighed 180 pounds, was piled on by four big Chicago Bears. When he got back in the huddle, he had a faraway look in his eyes and was muttering something about swimming at Santa Monica.

We finally won the championship in 1951 beating the Browns, 24–17. Our share for winning was $1,113 each. My biggest salary with the Rams was $14,000, and if you were married and had a child, it was tough to make it. I never went without a job in the off-season. We didn't make anything like the players do today, but I just have a feeling that we had more fun than they do. All of that money in their pockets changes a player's attitude. Maybe not the great ones, but it seems the average guy has lost the desire to work as hard as he should. We enjoyed the game and each other. I can't remember a time after a home game when the majority of the players and their wives didn't get together at a restaurant or somebody's home. Today they go out in twos and threes.

Nobody talked about drugs in those days, and for the life of me, I don't know how any of these guys today can stick a needle in themselves or sniff cocaine. I smoke a pipe and don't think I've ever inhaled that. Not many of the guys even drank hard liquor back then. There was only one league, and if you got dumped, there was no place to go.

During the 1953 season Hardy Brown hit me right on top of my head with a knee. My helmet was jammed down around my neck, and when I came around, I couldn't get up. My head was clear, but my body was out of control. I felt fuzzy for a few days and had some trouble focusing. Hardy was another one, like Sprinkle, who was as mean as I've ever seen but not really dirty. If you were partially tackled or slowed down in some way, he had a timing thing with his shoulder that was amazing. He wasn't a big guy, but when you were playing a team that had a man with that kind of reputation, you put your head on a swivel.

When we played the Bears later in the year, I got hit again in the head. I remembered returning to the huddle, but that was about all. Then in the 1954 all-pro game, Tommy James of the Browns and Em Tunnell of the Giants hit me at the same time. I went straight up in the air and came down on my head. They had to help me off the field, and I was out the rest of the game.

I guess a lot of people were worried about me, but the stories that had me walking around punchy after games were overdone. It was rocky sometimes, but football is a rough game, and everybody gets hurt somewhere along the line. At one point they sent me to a specialist and this cadaver of mine was all but dissected. I had lights shot into my eyes. I was put through reflex tests. The bottoms of my feet were tickled, and then they gave me an electroencephalogram. The technical verdict was a concussion with no relation to my other mishaps.

There was a rumor that I was going to retire after the 1954 season, and it nearly caused a riot. We had played our last game of the season at home against the Packers. As I started toward the tunnel, the fans surrounded me and I couldn't move. They started tearing off my uniform, and at first I was just about to panic. Then I figured the best thing to do would be to relax and let things take their course. It was lucky for me that they decided not to take my toes and fingers. Pretty soon I was standing there in the middle of all those people with just my hip pads on. The media and a lot of other people have always insisted that I was standing there in my jock strap, but my hip pads were still on. They took a picture of me standing there like that and I'll never forget the caption in *Look* magazine: SHORN RAM.

My last year of pro ball was 1957. I was thirty-three, coming up on thirty-four, and I had a good job offer from the Union Oil Company. When you're that age, you're pressing it to go another year, especially if you're an offensive end. By that time a game was a relief. If you had a coach that scrimmaged you, think of the running you did. You ran every pass play three times a day, and that's a lot of ground to cover. There's only so many miles in those legs, and I saw so many people who played one or two years more than they should have. That first year after I quit was tough. I'd go to the Rams' games and just sit there watching a defensive back. I'd be thinking, "Gee, I could beat him on a slant" or whatever, but you get over it, and that was the time for me to quit.

I worked in advertising for Union Oil for two years and also had a radio program. Then Dan Reeves asked me if I'd like to be the general manager of the Rams. Pete Rozelle was leaving to become the NFL commissioner, so I went there for nine years and then came to the University of Wisconsin in 1969 as the athletic director. The program was in bad shape when I got here, and a reporter said that I wasn't the first choice for the job. He said they would have preferred to sign Saint Jude, the patron saint of impossible causes.

When I look back even on my darkest days here, I'm still glad I came. What makes your job and makes your life are the people you work with, and we've got tremendous people here. I don't mean the rah-rah thing. I mean personal relationships and genuinely wonderful friends. Our academic standards discourage recruitment of some top-rated players, but I've tried to walk that fine line between our policies and the need for winning teams. Wisconsin coaches shouldn't be under the pressure to win bowls bids every year like a Woody Hayes or Bo Shembechler. You have to learn to walk away from anger. Somebody's always ready to get on you about some situation. He doesn't know any of the details, yet he knows exactly what you should have done. I don't complain if I've done something wrong. If I have a rap coming, that's fine. But sometimes these reporters give negative opinions without ever discussing a situation with you. They don't know the rules. They don't know the facts. It used to be that the good reporters supported the school. Not since Watergate. Everybody's got to be an investigative reporter. Maybe they think they'll get a Pulitzer Prize or something.

We've got a great program here, and I've had to go out and raise money. Personally I like to take money away painlessly. We have fourteen golf outings around the state every summer, and we take our coaches and staff along. We play golf, have a few drinks and dinner. In the meantime we're meeting the people, raising money, and everybody's had a good time. It all takes money. Crew is a beautiful sport with probably the best camaraderie, but it costs us $180,000 a year. We have to go all the way to one of the coasts to compete, and there's no way of charging for a race. That money has to come from someplace without a dime coming back.

Going into the Pro Hall of Fame was one of the highlights of my career. There were a lot of playing thrills along the way but that you didn't do on your own. Someone had to block, someone had to center the ball, and somebody had to throw it for you to catch. Going into the Hall, you do that on your own, and I think everybody chokes up when they make it. The other great thrill in my life was the All-Star game we played against the Rams in 1946. Otto Graham was the quarterback for the All-Stars, and I caught a sixty-two-yard touchdown pass from him and also ran sixty-eight yards for another. We ended up beating them 16–0, but it wasn't so much the game that I remember, it was everything that went with it. When they introduced the teams, they turned out all the lights in the stadium and had just one spotlight on you as they called your name and you run out on the field. Then they played your school song, and I can feel the chill that went through me when they started playing, "On, Wisconsin."

THE CROONING HALFBACK

ABISHA PRITCHARD

RUNNING BACK

Cleveland Rams 1942

Philadelphia Eagles 1942, 1946–51

New York Giants 1951

Look at Bosh on one play and he's making a sweep. Look again and he's the flanker. Take a further look and he's boring into the line. Glance at your program and see who the blocker was—and it's Pritchard. He's punted on occasion too. For a breather—he runs back kicks and usually finishes his sortie with a happy pat on the backside of the opponent who managed to stop him.

—Ed Delaney, Philadelphia *Daily News*

MY first name came from an uncle whose name was Abisha. I was one of ten boys, next to the youngest, and he told my parents that if they named me after him, he would give me my first pair of long pants. Well, he never gave me those trousers, so I never used his name. While I was growing up, my family used to call me "Bish";

they just dropped the *a*'s. When I was playing football in high school, a newspaper man named Morris Siegel—he used to write for a Richmond, Virginia, paper—did an article on me. He asked me, "What's your name?" I said "Bish." He said, "Bosh?" I said, "No, it's Bish." "Bosh?" "No, Bish." "Did you say Bosh?" Finally I said, "Call me Bosh."

My father was a farmer, and I was born in North Carolina. When I was four, he gave up the farm, and we moved to Hopewell, Virginia, twenty miles southeast of Richmond. Hopewell had about sixteen thousand people and only one high school. I played four sports for four years: baseball, basketball, track, and football. I weighed 155 pounds. The very first time I carried the ball I went sixty yards for a touchdown and it was like winning the Super Ball. For twelve consecutive years there was a Pritchard on the Hopewell team and my father never missed a game. My mother, on the other hand, never saw one of us play because she was afraid we'd get hurt. She finally went to Washington to see me in pro game, and then she was upset that she'd missed it all those years.

I had about thirty offers for scholarships, which was a lot in those days, and I was just about committed to go to Tennessee when the VMI coach came to see me. "It's about time you Virginia boys start to go to school in Virginia." I had never heard anything bad about VMI, so I decided to go up and look it over. After spending some time at the campus, I figured that if I was going to stay in the state, that was the kind of school I wanted to attend. I also talked to three other fellows who had made all-state that year; they were all backs, and we all ended up going to VMI. We had a good backfield but not much of a line.

VMI was military first, academics second, and football third. We only had about nine hundred students attending the school, and it was a very disciplined environment. I didn't want to go to a football factory because I wanted a good education, and I think things are worse today than it was then. Today some of these players are taking up bird watching, crocheting, canoeing, and I think it's a shame.

ABISHA PRITCHARD

There are no more amateur sports, and the presidents of the colleges ought to own up to it because I think they know what's going on. They're not kidding anyone because I think they know these players aren't going to classes and they let them get away with it. Look at these trips they take today; they're gone for days. When we went on a trip, we went for a weekend, took our books with us, and had to be back for classes on Monday. If you did miss a class, you failed if you didn't make it up. If you failed, you went to summer school, and I went to every summer school that VMI had while I was there.

My younger brother went to VMI, and he was captain of the baseball team. Another brother was one of the best basketball players that Hopewell High ever had. My older brothers never did anything with their football after high school because they had to work so the rest of us could stay in school. We didn't get meat every night, and a big meal for us was soup and cereal. My father died during my last year in high school, and he never knew where I went to college, which was a shame. I look back now and feel very proud of having gone to a school like VMI.

We played single wing in high school and college, and I was a tailback, running, kicking, and passing, until I went with the pros. Bill Dudley and I played opposite each other during my four years at VMI. He went to the University of Virginia, and we both played what they called the roving safety on defense, playing the ball. Punt returns, kickoff returns, we did it all. We beat Virginia two years and they beat us two years. Our freshman year, he kicked an extra point, which beat us 7–6 after I missed the extra point. Dudley didn't take a step on extra points; he just swung his leg, and if you had ten players on the field to choose from, and you didn't know Dudley, you'd probably rate him number eight. He ran funny, kicked funny, threw funny, but he would find different ways to beat you. Bill was one of the greatest competitors I ever played against, and we are still good friends today.

After I graduated, I signed with the Eagles and played one year. I actually started out with the Cleveland Rams, but I reported to camp late and they never gave me a chance to play. The Rams sold me to the Eagles for $100, and the Rams never beat us the entire time I was with the Eagles, which made me feel good. I showed up in Philadelphia on a Thursday and played the last quarter of that Sunday's game. I played five years of pro ball before missing a game due to an injury.

We had a so-so year, and when the 1942 season ended I joined the Navy V-12 program, as a physical fitness instructor. After my boot camp, I was sent to Villanova and was getting ready to play for the Eagles, actually the Steagles then, and the word came down that guys in the Navy couldn't play. We went all the way up to the Secretary of the Navy, but he said no football. They transferred me to Georgia Tech, and some of us did get to scrimmage against the varsity down there. That was when Eddie Prokop was their star player, and we usually managed to beat them.

Toward the end of 1944 I was transferred to San Diego, and while I was waiting for my orders to go overseas, I played for the San Diego Bombers of the Pacific Coast League. A lot of the pro players were playing for those teams at that time under assumed names. If you go to see "Crazylegs" Hirsch, ask him about a little guy who faked a punt in the end zone and threw to him about thirty yards down the field. That was me and he went all the way. I forget what name he used, but I took a chance and played under my real name because I didn't want to establish a reputation for "John Doe."

It may sound strange, but I probably had the greatest time of my life during World War II. I was living off the base, making $175 a week with the Bombers, and had a radio show at night. I was billed as the "Crooning Halfback," and there were pictures on the streetcars of me in my football uniform with a microphone. If we were ahead at halftime, I would sing with the orchestra. The war ended while I was still waiting to go overseas, and after I got my discharge I went back to the Eagles for the 1946 season.

We had a great team and won the championship in 1948 and 1949. In fact, we were unscored on in both of those games, and that was the first time it was ever done. One of the things that infuriates me about "Monday Night Football," or any game on television for that matter, is the fact that they never mention anything about those teams or players like Steve Van Buren. He had every record in the book at that time, but you never hear his name. This, to me, is one of the reasons why the work that the NFL Alumni is doing with the old-timers is so important. We're getting the names of the Ollie Matsons, Bulldog Turners, Marion Motleys, and Craylegs Hirsches the recognition they deserve. The NFL Alumni Project is to work with kids, giving something back.

You hear all sorts of things about O. J. Simpson and Jim Brown. They were both great football players, but I think that Marion Motley was a better all-around ball player than Jim Brown. Motley was backing up the line, and Jimmy Brown hadn't made his first block yet. Motley could block and he could run; I've seen five and six people bounce off him. They'd knock his helmet off, and he'd still be running. "Bulldog" Turner was one of the toughest players I ever played against. I'll never forget the first day I played against the Bears in 1942. I was playing defense and intercepted one of Sid Luckman's passes. That was "hog heaven," intercepting a Sid Luckman pass, and then the Bears tackled me. Bulldog took the ball away from me—in those days you could take the ball away until the whistle blew—and ran for a touchdown.

Scrimmaging against Van Buren was also tough because tackling him was like tackling a freight train. He was a fine runner when he came into the league, but he ended up running over people, something I could never do. Running a hundred yards straightaway, Steve could probably beat me by five yards. Running with the football, maneuvering, I was probably as fast as he was because I was small. The thing that made our team successful was the fact that Steve was billed as "Mr. Inside" and I was "Mr. Outside." Faking to me on the outside and then handing back to him or faking to him and then pitching it to me, it was hard to defend against. Today they say it wouldn't work because the linebackers have such lateral movement, but I think when you go one on one, it's to the runner's advantage. I'm sitting up there in the stands watching these games today, and there's a linebacker on the inside, and the end goes down the field—there's no way they can cover a swing man. Why don't they throw the ball around like Fran Tarkenton did? His teams didn't win any Super Bowls, but he gained a lot of ground.

Maybe the game has changed—I don't know, but today there's too many computers in football. A coach has to look at his computer: "Let's see, its fourth down and one—what am I going to do?" The computer says, "Kick the field goal." "Greasy" Neale would turn over in his grave if his team would kick the ball with fourth and one. He'd say, "If you can't make it, you don't belong out there." Lombardi said it best: "It's a game of blocking and tackling." You do that and you win football games. A team kicks off and the other team receives—they have four plays to gain ten yards or they have to kick. However you make that ten yards, that's up to you. None of that's changed, and I don't think a computer is going to tell a coach anything he can't figure out by himself if he really knows the game.

Today they like to talk about being "up for a game," and that's the most overused phrase I've ever heard. When that whistle blows, you should be ready to go. I was always ready to go the day before the game. Our club, especially the 1948 and 1949 championship teams—we knew we were going to win when we went out on the field. The only thing we didn't know was how bad we were going to beat them. Tommy Thompson would always say before a game: "We're going to knock their jocks off."

All that money they're making today! Based on the championship teams we played on, I'd have to be a $300,000 or $400,000 player today, and Van Buren would be making at least $800,000. Here they are, getting paid huge salaries to play something they love and these kids are walking out of camp. The Eagles' coach, Buddy Ryan, made a good remark one day: "All these guys walking out, there must be some really good-paying jobs out there that I don't know about." Somewhere along the line things got off the track and I feel that today a lot of the ball players are dictating to the owners. If you have an operation like the National Football League, any big company, you can't run things like that. Years ago, when Bert Bell was commissioner, he would say, "You play for this team or you don't play." A player couldn't go to another team and get more money. I realize that arrangement wasn't always fair, but that might be a better setup today because they're making more money.

Today everything seems to be wide open. In our day, some of the boys sneaked a few beers, but if you got caught drinking, Greasy would fine you $300. I have no sympathy whatsoever with athletes who abuse alcohol or deal in dope. They're told in high school, they're told in college, and again when they get into pro ball, you have a chance to become a millionare. If they can't exercise some discipline over themselves, and they get caught, "throw the book at them." As a former pro football player, I think we owe something to the public, to the kids today. I do a lot of speaking and I want the kids to look up to me. Some of the players today, nobody can look up to them, but I don't want you to get me wrong. There are many great athletes playing today, and the Eagles are an example. They run a class organization, and I don't know a bad egg on the team. It's just a shame that the few bad ones get all the publicity.

I'd also like to hear what Bert Bell would have to say about having a fellow like Jimmy the Greek on television during the game. Why should a handicapper, somebody whose background is strictly gambling, be talking about the game?

I follow the Eagles. I'm here for every home game, and the alumni are invited to one practice session during training camp. I still get out there and punt the ball, I've lost a little distance, but my hang time is better. I'm sixty-eight years old, but I feel like I'm forty and probably sound like I'm twelve.

It was a freak accident when I got hurt. I wasn't prone to injury during my career, and I think that was because I was a relaxed runner. If you're tight, that's when you're going to get hurt. I used to dive through the air, hurdle, and jump over people. We were playing the Redskins, and I was knocked out of bounds and fell over one of my own players. I probably shouldn't have gone back into the game, but my family had come up to Washington from Hopewell, Virginia, to see me play. After the game I went in to get my knee looked after, and the funny thing about it was that I came out with my hand in a cast. I had broken a bone in my hand, but the knee didn't appear to be that bad. I played the rest of the year, off and on, and the knee never did get right. It was a shame because I was having a great year. I was leading the Eagles; in fact, I led the league that year with a 6-yard rushing average. I was even ahead of Van Buren, and I won the Most Valuable Eagle Player Award that the Bakers' Club of Philadelphia gives out every year.

I tried to work the knee back into shape during the summer, and I was still having trouble when training camp opened. We didn't know how bad the cartilage had been damaged because my knee wasn't locking up on me. Usually if the damage is really bad, it will lock right up. I taped it up and was trying to play, and the night before we were supposed to open against the Browns, it locked up and I couldn't run at all. They operated on me the next week, and in those days you didn't come back the same year. That was the first year that the Cleveland Browns came into the NFL, and we were their first game. The defending NFL champions were playing the new guys in the league, and they beat us. Van Buren was hurt, so he didn't play; and Clyde "Smackover" Scott, who took my place, broke his shoulder in the first quarter. I'm not making excuses because the Browns had a great team. Otto Graham was throwing to Max Speedie, "Dub" Jones, and Dante Lavelli. That spread out our defense, causing us to cover one on one, and we just couldn't cover them. Otto Graham, he's still tops. I'm the toastmaster of the Pennsylvania Sports Hall of Fame Dinner, and he comes down and we have a great old time. Otto and I look a lot alike, and people used to get me mixed up with him. Somebody would come up and say,

"Hey, Otto, how are you?" I always tell them, "Fine," and they never known the difference. Otto and Richard Nixon—I look like both of them.

I didn't play at all during the 1950 season, and when I came back in 1951 we were going no place. We'd all grown old and sort of peaked out. "Greasy" was the kind of guy who didn't bring in a lot of new people, and our team had stayed intact for three or four years. The Eagles released me, and I played my last three or four games with the Giants. The first game I was with them, we played the Cardinals and I returned a punt for the winning touchdown. Charlie Conerly was the quarterback. Arnie Weinmeister was playing, if I recall correctly, and Kyle Rote and Eddie Price—they had some good players, but I was thirty-one years old and I figured if the Eagles thought I was through, I was through.

I didn't want anybody feeling sorry for me while I was a ball player. I think I could have played another year, but when you've lost that step, and you don't realize it until you see somebody who weighs about 260 pounds overtaking you, that will change your mind in a hurry. I saw Robin Roberts, as great a pitcher as he was, when he thought he could still pitch. Steve Carlton did the same thing more recently.

After I retired, I was vice president in charge of sales for Tel Ra Productions, which was the forerunner of NFL Films. Bert Bell gave us the rights, and we did all the pro football highlights. Then, when the NFL decided to form their own film company, they knocked us out of it. When that ended, I went into real estate and ended up working for John Canuso, a builder, as his customer relations manager. John built the first Ronald McDonald House at no cost to anybody because his daughter had leukemia. She beat the disease and he created a foundation, the Canuso Leukemia Foundation, and when the foundation began to grow, he moved me over to take care of that. I'm the executive director, and we raise money strictly for cancer research. We're one of the largest contributors to the Children's Hospital here in Philadelphia.

Even before I left football, I was a host once a week on a television sports show and a disc jockey on a three-hour request program on the radio. I've always been into music and have been a barbershop quartet singer for thirty years. We'd go into a club after a game to get something to eat, and if there was a microphone and music, they'd take bets as to how soon I'd be up there singing. I've also done some theater work in Philadelphia and New Jersey. I was Lieutenant Cable in *South Pacific.* He's the guy who takes his shirt off and walks across the stage. That was, of course, when I had a body. *Guys and Dolls, The Music Man, Most Happy Fella*—I've always had a little ham in me and enjoyed show business.

Having been a professional athlete helped me in business a great deal. I think I had a very good reputation, and if you've managed to maintain that, I think people will listen to you. I haven't played since 1951, and it's very flattering to walk down the street and have somebody say, "Hello, Bosh." I was lucky to play with a great team. Van Buren and Muha—what a backfield! Thompson? Anybody who doesn't like Thompson doesn't like apple pie. Pete Pihos, Jack Ferrante, and Neil Armstrong were great receivers, and I think Tommy Thompson should be in the Hall of Fame. They're putting some of these young fellows in there that don't deserve it as much as players like Tommy. As for myself, I don't think I have a chance to get into the Hall of Fame. When you're in the backfield with somebody like Van Buren, they only pick one, and he's the one who's going to get in. There was a magazine article written about me that was most flattering. It was called, "The Other Guy," and the idea was that I could have possibly become a major star if I had played somewhere else. But when you play with a team like we had, and somebody like Steve, it's hard to be number one.

I have no regrets and would have done everything the same way except that I would have cut back a little sooner at the sidelines in the game against the Redskins.

ROOKIES WOULD TREMBLE

EWELL DOAK WALKER

RUNNING BACK

Detroit Lions 1950–55

If there were a Mr. Everything Award for a nice guy and great athlete, I would give it to Doak Walker of the Detroit Lions. I don't believe Doak ever had anything bad to say about anyone. He never raised his voice, he never complained. He was Mr. Personality and Mr. Professional Football Man.

—Chuck Bednarik

I was born on New Year's Day, 1927, and it's been reported that my father went down the street telling everybody he had an All-American. In later years he would say that the story was exaggerated, but my mother always said, "Yes, he used to say just that, 'Mother, the boy will be an All-American one day. Wait and see.' " My father played his football at Austin College in Sherman, Texas, and was a letterman up there. When my father got out of school, he taught and coached at a prep school near Dallas. My mother was also a teacher. She taught in a little country school until I was born, and that took her out of the teaching business. My father ended up as an assistant superintendent in the Dallas public school system.

When I was growing up in Texas, football was the number one sport. California, Pennsylvania, Ohio, and Texas—those four states have always seemed to take their football very seriously. The powerhouse schools in my day were places like Amarillo, Waco, Wichita Falls, and Lubbock. They didn't go so far as to give scholarships to high school football players, but they did give jobs to their fathers. It wasn't unusual, if a kid was a good football player, for his father to get a decent job in the oil fields if he moved into that school district.

My football training began when my father started me drop-kicking the ball over the clothesline. I must have been two or three years old. We'd throw the ball back and forth to each other, and at the same time he was teaching me what a single wing was, what a double wing was—that kind of thing. It didn't register until much later, but I was learning the fundamentals as he played with me.

All of my schooling took place within a mile of my own home. My grade school was half a block away; the junior high and high school were about a mile walk, and SMU wasn't much farther. When I was in the fourth grade, my teacher asked the class to write a composition about a "great man." The other kids were choosing people like Lincoln and Edison, but I wrote mine on "The Great Fullback Named Harry Shurford." Shurford played on the SMU team that went to the Rose Bowl in 1936, and he was quite an idol of mine.

I played on the fifth-grade team when I was in the third grade. In fact, I played on that team for three years. We had a coach, uniforms, everything. In junior high we ran the same formations that the high school used, so it was really a farm club for the high school. They took a look at my neck in junior high and thought I'd make a good guard. On my first play from scrimmage, I intercepted a pass and took it in for a touchdown. That's when they decided I should be a running back. On defense I played safety and did that through college and into the pros, going in as the fifth man in the backfield.

EWELL DOAK WALKER

While I was in high school, I lettered in five sports: baseball, football, basketball, track, and swimming. Spring was a very busy season for me. With the schedules they have today, I don't think it's possible for an athlete to do anything like that anymore. The baseball season starts in the fall and the football season starts in the spring; there seems to be so much time involved for each sport that the only thing a guy can do is football and track. I was a good hitter and the Giants offered me a contract to play baseball but football was my first love. I just seemed to enjoy it more than the others, and I played four years of high school ball. That was commonly done at the time. I stayed over for a half year to play that extra year of football, and it really made a lot of difference in my maturity when I got into college.

The fundamentals that I had learned starting with my father and all the way through high school were solid, and it was a snap for me to play college ball. The most important influence on me at that time was my high school coach, Rusty Russell. In 1942 he came to Highland Park, my high school, from the Masonic Home, an orphanage over in Fort Worth. For years he had coached them into the playoffs, knocking off schools like Amarillo and Austin. Those schools had between three and four thousand kids to draw on. Rusty's school was so small that he only had fourteen players on his squad. They couldn't even scrimmage because there weren't enough players, but they'd sure knock your butt off in a ball game.

Those kids learned how to hit early and hit hard. Hardy Brown, who played for the 49ers, was one of the guys who came out of the home. His real name was Gordon Brown, but they called him Hardy. He went to Tulsa and when he started playing in the pros he became famous for "humping." Hardy would just wait for you and then spring and hit you with a shoulder, forearm, or anything else from the legs on up. That all started at the Masonic Home, and a lot of players respect Hardy. He had more knockouts than Joe Lewis.

Bobby Layne and I played together in high school. He was a year ahead of me and was a gangly, awkward kind of guy in high school.

Bobby wasn't very fast, but he had a great touch shooting a basket or throwing a baseball. He actually went to the University of Texas on a baseball scholarship, but that was only good for half his tuition, so in order to get a full scholarship he went out for football. The T-formation really helped make Bobby the great player he was because he was a fantastic passer. That came from his pitching a baseball. He never lost a game in the Southwest Conference in four years and was planning on going into pro baseball at one time.

There will never be another one like Bobby, that's for sure. He was a very warm, humble person, but he loved to go out and have a good time. The stories are exaggerated, as most stories are, and I should know because I was usually with him. Bobby would get all the bad press, and nobody ever mentioned that I was there. He wouldn't let anybody buy anything when he was out, and there was always a crowd with him because the freeloaders loved it. I always used to say, "Bobby, you don't have to do that, pick up the tab." He'd say, "Oh, what the hell, they all enjoy it." Like they say, Bobby always went in the front door and he always left by the front door.

After I graduated from high school, Bobby and I spent eight months in the Merchant Marine. We went to Florida for basic and then to Hoffman Island in New York for radio school. The longshoreman's strike hit the New York docks, and they sent us to New Orleans. When we got down there, we found out that only two guys had shipped in the last month and we were 103 and 104 on the list. The war would be over before they got to us, so we went back to school.

Bobby and I always hoped to play together at the University of Texas, but I decided to go to SMU. My father didn't come right out and say I couldn't go to the university, but he did convince me that I should go to school where I was going to make my home. Also, Rusty Russell had left Highland Park and had become the head coach at SMU, and that's what really made up my mind to go there. I only got to play in five games that year, but I did quarterback the

West in the East–West Shrine game. Then I was drafted into the Army and spent a year at Fort Sam Houston. When I got out of the service, I thought about transfering to the University of Texas but instead returned to SMU.

I played in '47, '48, and '49, and graduated in June 1950. I was an All-American all three years and won the Heisman Trophy in my junior year. At that time I probably didn't appreciate the Heisman as much as I do today. I'm sure it was big in the East, but to us it was just another award. You didn't have the television coverage that you do now, and I'm not sure the media in Dallas knew that much about it. Today I understand what it means.

That was a very romantic era in college football, right after the war and all, and I think people wanted to go where the action was. If a school had a winning football team, students flocked there from all over the country. I was probably on more magazine covers than any college football player that ever was involved with the game. Why they picked me, I don't know, but we did have two championship teams at SMU while I was there. We went to the Cotton Bowl twice; we won one game and tied the other. They'd call up and want a picture, so I'd go out and have a picture taken. I spent a lot of time having my picture taken, and it was a year-round thing. Of course, I'm sure that the publicity department at SMU had more to do with it than anybody.

It was a lot of fun being an athlete in those days. We all lived in the athletic dorm, and it was like our own little fraternity. You were very close because you lived, ate, and slept with the guys you played with. After classes we always hurried back to the dorm because there was always something happening, fun of some sort. The last time I went back to SMU was maybe six or seven years ago. It was homecoming. I was in a parade and they introduced me at halftime, but I don't go back that often. The school has taken the athleti dorm away from the athletes, and they've been shoved off parts of the campus. I don't know why they did that u school thought that the players were getting better food or treatment.

While I was going to SMU, I was thinking of a career in coaching when I graduated. Since both of my parents were teachers and I was a physical education major, it seemed the right thing to do. There wasn't any pro ball in my part of the country at that time, and I really hadn't thought much about it. Then I was drafted by the New York Yankees of the All-America Football Conference and by the Cleveland Browns. My rights came up in my junior year because I had spent the year in the service. "Bo" McMillin tried to get me to sign a contract with Detroit that year, even though he didn't have my draft rights. He created some phony award so I could come up to Detroit, and when I got there he tried everything in the world to get me to sign. I just flat wouldn't do it. My idea was that if he'd offer it to me then, he'd offer me the same thing when I graduated. Also, since the Browns had my rights, I figured I could play that against his offer.

Right after the 1949 season the two leagues merged and Detroit ended up with my draft rights anyway. The Lions drafted Johnny Rauch, the quarterback out of Georgia, and traded him to the Yankees for my draft rights. Bo McMillin made some kind of deal with Paul Brown, and that's how I ended up playing for Detroit. There were so many things that went on during those years. Lots of guys would go to training camp and get paid for signing a contract when they were still in school. If they didn't make the club, they'd go back to school and come back a year later and try to make the pro team again. The owners were pretty sharp operators—they had to be to stay in business. There wasn't any television money, and they used to say that George Hallas didn't make a phone call if he could use a letter with a three-cent stamp.

Just about the only people who thought I could make it in the pros were my father and Rusty Russell. Everybody else thought I [illegible] small and too slow. They asked Eddie Anderson, who [illegible] All-Star team in 1950, what he thought of me going into professional football, and he said, "If I could advise Walker, I would tell him to catch a train home instead of reporting to the Lions." Everybody thought it just wasn't my kind of game and I wouldn't be able to compete with the big, bad pros. In a way I understand how they felt because the type of guys who had played pro ball and the years of barnstorming around the country had left a bad taste in a lot of people's mouths. There were some pretty tough characters playing at that time, and I think I was very fortunate to go to Detroit. When Bo McMillin took over as coach, he started to build up a pretty good caliber of player. Most of us were college graduates, and there were a lot of lawyers and doctors on that team. It was during that era when the pro teams began to use the colleges as their farm clubs.

I should mention that at first my father wasn't too interested in my playing pro football. Not that he didn't think I could do it, but because he didn't want me playing on Sunday. He was a very religious person, and my family would open the church on Monday and close it on Sunday. Prayer meeting Monday night, youth night on Tuesday, choir practice; something was going on seven days a week. However, when the pros came around and started talking money and he realized that he wasn't going to be able to keep me from playing, he decided it would be all right. The way my father rationalized it in his own mind was that people who attended football games on Sunday could be doing a lot worse things. That was his analysis of pro football—good, clean family entertainment, especially if his son was playing.

I joined the Lions two weeks after training camp started because I played in the All-Star game that year. We played Philadelphia and beat them, 17–7. The Eagles were probably the only team we could have beaten because they were a running team. We had the muscle on defense and it turned out to be a real defensive battle. The All-Star game was a different kind of game because you were with such a great bunch of guys. They were all such good ball players that practices were a lot more fun than the game itself. The game was really incidental and I always felt the same about some of the Pro Bowl games I played in.

Bobby Layne, Cloyce Box, and I were roommates that first year, and I guess you could say that Bobby fathered me through that first year. That was his first year with the Lions, but Bobby had already played two years of pro ball with the Bears and the New York Bulldogs. Playing with the Lions wasn't that much of a change for me, as far as football went, but it was a big change as far as the players' attitude was concerned. I'd walk into the locker room after a practice, and people would be sitting around smoking and having a beer. That was a very different atmosphere from the one I was accustomed to.

Most of the time I ran scared. I guess I shouldn't say that, but I knew I wasn't going to hurt anybody if I ran into them. While I was playing, I weighed about 175 and I actually opened one season at 149. We played three exhibition games in Texas and Louisiana, and the temperature got up to 105 degrees. One thing about playing in that kind of weather, it really got you in condition, and at that weight, I'll grant you one thing, I could sure move.

My first salary was $12,500, and I got $10,000 for signing. I also got a percentage of the gate when we played exhibition games in Dallas, which usually got me $9,000 or $10,000. Real good money for that time, but I earned it. I played on offense, defense, kicked off, place-kicked, and was on all the special teams. Everything is so specialized today, even the backs. I see it here in Denver. They play one down and then sit one or two out. When you consider the actual time the ball is moving in a ball game, maybe five minutes, some of these guys are making all that money and probably don't play more than two, two and a half minutes at most. That's a pretty expensive player. I wasn't the kind of player who could have played on every other down. I had to play the whole game to get a feel for what was going on.

I especially haven't any sympathy for kickers today and just don't think they're all that specialized. You could take a big, healthy tackle and make a great kicker out of him. Then, you would have an extra man available to play if you needed him. These kickers today, they just kick, period. "That's not my job. Get them boys." I just can't picture anybody who considers himself a football player just doing the kicking. We would have never thought of such a thing, but I guess that's just my background.

I played six years of professional football and enjoyed every bit of it. Other than going into the Pro Hall of Fame, my most cherished accomplishment was the sixty-seven-yard run in 1952 that helped beat the Browns for the championship. That was a great thrill, and it's an incredible feeling to know you're the champions. The championship game was the Super Bowl of its time, and I'll remember it for the rest of my life. We were the world champions. We won games the next year just because we showed up. Teams were scared of us, and rookies would tremble when we walked out on the field. After a while we got a feeling for it, and it was funny because some of our mean old linemen would take advantage of it. They'd walk around scowling and spitting on the ground and scare the other guys half to death.

My last year was 1955. I wanted to get out while I still had all my teeth, both knees, and most of my faculties. I had played on two World Championship teams, made all-pro four times, and led the league two or three times in scoring. At twenty-eight I wasn't going to get any better and I figured I better get on with my life. During the off-season I had been working for the George Fuller Company, a big construction company out of New York. They offered me more money than I was making playing football, so it was time to get out.

After I retired, I found out it wasn't as easy as I thought it was going to be. It was especially tough because I really had no reason to quit other than going into a different business. I still found myself wanting to play, and I couldn't go to a game for five years. I wouldn't watch it on TV, wouldn't read about it, didn't want anything to do with the game. It just brought back too many good memories.

I spent six years in New York, and then Fuller sent me out here to Denver to do field work. I was here for a while and then went to Cheyenne, where we were building the launch facilities for the Atlas missile. Then they wanted to send me to Alaska, but I told them I didn't want any more cold weather and moved back to Denver and opened my own contracting business. While I was working for Fuller, I met some people from Fishbach and Moore, an electrical contracting firm working on the missile sites with us, and they contacted me about twenty-one years ago and asked me if I'd like to go to work for them. I've been with them ever since.

I actually wanted to coach when I quit. Halfway through the '52 or '53 season, SMU hired me to come and help with spring training. I was living in Dallas at that time, and Matty Bell, the athletic director, sent me off to do some recruiting. I guess that's what turned me off collegiate coaching. I went to call on two or three kids and met their families, and they wanted to know what they would get. I said, "Well, you get your tuition, room, board, and laundry money, whatever's normal." Then they wanted to know, "Is there anything else?" I said, "I don't think I want to have anything to do with getting you into SMU. Why don't you go to some other school where you can get what you're talking about." I went back and told Matty that he didn't owe me a damn thing because I didn't want any part of it.

They offered me the head coaching job in Detroit sometime in the early 1960s, but I didn't want it. I was honored and tempted, but I just didn't think I had the background. I'd been out of football four or five years and I also wouldn't have the power to hire my own assistants. During that same period SMU asked me if I'd consider a head coaching job, but when I told them how much money I wanted, and the privilege of hiring my own assistants, I never heard from them again.

Between jobs I coached with the Denver Broncos for one year, and that was a lot of fun. The old Cleveland end, Mac Speedie, was the head coach, and I was tickled to death when he asked me if I'd like to work with him. They fired Mac early in the season and gave the job to Ray Malavasi. He's a brilliant individual and very innovative. We didn't really have a quarterback—John McCormick could throw the ball as hard as anybody, but he never knew where it was going. We did have a bunch of smart kids who could execute what we were trying to teach them, so we won the last five games. If we'd beaten Oakland, we'd have been in the playoffs. Oakland beat us in the last two seconds on a field goal, and Lou Saban came in the next year with his own people.

I've still got a very strong relationship with the men I played with at Detroit. Maybe that's unusual among professional football players, I don't know. We used to go to training camp ten days early just to be together, and we weren't getting paid for it. Playing in the pros was a lot more fun than college ball because pros don't graduate. You could depend on a guy being there four, five, or six years, and we became very close. Families became close. I think some of the other teams were just there to pick up a paycheck and the hell with everything else. The Steelers, for instance, looked forward to a game so they could rest. They scrimmaged so much that they lived in their pads. Everybody wanted to get traded to Detroit because we seemed to have the unity and more of what it took to win. When Buddy Parker took over as head coach, we would always have a party after the game. There'd be a spread, all sorts of food, and beer if you wanted. If you had guests at the game, they could come too. It was really a way for Buddy to keep us together as a team.

I think just about everybody who played in my time had a lot of respect for each other. The way I always felt about it, I was taken care of as much by the other ball clubs as my own players. Maybe I was wrong, but I don't think so. There are always going to be those players who, because they can't quite make it any other way, are going to make up for it with other tactics. In our time the league controlled it, and if a guy was sadistic, he was eliminated somehow. Maybe by his own players. Everybody would say, "Oops, you're on your own." If a guy roughed up somebody on the Lions, we had a play we called the "Dead Dog." Say a linebacker would rough up one of our backs. Bobby would come back into the huddle and say, "Dead Dog, number thirty-three," whatever his number was, and when the ball was snapped, Bobby would go one way and ten other guys would run over number thirty-three. That got around quick, and it let that guy know he better shape up his act or he wouldn't be playing too long.

Don Colo, who played for the Browns, roughed me up on a play, unnecessarily. I was down, and he rammed his elbow into my face and rubbed it around a little bit. I just looked up at him and said, "Nice tackle." That must have melted him a little bit because I read an article later on in which he said that when I looked up at him and said, "Nice tackle," he was really embarrassed.

HOW'S THE CHEEK-BONE, TOY BOY?

TOY LEDBETTER

RUNNING BACK
Philadelphia Eagles 1950, 1953–55

Raising of the National Pro Football League player limit to thirty-three dressed players has added to the Philadelphia Eagles' football fortunes this season. This measure has brought a twenty-three-year-older who was a defensive gem in college but has turned out to be the Flock's best ground gainer at this early stage of the play-for-money campaign. He's Toy Ledbetter—a miniature Steve Van Buren—who delights in smashing vaunted opposing forward walls to shreds as he does his part to contribute to a victory.

—Ed Delaney, Philadelphia
Daily News

Toy Ledbetter, an Eagle halfback who runs hard with the ball, but who is otherwise inoffensive, had been tackled, and was halfway to the ground, when he was struck emphatically in the face by a shoulder belonging to Hardy Brown, a San Francisco defenseman. The right side of Ledbetter's face caved in so completely that Dr. Tom Dow, the Eagles' physician, described it as the worst face fracture he had ever encountered. To this day, Ledbetter bears the scars of the collision.

—Hugh Brown, Philadelphia
Evening Bulletin

IF you're looking for a journeyman ball player, that was me. All ball clubs had to have them because when I played there were only thirty-three or thirty-five players on a squad, so a guy like me had to do everything. I went down on kickoffs and punts, ran back kickoffs and punts, blocked on extra points, played some halfback and fullback, everything.

We were always so short of personnel; I remember we played the Colts in Baltimore one time, and all the offensive backs were hurt except me and the quarterback, Tommy Thompson. We had to put eleven men out on the field, so Greasy Neale put in some defensive backs and told them to just get out of the way when the ball was snapped. That's just what they did, they jumped out of the way and I would carry the ball. At one point I fumbled the ball on the goal line, and Greasy yanked me out screaming and cursing at me, but he had to put me back in because he didn't have anybody else. I finally did get a touchdown, and we wound up beating them. There were other times when we didn't have any defensive halfbacks, and I went in on defense. We played Chicago one afternoon, and they caught three touchdown passes.

I have no idea what kind of training camps they have now, but I know they were brutal in our time. I'd come in, overweight, white, and flabby, and there would be those kids with their goddamn long, lean bronzed bodies. That's one part of football that's really changed. You can't go in there waddling around trying to get in shape. Every year I'd look at those kids and think, "Lord God Almighty, what am I doing here?" Then they'd just slowly disappear, one by one.

We had a kid come in one year. He was about six-four, led the nation in offense, was tall, slim, broad-shouldered. He came out of California off those damn beaches. Everybody said, "There's your competition this year, Toy Boy." One morning I went out to practice and he wasn't there. I saw Vince McNally and asked him, "Where's your All-American?" He said, "I don't know where that son-of-a-bitch went. We went to his room this morning and his stuff was gone and so was he." I guess you had to have the staying power or whatever that made you last, and I never really understood those guys who left because I wasn't going to give up on it. Every year, here would come these goddamn kids, and one by one they'd just disappear.

My grandmother called my father her "toy boy" after he was born, and when it came time for him to have a birth certificate, she said, "Call him Toy," so it was Toy Ledbetter. I don't know why my mother made me Toy Jr., but she did, and people are always calling me Troy, Tony, and things like that. A lot of the guys who I played football with called me "Toy Boy."

As I recall, I went to twenty-one schools before I graduated from high school. My father was a construction worker on a road building crew, and when he finished a job, we'd move. He started when they were building roads with mules, and I've got nothing but admiration for him. I can remember that old man getting up at three o'clock in the morning and coming home late at night.

Since I was an only child, my sister didn't come along until I was twenty-one. I was a loner because we were never in one place long enough for me to make any friends. We lived in Texas, Kansas, New Mexico, Colorado, and at one point they were building a big lake near Durant, Oklahoma. I got there in time to play the last half of the basketball season and also ran track that spring. The next year was my senior year, and my father wanted to move again, but my mother finally put her foot down. "He's going to graduate from this school." So they moved and I got to stay behind and graduate.

The coach told me that if I wanted to play basketball, I had to go out for football. I'd never played a minute, but they had gotten me a job racking balls and cleaning up the pool room on weekends, and I was young. You didn't ask questions in those days. I told him I'd play, and it was hilarious when I went into the locker room for the first time because I didn't even know how to put the pads on. But I took to it and really liked the game. Even though I was small, I think I weighed all of 150 pounds, I did pretty good that year, made second-string all-state, and got so I could hold my own with much bigger guys.

My dad thought football was pretty dumb and didn't want me to play. On the other hand, I was my mother's pride and joy. She went to everything I ever did. After I was in the pros, my mother told me that my father used to get up and leave the room when the game would come on. They saw me maybe half a dozen times on television, and she said the old man would kind of stand by the doorway and look. The first time my mother saw me, she called from Oklahoma, and my mother didn't usually make long-distance calls. She was sobbing. "I saw you on television, Toy, and I'm so proud of you."

Several schools recruited me, including Baylor and Oklahoma, but I wanted to go to Oklahoma State because a couple of kids from Durant were there. It was called Oklahoma A & M in those days. They had a real good team and had been to the Cotton Bowl the year before. That was the era of Neil Armstrong and Bob Fennimore. I thought Fennimore was a monster because he was about six feet and weighed 195 pounds. He could run about a 9.8 hundred and you look now at the Herschel Walkers and kids like that who are running 9.2's and 9.3's. One year at Philadelphia we had what they called "The Elephant Backfield." There was Bielski, who

I think weighed about 220 and couldn't outrun a fat woman; Parmer, who weighed about 205, 210; and me at 200. Some "Elephant Backfield."

Oklahoma A & M was running the old single wing, and since I was such a little squirt, they made a blocking back out of me. In my third year they went to the T-formation, and that spring they tried me at quarterback. I was doing pretty good as far as handing off and running, but I couldn't pass to save my life. We had a little line coach, Toby Green, who was a peach of a guy but a little explosive. One of the old hands broke loose during an intersquad game, and I missed him by a country mile. Toby ran up to me and rapped me right on the shoulder pads and started cussing. I told him, "I didn't want this goddamn position anyway." That really pissed him off, and I lapped the field until I just about died. The last two years I played defensive halfback.

In my senior year I got a couple of letters from the Los Angeles Dons, but I never heard anything more, so when I graduated I got a job with my father running a Caterpillar tractor down in Fort Worth. We were building the turnpike that runs between Dallas and Fort Worth. One day I came in from work, and they said I had a call from Vince McNally of the Eagles. I called him back and he said, "Would you be interested in playing pro ball? A couple of our backs have gotten hurt, and we'd like you to come up to Philadelphia." It turned out that the Brooklyn Dodgers had drafted me and I didn't even know it. When the AAFC merged into the NFL, the Eagles wound up with my draft rights. Philadelphia had won the championship the year before and was going to play against the College All-Stars. Bud Wilkinson was coaching the All-Stars, and he was trying to run that split-T formation of his. Greasy Neale, Lord love him, was looking at the films, and I had two real good games against Oklahoma. I was, of course, a defensive ball player in those days, but I had to play offense and defense in those two games because everybody was hurt. Greasy wanted to know who in hell I was and ran me down by calling my coach, Jim Lookabugh. I got to thinking about sitting out in the 100-degree sun on that big Cat, and said, "Yes."

I got on a plane and went up to Chicago for the All-Star game, and of course I didn't get in the game. Then we went up to training camp, which was just outside of Duluth, Minnesota, and a real hell-hole. When I first got there, Greasy told me, "You're going to get an apartment at the such-and-such hotel." I don't remember what it was called now, but I found out why he wanted me to stay there. He wanted me to drive him to practice every morning, so I would go over and get old Greasy. He never did know my name that first year. He'd ask me, "Don't you ever say anything?" and I'd say, "No, sir," because I was scared shitless.

They were going to make a defensive halfback out of me, and I just couldn't play defense in the pros. "Birdlegs" (that's what we called Neil Armstrong), Pete Pihos, and "Black" Jack Ferrante would tell me which way they were going to break, and they could still beat me. Greasy just threw up his hands. "Ludbutter"—he never did get my name right—"you can't play defense, can you play offense?" The defense was working down on the goal line, and Greasy had me put in at halfback. They had drafted an All-American defensive end from Oregon, and I was supposed to step out and block him. He ducked about the time I came up and I split the side of his face wide open. It was sickening, and I really didn't intend to do it, but here comes Greasy, with his little fat belly bouncing and that baseball cap of his. "Who did that?" He wasn't looking at the poor bastard that was hurt; he just wanted to know who hit him. Old Black Jack said, "That kid did." Greasy said, "Let's run that play again and I want McDowell in there." McDowell was an all-pro, and I thought, "Oh, shit," because they knew what play was coming. I must have gotten lucky because I cut McDowell down, and they kept on running that play until I was exhausted. I imagine if I'd missed that All-American, I would have been back in Fort Worth running a Cat.

This was 1949 and they cut me anyway, just before the first

league game, but Vince asked me if I wanted to go to Paterson, New Jersey, to play for the Paterson Panthers. I said, "Ehhhh, where the hell is Paterson, New Jersey?" I got something like $500 a game and we played Jersey City, Richmond, teams like that, and I had a fabulous year, made all-league. I weighed 175 then and could run. I didn't mind Paterson because it was a chance to play ball and make some decent money. Actually, if the truth were known, I made more money that year than I did the following year with the Eagles. After I had a couple of good games, I told the guy who owned the team that I wasn't making enough money and I was going home. He put me to work with his construction company, and I think I was making twice the $5,000 that the Eagles ended up giving me my first year.

I was still marginal in 1950, but then "Smackover" Scott broke his shoulder and I played that season and was drafted by the Army just before the last game of the season. I went to Fort Sill, Oklahoma, for basic and they put me into an observation battalion and sent me to Germany for eight months. They wanted me to come up to Frankfort and play football, but our colonel was a former ballet instructor and he hated my guts. He said no, and it was really a miserable existence.

I came back in October of 1952 and called the Eagles. Vince told me, "Toy, if you want to come back, you can, but we've only got about six games left and we're having a horseshit season." He asked me if I was in any kind of shape, and I told him that I wasn't. "Why don't you go home and get in shape and come back next year?" That sounded like a good idea, so I went back to Oklahoma and got a job with an oil company and worked there until the 1953 season started.

Our very first game that season was against the 49ers. We didn't wear face masks in those days, and just before the first half ended, Hardy Brown busted my cheekbone with that goddamned shoulder of his. It severed the nerves, so I wasn't really in any pain. I remember getting on my hands and knees trying to find the football while everybody tried to get me off the field. The 49ers had a defensive end by the name of Charlie Powell, a big colored kid who was supposed to be a boxer, and we had Bobby Walston—he was a Golden Gloves boxer—and the two of them were fighting. It was a little wild out there for a while. Of course I didn't play anymore, and they didn't want to leave me out in San Francisco, so I flew back with the team. They operated on me during the week and put the bones together, and I spent the next weekend in the hospital. Two weeks later I was sitting on the bench and we were getting down toward the goal line. Jim Trimble turned around and said, "Can you play?" I said, "I still can't see out of my left eye, and I don't even have my pads on." He said, "Okay," and when we went in at half-time, the next thing I knew, Freddie Shubacker, the equipment manager, came over to me with a helmet with one of those bird cages on it. "See if this fits." I said, "What the hell is this?" "Jim said for you to try this on and get your pads on, too." Sometime during the second half he sent me in and I caught a pass. I was scared to death.

The next week the Eagles sent me to Chicago, and Wilson, the sporting goods company, made a mask for me. It had a steel bar that was covered with rubber and a plastic shield to protect one side of my face. When the Browns came into Philly, Otto Graham came into the locker room to see my mask. He had gotten his cheekbone busted pretty bad and was still on the inactive list, so I guess they made him one like I had. From what I understand, they've got Otto's in the Football Hall of Fame and they're calling it the first plastic face mask; it's a minute point, but mine was first. The NFL Alumni sent out a questionnaire a few years ago and asked if we had any mementoes of our career that we would like to donate to the Hall of Fame. I sent them my face mask, and I don't know what they did with it; probably they put it in the basement.

The next week we were playing the Giants, and we were down on the goal line. I started off-tackle, and Arnie Weinmeister reached over and grabbed that mask and started popping my head back and forth as hard as he could. He didn't care whether I was hurt or not

—he just didn't give a shit. There were no rules against that kind of crap, and old Lum Snyder and some of the other Eagles were kicking Arnie, trying to make him let go. The fans came out of the stands and were threatening to kill Weinmeister. He was laughing because he was just tickled at what he did. My surgeon came down out of the stands and they took me into the locker room, all that bullshit. Arnie wasn't dirty—he was just a good tackle and a tough son-of-a-bitch.

Hardy wasn't actually that dirty either because he was right up front about it. Guys like Bucko Kilroy and Ed Sprinkle, they were a little sneaky. In those days they didn't slip the tackles out on the defensive ends, they put us halfbacks out there and Sprinkle would just eat us alive. That goddamn guy would get you down, and he'd hold you and step on you, do it anyway he could. Bucko, well, he was just Bucko. When he started with the Eagles, he played offensive guard, and I just hated to see him come in because Bucko never blocked anybody. He was pretty fast for being so big, and he'd be the first one in the end zone. Then he'd turn around and look back and wonder why you weren't there with him. Goddamn, he looked so pretty wheeling around there, that little old blocky body of his, but he just wouldn't block, so they switched him to defense and he found his niche. He liked playing nose tackle because he could hit somebody and then fall on them and stick a knee in them or something like that.

We had a lot of characters then—the Bobby Laynes, the Buckos, the Ed Sprinkles. Maybe Joe Namath was the last of that type of guy. We laughed at them when they carried on, but we also laughed with them because they were good ball players, and in our own way we were proud of them, they were part of us. But the guys playing now, I'm not so proud of some of those people. They get their names in the paper for the wrong kinds of things. I don't even want to watch them, don't want to talk about them or hear about them. My kids tell me, "You're old-fashioned, Pop." Maybe I am.

After every game we'd unwind and get drunk on our keesters.

Not everybody, but probably 70 percent of the team, and we'd all go together, but I don't remember any drugs. It just amazes me how many seem to be involved today. But these kids have got so much money and they're in the limelight so much, everybody wants to be seen with them. Even in my day there were people who wanted to be around ball players, and it didn't make a bit of difference whether you were a hockey player, a basketball player, baseball, football, whatever. Everybody's got their groupies. They're buying you drinks and inviting you to parties—I can imagine what it's like now.

I was the only single guy on the whole ball club, and I used to go out a lot because I was bored, I had nobody to go home to. I was hustling some old gal, good-looking shiny thing, and come to find out she was a racketeer's girlfriend. He was down in Mexico or somewhere until something blew over. I was just a hick kid from Oklahoma, and all I knew, she was good-looking and we were getting along just fine.

Bert Bell called me into the league office, and he said to me, "I want you to stay away from that broad." I said, "What broad?" He just shook his head. "And I want you to stay out of the goddamn bars once in a while." I didn't think they'd care if I went in those bars, but they did, and Bert laid down the law. Like I said, playing football gave you a little notoriety, and you could walk in the bars and nightclubs, and they would sit you down and buy you a drink. I enjoyed it, Jesus Christ, I enjoyed it, and I can see where these kids today must be able to have just about anything they want. They sing Rozelle's praises, and he has done a lot, but Bert Bell was very shrewd and a fantastic guy. Without him, I doubt that professional football would be the game it is today.

You also had people like Paul Brown. We always ended up second against the Cleveland Browns, and I can remember when we played against the Browns, we all disliked him. Not only did he kick our ass, he was so cold and unemotional. I don't know if they had computers in those days, but Paul Brown had a computer in his head. When Paul was coaching Cincinnati, they were playing the Broncos here in Denver, and I ran into him in a hotel lobby. I introduced myself and he said, "Oh, yes, I remember you." We got to reminiscing, and he said, "You always tore up our punts and kickoffs so goddamn bad." I said, "Well, if you recall, the last time we played Cleveland I sure didn't." He said, "Yeah, and you know why? I had two linebackers on you." I'm not knocking our coaches, but I don't remember them ever thinking about things like that. I did get down on punts real quick and was elusive enough that I'd usually get the ball carrier. I think I'm onc of the few people who ever tackled Ollie Matson on the ten-yard line, and he was a great runner. Most teams would never think anything about trying to stop me, and I'd get down so fast that the runner wouldn't get a chance to get loose. Paul Brown did.

While I was playing football, another guy and myself had put a little drilling company together. In Colorado, the business was going good, and I had also met my wife, Barbara, a Continental stewardess, and I didn't want to play any more football. It was taking me all week long to get ready for the game on Sunday, and I was just so goddamn tired of football. I had never argued my contract with McNally because he was as tough as whale shit and he kept sending me contracts and I kept throwing them in the drawer. Finally he called and I said, "Damn it, Vince, I've got to quit sometime." "Toy, you've got to come back. We've got Hughie Devore as our new coach, and he's got to have some veterans." Finally he made me an offer I couldn't refuse, and I also thought I could talk to some people I knew in Philadelphia about getting some oil-drilling money.

Training camp was miserable, and I guess I was a little cocky and got in a little hassle with some backfield coach they hired that year. At halftime during an exhibition game, I stopped to talk to somebody on the sidelines, and he came up and grabbed me by the arm and said, "Get your ass in the dressing room." I said, "Don't ever touch me again," and quit after that game.

I went back to Colorado and continued to work in the oil business, full-time. We were going great guns, and I thought that I'd found the easiest way to make money I ever saw in my life. Then, about 1960, we went broke and I went into sales. About 1978 I had a little heart attack. At that time I was working for a ceramic company, as v.p., and general manager. I was completely out of shape, was smoking a pack of cigarettes a day, and had gotten extremely heavy. They wanted me to stay in management, which was causing all my problems, so I resigned from the ceramic company and went back into the oil business. It was great up until about 1984, and then I don't have to tell you what happened. I tried to tell those people a year before it happened that this thing was going to hell in a handbag, but they didn't want to listen.

I haven't really done much of anything since then except play a lot of golf. A friend of mine has a company that builds these convenience stores, and he asked me if I'd like to do some consulting work. For the last year or so, I've been helping him look for sites in Colorado and trying to set up some oil deals for him. He's a great friend, and that's stopped the outgoing cash for a little bit. I still have a lot of friends who are working as checkout clerks in grocery stores, and if the oil business doesn't come back soon, I'm going to run out of time.

As far as the Broncos go, these fans are fantastic. The fans in Philly were tough. We were playing in old Connie Mack Stadium, and even though the damn thing only held about 30,000 people, it was half empty every time we played. If you won in Philadelphia, fine. If you didn't, the fans wouldn't come out. These fans out here in Denver, win or lose, they fill the stands. My wife, Barbara, likes to go to the games, but I just won't go because I hate the crowds more than the traffic jams. Those people sitting around me just drive me crazy, so maybe twice a year somebody will con me into going with them, and then I want to leave early. Those people are probably the best football fans that I've ever run across, but they're also crazy.

TOY LEDBETTER

When they first started the franchise here, they had a couple of ex-Eagles playing for them that first year. I went over to the locker room one day to see Frank Tripuka. Frank and I had come up together in 1949 with the Eagles, and Bob Hudson was also here. He played defensive halfback for them. When I walked into the dressing room, I heard this cackling over in the corner and it was Hardy Brown. He played linebacker one year for the Broncos. "How's the cheekbone, Toy Boy?" He was like Bucko; he beamed when he hurt someone, and I think Hardy remembered every hit he ever had in his entire career. I went over and shook hands with him, and he said, "No hard feelings." I said, "You asshole."

A STEEL-DRIVING MAN

JOHN HENRY JOHNSON

RUNNING BACK

Calgary 1953

San Francisco 1954–56

Detroit Lions 1957–59

Pittsburgh Steelers 1960–65

Houston Oilers 1966

If I was going down a dark alley where hoodlums hang out late at night, I would rather have John Henry with me than anyone else on earth. He was just a helluva nice guy. But he hit like a tornado—all over you at once. And he was absolutely fearless.

—Leo Nomellini

John Henry told the Captain,
A man ain't nothin' but a man,
And if I don't beat your steam drill down,
I'll die with a hammer in my hand,
Lawd, Lawd,
I'll die with a hammer in my hand.

—Folk Song

JOHN HENRY JOHNSON

THE people from the Hall of Fame called me in January and told me there was a possibility I would get in. I was starting to think that I wasn't going to make until I was dead. After not getting in for so many years, I figured they'd wait until I died. Then everybody would feel sorry for me and say, "Well, let's put old John Henry in there." I'd have been in the Hall, but it wouldn't have done me a damn bit of good. The last three or four years I had been a finalist, and the first couple of times I got real high-spirited, expecting it to happen. But each year I didn't make it and that knocked me down a little. This last time I wasn't going to do anything but wait and see. Then it came true.

Let's face it, my stats were just as good as anybody who was in the Hall. I had almost 7,000 yards rushing and was number three or four the year I retired. My stats are better than thirteen running backs who were already in there—Ollie Matson, Lenny Moore, John David Crow, just to name a few. Frank Gifford had 3,600 yards and Paul Hornung had 2,000 yards carrying the ball, or something like that. They were in, and I was still on the outside with over 6,000. I'm not trying to take anything away from anybody, don't get me wrong, but I can't think of any other yardstick they can use except the total yards you gained. It may have been that guys who played in New York and Green Bay, places like that, got a lot of press back in those years, because their teams were winning. They were better known than I was, but I thought you were supposed to make it on your own merits, not on what your team did.

The ceremony itself was fabulous, just fabulous. Art Rooney was my presenter, and that made it a real historical moment because he's a historical guy. Mr. Rooney is the grand old man of football and one of the nicest owners I ever played for. He was interested in you as an individual and helped you any time he could if you had any problems. He was a different kind of owner because he appreciated the players. I used to talk to Mr. Rooney all the time about not getting in, and I know he put up a fight for me with the people at the Hall of Fame. There was never any question that he should be the one to present me.

My father was a railroad man, and he named me after that steel-driving man, John Henry. I was born in Waterproof, Louisiana, down near Natchez, but actually I grew up in Pittsburg, California. I had four brothers and one sister. I was the baby. My father died when I was very young so my mother and one of my brothers, Milford, moved out west. Growing up in California was nice because it gave me a chance to go to school and develop myself. The school system was good and I got a good education.

We moved out there around 1945 or '46, and I played a little bit of football in junior high school. I didn't start to play serious ball until my sophomore year in high school. My first year I played offensive end; then they moved me to fullback, and I've been a fullback ever since. We won the championship two years out of the three that I played in high school, and I made all-county and all-California. We had an excellent coach, Buck Weaver, and he had a lot of influence on me, on the way I think and behave. Coach Weaver was always checking up to make sure you were hitting the books and keeping your grades up. He also helped me pick the college I went to, St. Marys.

I got thirty or forty scholarship offers, and Coach Weaver thought I would be better off going to a small school. It was only twenty miles from my home and looking back on it now it was a good place for me to go. Also, a lot of St. Marys' alumni lived in the Oakland area. They were running quite a few of the companies around there, and I figured that would make things easier for me after I got out of school. I could get a job. After I had gone to St. Marys for two years, they disbanded football. The school wasn't making any money. I transferred to Arizona State, and that was quite different. It was a big school and I was living on campus. I really enjoyed it out there and we had a good football team. We won our conference two years in a row.

At that time we were still playing both ways; in fact I did that my first couple of years in the pros. On defense I played corner or linebacker, and I always liked that. It gave you a chance to get people back for what they did to you when you were running the ball. When I got the opportunity, I'd give them back everything they gave me. Double.

The scouts began to come around in my junior year and started giving me questionnaires to fill out. By the time I was a senior, I was getting so many of them I figured that I was probably going to get a chance to play in the pros. The Steelers drafted me as their number two pick, but I didn't want to go to Pittsburgh because I thought it would be too cold. They traded my rights to the 49ers, but in the meantime I had gotten a good offer from Calgary, so I decided to go up and play in Canada. It was a little different kind of football. The field was bigger and they passed most of the time, but I enjoyed it until it started to get cold. I had a good year up there, and the 49ers were hearing all about the good things I was doing, so I decided to come back and play for San Francisco.

I was with San Francisco for three years. We had a good offensive team, but we weren't too hot on defense. Oh, we could sure score points, but it's defense that wins games, not offense. Can you believe we lost a game, 55–54? It was exciting playing with Y. A. Tittle, Joe Perry, and Hugh McIlhenny. They called us the "Million Dollar Backfield." I'm still looking for the million. My first salary was $15,000, with a $3,500 bonus, for a number two draft choice. When I retired, I was making $40,000. People ask me what I think about the players of today compared to my time. I tell them that there are only two differences. One, the guys are bigger and maybe some of the linemen are a little quicker. Two, and this is very noticeable, they make more money.

We were losing a lot of games at San Francisco. They decided that there were too many running backs, so I was traded to Detroit. I wasn't getting to carry the ball very much at San Francisco, so I was glad to go. The first year I was with Detroit, we won the championship and I had a good season running the ball. When I was at Detroit, and even before I got there, we were always beating Cleveland. That was during the Otto Graham and Jim Brown years, when they had some real good teams. One of the games I remember most was against Cleveland because I gained over 200 yards. It seems that some teams have systems that match up against other teams because they never have any success against you.

I always used to have a lot of fun playing against Cleveland because I was always very successful. They had a couple of huge defensive tackles, and we would always have a big intimidation battle going on. People would step on your hands, bite you, twist your legs in pileups, scratch my eyes, and if I was on the ground they'd be choking me. All those things used to annoy me. Bob Gain was good at stepping on your hand while you were getting up. He'd step right on my hand and then say, "Excuse me, John, I didn't mean to do that." Then he'd hit me with an extra blow after I was down. "John, I'm sorry. I didn't hear the whistle." We had a lot of fun.

Being a back, all of the defensive men liked to try and intimidate me. They were always trying to show you that you weren't going to get away with what you did the last time. They'd be doing all sorts of things to you. About a month ago I saw Sam Huff at a golf tournament. We were talking and he was telling me about the things I did to him. I said, "Hey, Sam, you seem to forget that you did a lot of things to me. Twist my arm, hit me when I wasn't looking. You seem to forget about that." The Eagles had some guys who would do anything to stop you. There was Kilroy—we had quite a few run-ins and he was tough. They had another guy, Wayne Robinson—he'd hit you in a minute. Better not turn your eye away from him. You had to look him right in the eye when you were coming through a hole or going out for a pass. Turn your back on him one minute, he'd put the club on you. Ernie Stautner, who played with me at Pittsburgh, was another one. Ernie was taped up like a mummy, and he'd use that right arm to beat a guy to death. He was small for a tackle, but for a guy who weighed 230 pounds he was really tough.

We were playing Cleveland and Ed Modzelewski came in, trying to block a punt. I hit him right in the mouth, and Paul Brown was over on the sidelines yelling at me. "Johnson, you've hit everybody in the league." I told him that we had a tie game going because everybody in the league had hit me. Another time I blocked a defensive back who played for the Giants, Eddie Hughes. I broke his cheekbone, and he was real nice about it. When I visited him in the hospital, he told me, "Nice block."

The last year I was at Detroit they got a new coach, and I was playing defense all the time. I wanted to play some offense. Then the Lions traded me to Pittsburgh, and that was the best thing that ever happened to me because I really got a chance to run the football. I really enjoyed playing in Pittsburgh, playing ball with Bobby Layne again, and Buddy Parker was a great coach. I had my most productive years when I was playing for Buddy Parker and I learned more about football from him. He was one of the most knowledgeable football people that I was ever around. He wanted effort because he felt that if you did what you were taught all week, and put out a great effort, you would win more than you'd lose. Buddy would fine you in a minute if he didn't see you put out a good effort.

I played with the Steelers for six years, and we didn't win any championships, but we were quite competitive. Our problem was that we didn't have the depth of maturity to go all the way. We were as good as any of them until somebody got injured. While I was with the Steelers, we won nine or ten games a couple of years and won our division. Pittsburgh's training camps were always tough. We scrimmaged every day, and I always thought we scrimmaged too much. But later on in the year, when everybody else was getting tired and going down, we were always getting stronger and stronger. If you could survive the first few games, you knew you could make it to the end of the year.

We always had a tough series against the Eagles when I played with Pittsburgh. It was a real state rivalry, and they used to call it the "Battle for the Brown Jug." The Eagles had some great defensive guys, and they also had some good backs like Clarence Peaks and Tom Brookshier. It was war when we played each other. Who could last the longest? There were a lot of fights on the field, particularly when we played in Philadelphia. We actually had three or four riots. I remember one game where just before halftime a big fight started, and the fans came running out on the field. The poor band was all lined up to march, and those fans were taking their drums away from them and throwing them at the football players.

My last year was with Houston. They got a new coach at Pittsburgh and we were losing a lot of games. When you're playing on a team that's losing, everybody starts blaming everybody else, and I guess it was my turn. The Steelers traded me to Houston at the end of the 1965 season. I played that last year, but I didn't do much. George Blanda was the quarterback and he threw the ball every down. I didn't get a chance to run the ball, and all I had to do was block. I wasn't even getting my uniform dirty. At the end of the year I quit because I was starting to feel old, and it was just getting tough to play. We won the first three games when I was at Houston, and then we lost the next eleven, something like that, and it just wasn't much fun anymore. Fifteen years is a long career for a running back, and I figured I should give it up and get established in my other life.

Playing football, being an athlete, period, has its good points. It makes you disciplined and teaches you how to work together with people. You learn how to organize yourself for whatever you're doing, a lot of the little things that you need after you get through playing. I always worked while I was playing football, usually in public relations, and I spent twelve years with the Carling Brewing Company. Right after I quit football, I got a job with Columbia Gas. They have offices all over the place in Ohio and Pennsylvania, and I was always on the road. Banquets, conventions, I was always giving speeches.

After twelve years of that, I started the John Henry Johnson Foundation. I'd go around to recreation centers talking to kids, and I made a lot of speeches to various groups. During the summer I ran a football camp, and we'd take city kids out there and give them a little football instruction. I'd invite some of the guys I played with, and we would have a real nice time with the kids. I did that for about five years and then came to work for the Allegheny County Community Services Department.

I actually have two jobs right now. During the winter I work in energy assistance. That helps out people who have high utility bills and can't pay them. The rest of the time I'm out in the high schools and youth clubs making speeches about drugs. You'd be surprised what some of these kids will tell you. It would shock you. They don't talk to the teacher, but they come up and confess to me. The teacher is saying, "I didn't know that kid was doing that." Some kid will be standing there telling me, "I take this drug on Monday and that drug on Tuesday," and the teacher is standing there with his mouth open. I ask them how they get the money for this stuff, and they say, "I steal it." They steal money out of their mother's pocketbook. They even steal things out of the house and sell them. The young girls are working as prostitutes. It's amazing and very sad, the things I've heard.

We don't have a follow-up procedure, but I hope that what I'm saying will make a few reconsider what they're doing. When they introduce me, they read all of my stats and it kind of impresses them. Most of them already know who I am because they're sports fans. We usually have a question-and-answer period, which is the best part of the program. Sometimes it gets pretty hot, but I get a chance to talk directly to them and tell them exactly how I feel about things.

In my time we didn't have much of that sort of thing going on. There were a few, but I don't think they were into drugs. You'd see pills around, bennys and that sort of thing. We also had a few big drinkers and everybody knew who they were. They always seemed to be ready to play hard on Sunday, though. "Big Daddy" Lipscombe was a drinker, but he was an excellent football player. It was a tragedy the way he died, and to this day I don't believe he did it to himself. He was a guy who was always laughing about something. You'd always hear him talking to somebody on the field. "Trying to trap the Daddy, huh? I'm waiting for you. You just forget about trying to trap the Daddy." He could get a lot of guys boiling talking like that, and he could do what he said he could do. Daddy was big and strong enough to get the job done. He also had a fear of needles that was on the fanatic side. He wouldn't let them give him a shot when we got in those big lines so they could give the whole team cold and flu shots. They couldn't tie him down to give him a flu shot. A man who has that kind of fear of needles, he's not going to shoot himself with no dope. That doesn't jive. I think somebody shot him up while he was sleeping. Got him drunk and shot him up to hook him. They didn't want to kill him; they wanted a customer. That was a big tragedy. I've seen a few, and that was the worst because I was real close to Big Daddy. He was my friend and buddy.

At one time I had aspirations of being a coach, but I never got the opportunity. During the summer they always used to call me from Arizona State, and I would go out and work with the backs. I always enjoyed that and think I would have made a good coach. The way it looks to me, coaching is a friendship kind of thing, and whoever the coach is, he gets his friends in. They seem to have their own fraternity. We don't have too many blacks in the coaching or management professions right now, but we do have 50 percent of the players. We're good enough to play and win for them, but we're not good enough to coach and direct the game. They fire ten or twelve coaches every year, and all I ever asked was the chance to coach. If I failed, fire me.

One thing I have to say, I don't think these young black players in the game today have any idea what we had to go through. They might have heard a little bit, but when they came in, we had their beds made for them and it was a lot easier. Some of the guys who came before I did, the problems and discrimination they had to go through, it was rough. When I started playing, that kind of thing was sort of on its way out. People were starting to accept the fact that we were good football players and we could contribute to the game.

When I was raised up, I always played with white kids. But whenever white kids bothered me, we'd fight. I didn't take nothing from anyone. In a football game, though, I hit the black guy as hard as I hit the white guy. I didn't think about color when I was playing. On occasion I'd get a little trouble. I was called a "nigger" a few times, and all that would do was make me play a little harder, hit them harder. I ran over guys if they got in my way, but I had a few moves, too. I believe the quickest way down the field is straight, and they taught me to run north and south. I didn't fool around too much, and I didn't take no pity on them—just rolled them little backs up if they got in my way.

There was only one racial thing that I really remember. We went to Oklahoma when I was playing with Pittsburgh to play an exhibition game, and they told us we had to stay in a black hotel. I said, "Hell, I'm not going to play. If I have to stay in a black hotel, I'm not going to play." There were so many black guys on the team that if we didn't play, they wouldn't have a game. Whoever it was that didn't want us in their hotel got the message and changed their mind. Economics. You can change a lot of people's minds with the dollar.

The most important thing that I got from football was the friends I made. I go to these golf outings and run into guys I played with and against, and we go out and have a nice time—socialize and laugh and tell war stories. Those defensive guys I played against are always teasing me about my golf game. Art Donovan, he's always on my case. Chuck Bednarik, Sam Huff, we have a nice bond. Even though we fought on the field—I really went head to head with some of those guys—we could always go out and forget it after the game was over. There are a few guys who are still holding grudges from way back, but just a few.

IRON MEN

If I could write my own inscription, it would say: "An excellent" —I'm writing my own, now, so I've got to make it sound good— "an excellent football player, a great blocker, a good pass catcher, and a good runner." But most of all I want to be remembered as a man who loved the game.

DON'T ROUSE THE SLEEPING DOG

MARION MOTLEY

RUNNING BACK

Cleveland Browns 1946–53

Pittsburgh Steelers 1955

Marion lived right near me. One day after practice I was counting my pennies and trying to figure out the cheapest way to get home. Marion didn't say a word—except "Get in"—when he pulled up his car. So every day we used to drive to practice together and drive home, one of the greatest stars in the game and a guy just fighting to stay on the club. But that's the way he was. If you were his teammate, he would do anything for you.

—Joe Spencer

THERE were five of us in the Damon Runyon game that they had down in Houston in 1949. There were three black players from the Cleveland Browns—Bill Willis, Horace Gillom, and myself—and two black College All-Stars, Buddy Young and Joe Perry. We couldn't stay with the other players because blacks weren't allowed in the hotels, so we all stayed in a private house. The All-Stars were at the Shamrock Hotel, and when Young and Perry went there to practice they would have to go to the back of the hotel, enter through the coal room, then through the swimming pool and get dressed in the basement. Then they would have to go out the same way to get to the hotel lawn where the team was practicing.

The day of the game it was raining so hard you could hardly see across the street. We couldn't ride to the game in the bus because the teams were staying on the other side of town, so we caught a cab. We got to the gate we were supposed to go in, and there was this little old, squatty kid in charge. We told him we're players and he said, "Don't no players go in this gate." I said, "But this is where our coach told us to go in." Again he said, "No players in this gate. You go up to the other gate and see if they'll let you in there." I don't know if you've ever been to Rice Stadium, but it's two city blocks long. We walked to the gate at the other end, where they said we couldn't come in, and turned around and came back. None of us brought our raincoats with us to Houston, so we had to buy one there and mine hit me right around my ass. By now I was soaking wet, and when we got back to the first gate, I said, "Why don't you let us come in out of the rain and when our coach comes along he can verify who we are." That little bastard said, "Goddamn it, didn't you hear what I said? No players come in this gate."

All right, just as I was about to turn around, get in a cab, and go back to the house and say, "Fuck this game," Paul Brown and the team drove up in the bus. I just lay back and sure enough, they got out of the bus and started heading in the gate. Paul saw the three of us and yelled over, "Motley, what are you guys waiting for?" I said, "We've been standing out here in the rain for an hour. That little stubby son-of-a-bitch standing right there said no players in this gate." Paul said to the guy, "Did you tell him that?" and that stubby bastard looked at him and said, "Oh, is he with your team?" I was so mad I went looking for the guy who was running the damn game and finally caught up with him. I told him, "You got a stubby son-of-

When John Henry Johnson was inducted into the pro football Hall of Fame in 1987, a lot of people, including Steelers' owner Art Rooney, said, "It's about time." One of the most formidable runners in NFL history, John Henry was characterized by Bobby Layne: "He went three ways: offense, defense, and to-the-death." In his acceptance speech at Canton, Johnson spoke of his playing days: "Old-timers were driven by pride and not dollar signs. They looked at fame as something to be earned by performance and not press clippings."

Looking more like a dancer than a football player, Elroy Hirsch demonstrates the style that earned him one of the most famous nicknames in the NFL—"Crazylegs." Asked about Hirsch's unique style of running, Norm Van Brocklin said, "You've heard about the guy who zigged when he should have zagged? Well, Elroy also had a zog and a couple of varieties of zugs when he got rolling full-tilt."

Maybe the most celebrated "little man" to play pro ball, Eddie LeBaron proved that his size didn't mean a thing. One of the most gifted ball handlers ever to play the game, LeBaron learned how to get around rather than over the BMFs he was playing against. "I made the mistake one day of trying to straight-arm Len Ford of the Browns, who was something like six-five and 220. My hand got inside his face mask somehow, and he bit me. I was careful after that to make sure where I put my hand."

In 1942 the Philadelphia Eagles spent the magnificent sum of $100 to pick up Bosh Pritchard from the Cleveland Rams. There was never any doubt that the Eagles got their money's worth, because the crooning halfback could do it all. Besides the usual running, catching, and kicking, this versatile individual could also go out at halftime and sing a few tunes.

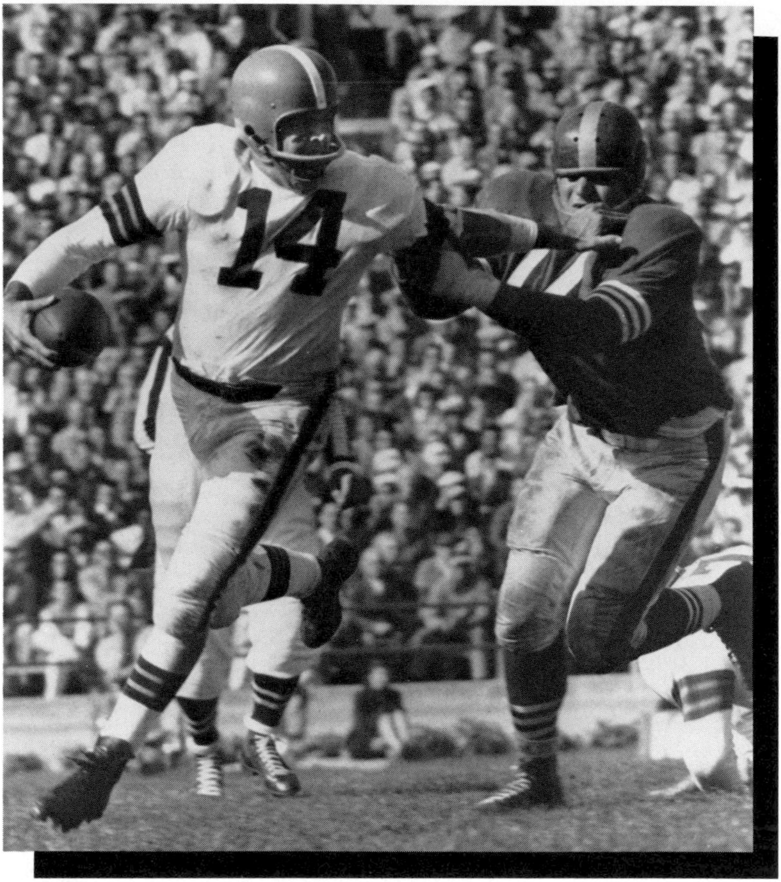

Otto Graham helped make the forward pass the ultimate weapon during the ten years he played for the Cleveland Browns, but he was no shrinking violet. Not afraid to run the ball, Graham scored three touchdowns by himself when the Browns beat Detroit in 1954 for the title. Whether Graham was the best quarterback to play the game can be endlessly debated, but he may the closest thing pro football ever had to Babe Ruth. (PHOTO BY FRANK RIPPON/NFL PHOTOS)

When Redskins' owner George Marshall saw Jim Ricca stop 230-pound Villanova fullback Ralph Pasquariello single-handedly, he knew he had to have him. It helps when the boss likes you, but Ricca found it rather disconcerting when Marshall would breeze into the locker room and say, "Hi, Jimsie." Today Ricca is president of the Washington Redskins Alumni Association, helping players from his era whose luck has run out. "It may sound corny, but I owe something to the guys who were there alongside me."

The juggernaut known as Marion Motley gains yardage against San Francisco during the 1949 season. Maybe the best all-around player in NFL history, Motley helped the Browns win four championships with his hard running and devastating blocking. When asked to describe Motley, Paul Brown said, "Nothing devastates a football team like a selfish player. It's a cancer. The greatest back I ever had was Marion Motley. You know why? The only statistic he ever knew was whether we won or lost. The man was completely unselfish." (PHOTO BY FRANK RIPPON/NFL PHOTOS)

Packers' quarterback Bart Starr is just about to find out why Joe Schmidt was considered *the* middle linebacker of his era. Van Patrick, who broadcast the Lions' games, said of Schmidt, "He makes so many tackles, it's actually embarrassing to broadcast the games. I have to keep calling Joe's name so many times during an afternoon that I figure the fans who are listening think I'm making it up."
(PHOTO BY MALCOLM EMMONS/NFL PHOTOS)

One of the classic combinations of all time...Bart Starr takes the ball from Ringo. The center of Lombardi's legendary Packers, Ringo remembers those years well. "Vince made us believe that the only reason we ever lost was because the clock ran out on us. He used to take out films of other teams and tell us that they were trying to copy us. Then he'd say we shouldn't worry because they couldn't be like us, even if they tried. I think Vince was right—I don't think there was anybody like us *ever*."
(PHOTO: NFL PHOTOS)

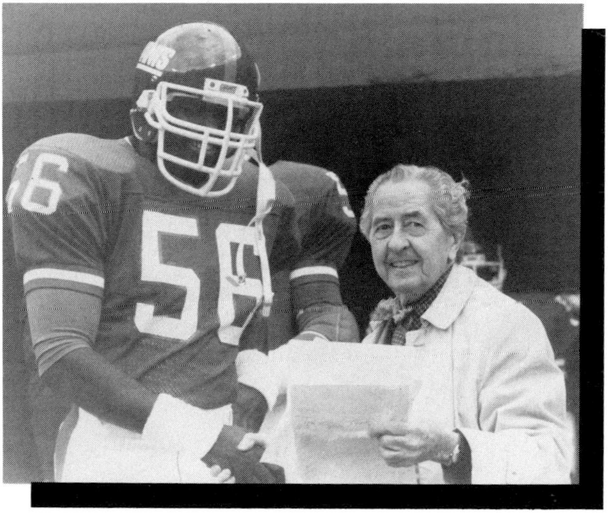

Cy Fraser introduces Lawrence Taylor at the Meadowlands during the 1987 season. Starting in 1936, Cy has worked for the New York Giants on game days, following them to five stadiums in three boroughs and three states. His memories of more than five decades of Giants' football include such things as a great catch by Frank Gifford that helped win a championship and the excitement of the Super Bowl season. Cy also remembers going to see John McVay for the lineups and having him say with a smile, "Cy, who would *you* want to start?"

Toy Ledbetter has the map of the NFL embossed on his face. The "journeyman ball player," Ledbetter typifies the majority of players in the NFL when there were only thirty-three players on a squad. "A guy like me had to do everything. I went down on kickoffs and punts, ran back kickoffs and punts, blocked extra points, played some halfback and fullback—everything."

In a business where people come and go before the ink is dry on the media guide, Jim Gallagher is an exception to the rule. He has worked in the Philadelphia front office for almost forty years. In addition to his abilities as a public relations director, he obviously has many skills, but most importantly he's a nice guy. The Philadelphia Eagles Alumni chapter states, "Jim should be cloned so he could continue to help players for eternity."

a-bitch out there who had us walking the whole length of Rice Stadium in the pouring rain because he didn't want to let us in the gate." He told me to show him the guy and fired the little bastard on the spot.

The reason they played that game in the first place was because Texas was trying to get a pro team down there, and I told him, "You want to get professional football down here and if you do, you're going to have black players. Unless you change your ways, there's going to be hell to pay. You guys ought to get yourselves together."

When I started playing football in Canton, Ohio, there weren't that many black kids playing, and you had to be three times better than the white kids to make the team. If you weren't hurting somebody, they wouldn't let you play and it made you so mad you ended up taking it out on somebody. I had a friend ahead of me in high school, and he was a very light-skinned guy. They were playing some team in southern Ohio, and the guy he was playing against said, "Hey, I hear you got a nigger on this team. Where is he? When is the nigger coming in the game?" My friend didn't say anything, but he sure beat that guy's ass during the game.

My family is originally from Albany, Georgia. That's where I was born. My father was a molder in a foundry, and when some of my relatives migrated up to Canton in the 1920s, my parents brought us along. I was two years old when we moved and had three brothers and one sister. I was the only one in my family who played sports, and I almost didn't get to do it either. When I went out for junior high football, they didn't give me a suit, so I stood around for two weeks in a pair of World War I khaki pants my uncle gave me, waiting for a chance to play. Three days before our first game the coach asked, "Who hasn't been in yet?" I said, "Me," and they put me in on defense. I was playing tackle, and they were really going to use me for fodder because I didn't even have any pads on. Well, nobody could block me. I was knocking everybody down and broke up every play they tried. That damn coach said, "Where in the hell have you been?" I said, "I've been standing right here." He told the manager to make sure I got some equipment the next day.

I played my high school ball at McKinley in Canton, and shortly before I graduated I got a letter from Clemson University asking me if I'd like to come and play football for them. I wrote back and told them, I think you might have made a mistake because I'm a black player. I never heard another word from them, and I went down to South Carolina State College, which was an all-black school.

After I'd been at South Carolina for about three months, I got this letter from Jim Aikens, who had coached at my high school. He'd moved to Akron University before I was on the team, and while I was playing at McKinley he had scouted me. Aikens told me that he had left Akron and was now at the University of Nevada, in Reno, so I changed schools in the middle of the season. After growing up in the North, I didn't like being down in Orangeburg, South Carolina. No, sir, I didn't like that at all.

We played one game against the University of Idaho, where I was the only black player on the field. The fans were calling me all kinds of names. "Alligator bait," "Nigger," "Get him off the field," "Kill him." Idaho's coach was a guy named Francis Schmidt, who at one time coached Ohio State. Before the game started, he told Aiken that I couldn't play. He just flat-out said, "Marion can't play." Jim said, "You mean to tell me that after getting me all the way up here, you're not going to let him play? What kind of shenanigans are these? This is bullshit." Jim was about five-seven and maybe 135 pounds, soaking wet, and all of a sudden he wanted to fight Schmidt. I had to grab Jim and put him under my arm with his feet off the ground. He was yelling, "Put me down, put me down. I'll kill that son-of-a-bitch." After he cooled off, I put him down and he said, "Motley, you go out and tell our football players that we're going home." Right away Schmidt said, "Oh, no, you can't do that." He was afraid of all those fans who'd come to see a game. "We have to come up with a compromise." They messed around and finally

Schmidt came up with "Motley can't play the first half, but he can play the second." Some compromise.

They were supposed to beat us 28–3, something like that. Idaho was in the Pacific Coast Conference, and they played Southern Cal, UCLA, teams like that. We had a small ball club, but we were building a name for ourselves. When I started the second half they were leading 6–0, and the first time I touched the ball I went to the goal line. I put the ball down, and when I turned around the referee was telling me to bring it back. We were penalized five yards for offsides, and about four or five plays later I took the ball to the five-yard line. The referee called it back again. In the last quarter I ran another touchdown in, and they called that one back too. Idaho beat us, 6–0.

We played another game at Brigham Young University. After we got there, I was walking down the street with another guy and some little kids came running up to me and said, "He ain't got no tail. I thought you said he had a tail." I told the little bastards to get away from me or I was going to kick them in the ass. Then I ended up going back to the hotel and sitting in my room until game time because I didn't want to get mad at little kids who were just repeating what their ignorant parents were saying.

I spent three seasons at Nevada and hurt my knee, so I came home to Canton and got a job with Republic Steel. My knee was pretty bad because the muscle around it had been torn, but I was burning scrap iron with a torch, and it got awful hot where I was working. All of that heat seemed to help the knee, and it healed up just fine.

I was inducted into the Navy on Christmas Day, 1944, and went to bootcamp at Great Lakes Naval Base. Paul Brown found out I was there, and he asked me to come over so he could see what size I was. Paul coached at Massillon High when I was at McKinley, and they were real rivals of ours. He thought I'd be out of shape like some of the other guys, but I was a mean, 225 pounds at that time. He was elated over the fact that I hadn't gotten fat, and he put me in what they call ship's company. That meant I could stay at Great Lakes, and I played football for Paul during the war.

When I got out of the service, I wrote and asked Paul for a job. He turned me down and wrote back that he had enough backs. Then they got Bill Willis, the first black to play in the league. He walked on and asked for a tryout, and since Paul had Bill at Ohio State, he knew the quality of ball player he was. Bill made the team the first day of scrimmage.

About a week later Bob Voigts, one of the Browns' assistant coaches, called me and asked me if I'd like to try out. A few days later and he would have missed me because I was all set to go back to the University of Nevada. I told him yes, and one of my cousins drove me up to the Browns' training camp at Bowling Green University. I got there just before practice, and after they gave me my equipment we went out to the field and immediately ran wind sprints. The only back that could beat me was Bill Lund, and he had been on the track team at Case University.

Paul put me on the second team, and I could feel the animosity among the other backs. Bill Willis and I were rooming together and I told him, "I hope Paul takes me off that second team and puts me on the third or fourth because I can understand why those guys are mad. They've been here four weeks, and I'm here one day and they put me on the second team. I hope Paul puts me back and when we start scrimmaging, then we'll decide who it's going to be." I think the Lord must have heard me that night because without my saying a word, Paul put me back on the fourth team. I was comfortable and everybody else was comfortable. One day we had a scrimmage, and I was playing linebacker and making a few tackles and hitting people, and somebody asked Bill Willis if something was wrong with me. Bill told him, "Nothing's wrong with Motley, he's just trying to make this team." Gene Fekete was supposed to be the starting fullback that year, but he hurt his knee in the first game of the season, and from then on I was the first-string fullback and I also played linebacker.

MARION MOTLEY

A lot of people don't know this, and they always talk about Jackie Robinson being the first black in professional sports, but Bill Willis and I were playing at Cleveland in 1946, a year before Jackie got to Brooklyn. The reason he got hired, Branch Rickey made the statement that if Bill Willis and Marion Motley can play a contact sport like football, Jackie Robinson should be able to play a noncontact sport like baseball. I give Paul Brown credit for Bill and myself getting a chance to play football. At that time the league had kind of an unwritten rule about blacks not playing, but Paul didn't think too much of a rule like that. He was taking a chance in those days because a lot of people didn't want black players doing anything in pro sports.

Paul talked to Bill and myself and he told us that people were going to be laying for us. "They're going to call you names and they're going to try to hurt you. It's up to you to take it and take whatever they give out." It was rough. I'd be on the ground, and they'd step on my hands with those damn old cleats. My hands were always bloody, but if either Willis or myself had been hotheads and gotten into fights and things like that, it would have put things back ten years. Blacks would have never been accepted like they were. Sometimes I wanted to just kill some of those guys, and the officials would just stand right there. They'd see those guys stepping on us and hear them saying things and just turn their backs.

That kind of crap went on for two or three years until they found out what kind of players we were. They found out that while they were calling us "niggers," I was running for touchdowns and Willis was knocking the shit out of them. They stopped calling us names and started trying to catch up with us.

Our last regular game my rookie year we were going to play the Miami Seahawks, in Miami. I got a letter: "You black son-of-a-bitch, you come down here and run across our goal line, you'll be a dead black son-of-a-bitch." I showed the letter to Bill Willis but otherwise kept it to myself. About a week later, I went to see Paul and told him, "I've got something to show you." He looked at the letter and couldn't believe it. "Well, Marion, what do you want to do?" I told him, "Paul, I'm not going and I don't think Bill wants to go either." He was agreeable and said, "I can understand your feelings. You both stay here and when we get back, we'll go on from there." The Browns went down there and beat the shit out of them, 60–7, something like that.

There are three games that really stand out in my mind, and those are the ones that I always tell people about. The first was in 1948 when we played the Yankees in New York. That was in our dynasty days, and at one time during the game we were twenty-eight points behind. We scored just before the half, so it was 28–7 when we came out for the second half. I scored the next three touchdowns and we ended up beating them. We played three games in seven days that year. The Yankees on Sunday in Yankee Stadium, the Los Angeles Dons in Los Angeles on Thanksgiving Day, and San Francisco the next Sunday. That was the year we didn't lose a game.

Then there was the game we played against the Eagles when the leagues merged in 1950. Greasy Neale was telling everybody, "The high school kids are coming to play the pros." You know what I think gave us the incentive to go out there and play the game we did? A Philadelphia *Enquirer* sportswriter came up to live with us the three weeks we were in camp, and he was going to write a story about it. He used to get the paper sent up from Philadelphia every day, and he'd cut out the sports column. Pretty soon the board was full of those articles, all of this shit about how they were going to do this and that to us.

When we walked out on that field that evening, we wanted to beat them because we wanted that guy to have to eat his words. We kicked off to the Eagles and held them, and then they kicked to us. A little back we had, "Dopey" Phelps, went all the way in for a touchdown, but they got Lenny Ford for holding. The Eagles kicked to us again and Phelps took it to the thirty-five. From then on, the Eagles couldn't do a thing.

We beat them throwing the ball in that first game, and Greasy

Neale started saying that we weren't nothing but a basketball team. The next time we play them, we never put the ball in the air and beat them again. We ran that ball right down their throats. That's the kind of guy Paul Brown was, stubborn, especially if he got something in his mind. We were on the side lines screaming, "Throw the ball, throw the ball," but he wouldn't let Otto throw it one time.

The third game would be the championship game that same year. Late in the fourth quarter we got the ball on an interception, and Groza kicked the field goal with twenty-eight seconds left in the game. I was somewhat of a goat in that game because I fumbled and they scored. The ground was frozen, and we came out in our cleats and Los Angeles was wearing gym shoes. We finally had to go to the gym shoes, but before we did, I was running up the sidelines with the ball. When I went to stop my feet skidded, and when I tried to catch my balance they knocked the ball out of my hands. Larry Brink took it into the end zone, and that made it 28–27 in favor of L.A. We fought back and stayed in the game and won it on Groza's kick, 30–28.

I think I would fit right in with the backs they have today because when I was playing, Norm Stanley from the 49ers and myself were the two biggest backs in the league. I weighed 230 at that time, and most of the guys weren't that big. Take Buddy Young. I don't think he ever got over 160, but he was a hell of a football player and he could knock you down if he got the chance. One time we were playing the New York Yankees, and at that time they were using the single wing. Every once in a while, however, they would go into the double wing and I would see Buddy running with the ball toward me. Then he gave it off to Lowell Wagner and Wagner went the other way. I forgot about Buddy and took after Wagner. The next thing I knew my feet were eight feet up in the air and I landed right on top of Buddy. He had made a loop, and he came right around and hit me. When I found out it was him, my feelings were hurt, so I just spread my legs and arms and wouldn't let him get up. You can imagine what he said. He was calling me all sorts of names. "Get up. Let me up, you big bastard."

After the game I was talking to Buddy's mother, and all of a sudden I felt somebody beating on me. It was Buddy's sister, Claudine. They were twins. His real name was Claude and she was Claudine. "What do you mean by falling on my brother like that? Why didn't you let him up?" I said, "Are you kidding? I wasn't going to let that little son-of-a-bitch up after he done almost killed my ass out there. I didn't want anybody to see who hit me."

I never had anybody that I really had a thing with, but there were a few who were really tough to play. The Giants had Arnie Weinmeister, and they said at the time he was the strongest man in football. I don't know about that, but he was strong, big, and fast. Arnie was a hell of a football player, even if you didn't bother him, but get him mad, he'd kill somebody. We had a guy by the name of John Sandusky, who coaches now for the Lions, and John played tackle, so he was in front of Arnie. He couldn't block Arnie, so he swung an elbow at him and missed. Now Arnie had a voice like a lady, real high, and here's my right hand of God, he said, "You son-of-a-bitch, I'll kill you. Swing an elbow at me, will you? You've got a bad afternoon coming." The next play he took his arm and hit John so hard he drove him right into the ground. Now he was after Otto, and I didn't even get to the defensive end like I was supposed to. I had to get Arnie. Arnie and I were going at it, and when we had a time-out, I went over to John and said, "Haven't you heard about the sleeping dog?" He said, "What the hell are you talking about?" I said, "If you see a dog sleeping, let that son-of-a-bitch sleep. Don't rouse him. Arnie, he was asleep for a while, but you went and woke him up. I'm going to have him all afternoon because you aren't blocking him worth a damn." I mean, he didn't block him once after that. Arnie kicked him, punched him—he did everything he could to John. He'd have been better off if he'd hit him with that elbow.

Hardy Brown was another mean one, and he put more football players out of the game than anyone else I know of. He had that hitch of his, and he would hit people and just put them out. I don't mean just out for a season; I mean completely out of football. I played against him for years and always stayed out of his way, but he finally caught up with me on a kickoff or something and stung the shit out of me.

In 1951 I hurt my knee. It was a real fluke accident. We were practicing a reverse body block, where you step in and put your knee between the guy's legs and then let your leg whip. Tony Adamle and I were working together, and his knee hit my knee; that was the beginning of my problems. The ground was very hard, and before the practice was over my knee was swollen up like a balloon. During training camp in 1954, I was running downfield on a kick and felt something tear in my knee. I stayed out that year and knew Cleveland wouldn't want me back. They had all those young backs like Curley Morrison and Dub Jones and Chet "the Jet" Hanulak, so they traded me to Pittsburgh in 1955. I hurt my knee again. Since I was thirty-five years old, I quit.

When I finished playing, I asked Paul for a job coaching, but he said I didn't have enough experience. That's the kind of bullshit you got. For years after I quit, the Browns used my moves to teach my pass possession block, the trap, and the draw play. We basically had four plays that I did, and that was all—an end run, a buck up the middle, a trap play, and a screen pass. I'd only carry the ball eight or nine times a game, and I always thought I could have carried it a lot more, but Paul Brown was the coach and he was also a winner. He didn't need any advice from me. I was the first back to ever run the draw play, and the Browns told me I didn't have enough experience to coach. Paul also made some statements which I will never reveal, but they left me with a bad taste in my mouth for a while. I was very bitter for many years, and then I thought to myself, "There's no use going around carrying a chip on your shoulder, Marion." Today Paul and I are very close friends, and he's kind of mellowed.

When Otto Graham was coaching at Washington, I asked him for a job and he told me he had all the coaches he needed. He hired a defensive back to teach his offensive backs, and that's why Otto's backfield never moved the ball. Here's a guy played defensive ball all his career, and that would be like me trying to teach deep backs. Although I played defense, I don't know what to look for. You see an end or back move, your mind has to click right away or else you'll get burned. The same on offense. You have to know what you're doing or you can teach a runner a lot of undesirable habits. If I'm going off-tackle, I don't go full speed because if I do, and I get ready to cut, I'm off balance. You go three-quarters speed, and when you see the daylight, you have the extra speed to turn on. There's all sorts of things—how to get through the line, keys to look for—but I'm not mad at anybody anymore. I'm living and I've got a good livelihood.

When I left football, I went to the post office for a couple of years, and then I sold whiskey and worked for a construction company as their safety director. Then I was with the Ohio Lottery for about eight years until the Ohio Department of Youth Services asked me to come to work for them five years ago. Today I'm working at the Indian River School, which is a maximum security boys' industrial school. We handle them up to eighteen years old, and sometimes we get them as young as twelve. We have eight institutions in Ohio, two maximum-security and the rest semimaximum, and I'm involved with recreation. We put on a lot of intramural tournaments between the eight institutions. Basketball, softball, volleyball, and things like chess. At one time we had boxing and football, but those had to be cut out because of the injuries. A kid would get his leg hurt or arm broke, and it was quite expensive. Most of the kids stay about nine months, but we have a few felony-one and felony-two inmates who are here for quite a while longer.

I enjoy working with them, and so far I've been very fortunate because I think I relate to them and they relate to me. They know who I am, and if they don't, they find out very shortly from the other kids. They find out where I'm coming from and usually call me "Mr. Motley." You can see what drugs do to them in their faces and bodies, and they are always talking that sly talk: "Yeah, man" and all that crap. I tell them, "You better be trying to get yourself some education and make something of yourself. Otherwise, you're going to be in these kinds of places for the rest of your life."

A lot of these kids want to know what I think about football today, and I don't think there's a real way to compare the game today with the one we played. Our hands had to be on our chest, and if they moved from there, you got called for holding and it was fifteen yards. Another thing, the blocking is atrocious today. I don't care how strong these kids are, that doesn't make any difference. You can't just take your hands and push the other guy and expect to get him out of there. That's the reason you see so many field goals kicked today. They get down near that goal line and want to push and don't go anyplace. Down there we used to eat dirt. You'd root your way in, down on your knees, and use your shoulders and hit that guy. Guys who are playing today don't want to do that.

As far as runners are concerned, I don't really try to evaluate ball players. How would it look if I was talking to people, saying, "This guy was no good or that guy was no good." Look at Jim Brown. He was a great football player, but he just can't seem to get over a lot of things. He goes around making these statements, and he doesn't need to do that because he's got the name and nobody's going to take that away from him. He jumped on that Harris boy like that, and that was bullshit. I don't put anybody down because today I couldn't run across the street. My old lady walks five miles every day, and she tries to get me out there with her. I just can't keep up. She gets that little old gait of hers going and walks away from me every time. Sometimes I go shopping with her, and when we go into the mall, I always find one of those benches. I sit down, light up my cigar, and don't even try to keep up with her.

P A R T

V

BACKUP

HEY, DANNY, PICK UP THE WHITES

DANIEL M. ROONEY

PRESIDENT

Pittsburgh Steelers 1975–

In this business, ego can be a narcotic, and if people have any tendency it's usually to go the other way. Dan is a rare exception; you just don't run into very many sports figures who have it under control the way he does.
—Pete Rozelle

THERE have been times when it was tough to be Art Rooney's son. I went to North Catholic High School and played three years of football. Before I got there they wrote a story about me in the local newspaper. The headline read NORTH CATHOLIC HALFBACK PROBLEMS ARE OVER, complete with my photograph. Somebody at the paper must have thought that since I was Art Rooney's son, and he owned a professional football team, I would be the next Red Grange.

I've been president of the Steelers since 1975. One morning my father walked into my office and said, "As of now you're the president," and that was that. He still comes to work every day and likes to give his opinion. Occasionally my father still thinks I'm a kid, but over the years we've worked things out. I understand his point of view. He understands mine. My father is, and always has been, a politician. That's where the differences come in. It drove me crazy sometimes. We would plan to do something, make some changes, and he would say, "What will people say?" I'm not always interested in what people think because I'm running a business. In some regards, that isn't always a pleasant way to do things, but my philosophy is that you have to do what you think is right and logical, even if it's something as unpopular as raising ticket prices.

A lot of people think my dad was part of the original group that started the National Football League, but that isn't true. He's considered one of the pioneers because he was there when the game really began to grow in popularity. The league played its first games in 1920, and at that time Pennsylvania had blue laws. They wouldn't allow teams to play on Sunday. In 1933 the laws were changed, and Pittsburgh and Philadelphia came into the league. My father started what was then called the Pittsburgh Pirates, and Bert Bell created the Eagles.

They called the team the Pirates because baseball was a well-established sport at that time, and the name seemed to put pro football on the same level. By 1939 the game was starting to get credibility, and it was obvious that they needed their own identity. There was actually a contest to name the team, but I've always had the feeling that they knew what the name was going to be ahead of time. Pittsburgh, of course, is the steel city.

My father grew up in Pittsburgh, and they came to him when they wanted somebody to start a team because he was a promoter. They needed somebody who knew the ropes. He had been a baseball player and was involved with both semipro baseball and football. He also promoted fights and was connected with horse racing. When he was a boy, he actually lived in a house that was right where Three Rivers Stadium stands today. That, of course, is all gone, but the house that he raised us in is still there, and he lives in it to this day. You might say that we're kind of planted in the Pittsburgh area. My parents tried to give my brothers and myself a sense of values. We lived comfortably, but they tried not to spoil us.

I was one year old when my father started the team, so I really grew up with the Steelers. When I was about five years old, I began to go out to training camp with my father. One of my early memories is having my nose broken. We were playing that old game where you put your hands between your legs and somebody pulls them and you do a somersault. I forgot who the player was, but he didn't pull hard enough and I landed right on my nose.

I was fortunate in that my father was not the kind of guy who watched me all the time. When he took me to training camp or on a road trip, he just dropped me and the football players became what we would call today, my baby-sitter. Until I got to be about seven, I used to stand on the sidelines and one of the players would watch me. When he went in and took his turn, he'd tell a guy coming out, "Watch Danny," and that guy would keep an eye on me. We traveled to the out-of-town games by train, and I would sit with the players and listen to their stories by the hour. When I got into school and started bringing my books along, they would help me with my homework. My father was very involved with the players, and we would have some of them come to dinner in those days. We had a player by the name of Ed Karpowich, and he even took care of us in the off-season. One winter we went to Florida for a vacation, and he went with us.

Spending time like that with the players has really helped me in the position that I have today. I got to know them as real people, so I have a real appreciation and fondness for football players. It has always been fun for me to spend time with them, and that's one of the things that spans the years. People talk about today's players and the fact that they just play for money. I don't believe that, because if it wasn't fun they wouldn't be playing football. It's too tough. If you don't have that kid in you, that basic enjoyment of the game, you can't play. Everything that we hear about today—the money they receive, the union, the agents—all of that messes them up. But the fact that a guy is being told he isn't getting enough money, that doesn't matter when he's playing. He isn't worrying about that on Sunday. It's during the off-time that he may get mixed up. What I'm saying to you is that today's players are basically the same kind of kids that I spent time with when I was growing up, the kind of guys who have been playing this game from its inception. They play because it's fun, challenging, and because they enjoy the feeling of being part of the team.

One of the players I became good friends with was Jim Finks. We got along very well. He came to the Steelers in 1949 and was the quarterback at that time. I was a high school quarterback, so I really had an affinity for him. He gave me a lot of advice and was a very patient guy. I did pretty good in high school, and in my senior year we won the Catholic championship, but I was beaten out for the All-Catholic honor that year by a junior who went to St. Justi's High School. I have always wondered how they could pick that kid from a much smaller school. His name was Johnny Unitas, and it just proves that reporters are right once in a while.

One of the other players I remember well is a fellow by the name of Armand Niccolai. He played for the Steelers from 1934 to 1944, a pretty long career. Armand still lives in the Pittsburgh area and comes to all our games. When he retired from pro football he became a high school football coach. My high school played his team and during the game I got into a fight with one of his players. I chased the kid across the field and right into their locker room. Armand came in after us and grabbed me. "Are you crazy? You could get killed coming in here like this."

After high school I went to Duquesne University and only played freshman football. That was around the time that a lot of Catholic schools did away with the game because it was costing too much money. I majored in accounting, and that, obviously, has been very helpful in this business. When I graduated in 1955, I came right to work for the Steelers and have been here ever since.

As I said, I have been involved with the team since I was very young, and when I was about eight or nine I started doing odd jobs at training camp. I'd do anything. Somebody would say, "Hey, Danny, pick up the whites." That's what we called the towels. I'd gather them up and take them into the locker room for the trainer. Then, when I got to be thirteen or fourteen, I became what is known today as a ballboy. That was exciting because I got to stand on the sidelines during the games. I did that until I was about nineteen, and then I became the training camp manager. I actually signed a football player before I was old enough to legally do it. We sat down together and negotiated his contract, and when it came time to sign I had to go to the coach. I told him, "I'm not twenty-one. You'll have to sign this guy, but all the work's done."

Even when I got into college, I wasn't thinking of making the Steelers my career. When people asked me what I wanted to be, I usually told them that I was interested in becoming an architect. One of the players, a quarterback from Notre Dame by the name of Joe Gasparella, had studied architecture, and we used to talk about it a lot. While I was going to college, I started to get more involved with the business end of the team, and that's what may have changed my mind. I was working in public relations and producing the programs for the game. Sell the ads, deal with the printer, create the layouts, actually publish the whole thing. Just before I graduated from college, my father bought a horse track. He asked me if I wanted to get involved with that. I told him that I would rather work with the football team and started working full-time in the scouting area.

At that time scouting was a lot different than it is now. We'd contact every college in the country by mail or phone and ask them who their best players were. Once in a while we'd go to games, mostly bowl games, but it was more from a conversation standpoint.

As time went by, we started to get more refined and began to hire scouts, things like that.

Then I got one of the big breaks of my career. In 1957 we hired Buddy Parker as the head coach. Buddy had absolutely no interest in the front office. In fact, I think he thought of it as a necessary evil. That was the era when the league was really starting to gain popularity, and my father started to take me to league meetings. People began to know who I was. When they had some business with the Steelers, they would talk to me. I began to make decisions, and after a while I was the guy that people would ask for. Buddy thought that was fine because he didn't want anything to do with the day-to-day headaches. It really worked to my advantage, being exposed to the problems surrounding the business right from the onset. If I had my druthers, I would have preferred to be more involved with the players, but this is more to my advantage. It's where I belong.

I always thought that professional football was a great game and had the potential to be well received. I can't say, however, that anyone ever though it would go to the heights that it has today. Television really brought the game to the general public, and that was good for everybody. Good for television because it gave them an exciting new product. The players benefited because they became household names. It helped the owners because we had a new market for the game. The transition wasn't something that happened overnight, and if you had told me in 1955 that the Super Bowl would be the hottest ticket in the world I wouldn't have agreed with you—especially if you could have seen the size of our offices back then. We had a couple of rooms in the old Roosevelt Hotel, and we operated with an organization of ten people. Today we have almost fifty.

My father likes to tell a story about how tough it was in the old days. The Steelers played an exhibition game in Chicago, and after the game was over, my dad and George Halas got into an argument over $500. That was big money in those days. George got mad and told my father, "I'll fight you for the money." Day didn't want to fight Halas, and he needed the money, so they argued for a while and ended up splitting it fifty-fifty. When he was leaving Halas's office, my father told him, "George, don't be too sure who would've won that fight."

Another time—this wasn't even that long ago—the Philadelphia Eagles were in terrible financial trouble. We played them in Philadelphia, and visiting teams in the NFL collect forty percent of the gate receipts from the hometeam. Somebody from the Eagles came to see my father and told my father, "Don't cash this check." We hung on to it so long that we had to have a new check issued.

The business end of professional football has become very complicated, much more so than in past years—agents, the union, strikes . . . I'm not saying that I enjoy all of it, by any means, but it's still a great way to make a living. I hope we can get things worked out between the players and management. The issues aren't straightened out yet, and if we don't work them out in the near future, I think there will be a change in our relationship. What they're trying to get, of course, is free agency, and I don't think that will work. Money is already a disruptive element for the players, and if they can start moving around, I don't think it's good for anybody. When I say that, everybody's first reaction is, "All you're trying to do is save money." What I'm saying is if we get the players moving around from team to team, the fans are going to lose their identity with the team.

This is a very fragile industry. You're talking about people's emotions and choices, and if they get to the point where they feel that they'd rather do something else, we're in trouble. We had the most no-shows we've had in a while last Sunday. The demand for tickets was good, but when it came to the season's-ticket holders, the no-shows went up to 12,000. They found something else to do. I attribute much of that to the strike and the turnoff for the fans. They were upset by the idea that these guys who are making all this money went on strike. My father thought they were crazy because he cam remember when they weren't making anything. It's just not a good thing to have happen to this game because you're going to get a lot of residual problems. There is plenty of money in this game to take care of everybody more than comfortably. You can't let any one segment get out of line.

There have been some great characters in this game, and they each made their own contributions. George Marshall was a phenomenal guy. Every year he would take his band on two trips. They would always go to New York and one other city. When he'd come to Pittsburgh, they would get off the train and march right up Fifth Avenue, all the way to the stadium, playing "Hail to the Redskins." When the players say, "We are the game," they should take into consideration that this kind of color and excitement also helped make the game what it is.

I really looked up to Marshall because my father always used to tell me stories about him. Then, when I was just getting involved with the Steelers, I got to know him. I was sitting in his office before a game, and it was raining like the dickens. The band director came in and said, "Mr. Marshall, it's raining." "So?" "Should we wear the headdresses?" Marshall gave him that look of his and said, "Young man, we are in the entertainment business. We wear our costumes when we perform. Get those headdresses on." That was the kind of guy he was. People said he was prejudiced because the Redskins were the last team to hire black players. My father used to say, "George Marshall isn't prejudiced against anybody. He's prejudiced for the Redskins."

My father went to Washington to see a game on December 7, 1941. Marshall was in charge of everything when they played in Washington. He had phones to the bench, another one to the band, everything. At one point during the afternoon, a guy came up and said, "Mr. Marshall, the military wants to make an announcement over our P.A. system." Before the guy could say anything else, Marshall said, "This is the Redskins. We don't let anybody make announcements over our P.A. system. Tell them no." About two minutes later, in came the military police. "Mr. Marshall, we are taking over your P.A. system." At that point he decided it was time to let them use it.

The owners also have a responsibility to the game. They can't be looking for too much of a return, monetarily or publicity wise. Most of the people who are in this business are in it for the right reasons. For instance, Pat Bowlen of Denver is a fine guy who has made a big contribution. He really wants the team to be successful and isn't antiplayers. Pat's trying to do something for the entire Denver community, not just his own interests.

If you talk about the Steelers and what they did for the city of Pittsburgh, the team really helped bring this area together. Everybody lives in these little communities, the Monessens, Monongahelas, the New Kensingtons, places like that. Each of these towns usually has its own ethnic makeup and they all have their own football team. On Friday night those games are the main attraction and there are some incredible rivalries. The Steelers brought them together and unified these little towns, gave them something to root for together.

The fans here in Pittsburgh are the most knowledgeable football fans in the country. They like to express their feelings, and they'll boo anybody if they think they deserve it, but they're really good about it. I think one of the greatest tributes I've ever seen from any fans was when we were just starting to get good in 1972. We played the Miami Dolphins at home for the American Football Conference title and lost. At the end of the game, even though we'd lost, the fans gave the team a standing ovation for their effort.

I'm involved with our fans in many different ways. Next year I'll be president of the United Way in Pittsburgh. On Monday I have to give a speech to the National Conference of Christians and Jews about the human relations involved in professional sports. My wife is on more charitable committees than I am. What I'm saying is that we are a part of the community and that has filtered down to the players. I'm in the media, not often in a good way, but I'm in there and because of that I'm visible. The local media in Pittsburgh has always been very good to us. We don't have any real problems with that. They're critical at times, and probably deservedly so, but I have no beef with the media.

Our games with Philadelphia always seemed to mean a little more to us because we were playing for the bragging rights of Pennsylvania. The Eagles had a player in the 1950s by the name of Bucko Kilroy, and I remember him well. He got into a lot of trouble because he was considered a dirty player. We had two guys on our team who were on either side of his dispute. Elbie Nickel, who was an offensive receiver, said that everything they said about him was true. Bill McPeak, a defensive end, said he didn't think Kilroy was so bad. Those two guys would get into arguments, and Nickel would say, "Kilroy's a big stiff. He's a dirty so-and-so," and McPeak would say, "Oh, Bucko's not such a bad guy." Finally Nickel would say, "You're just saying that because you don't have to play against him. You don't have to face that SOB."

I've been asked a lot of times who I think was the best team that ever played the game. I'm sort of prejudiced toward the Steelers of the 1970s, but you have to look at the whole history of the NFL—the Green Bay Packers in the early years, the Bears of the 1940s; Lombardi's Packers of the 1960s and then our own Steelers in the 1970s. All of those teams did what they were called upon to do. People will say, "Oh, they only played twelve games back then, and there was only one championship game." Hey, they won the championship and the competition was just as tough, maybe tougher. In their own time they were the champions.

It's the same with players. I don't really have a favorite player because again you're talking about different eras and traditions. Let me say this to you, there have been guys who have made an impression on me, more than others, and not always on the football field. One of them was Joe Greene. I remember people used to say that black guys can't be leaders. Joe was the best leader I've ever seen. He was such an important part of those championship teams, on and off the field. And there was Rocky Bleier, the Vietnam veteran. I remember the great plays he made, but more than that I think of the pain and suffering he had to live with. The equipment guy had to come to me at one point and say, "You'd better get him out of there. That poor guy is really hurting."

Another guy was Jack Lambert. He expected everybody, including me, to do their job. If you didn't, he'd come and tell you about it. He was a tremendous player, but more than that a great human being. Five years ago, on the Steelers' fiftieth anniversary, we brought back as many members of the first Steeler team that we could get together. We had all sorts of special events for them during the weekend, and that was a lot of fun. At halftime we brought them out on the field and introduced each man. One of the most significant moments for me came after the introductions when those ex-players were all standing along the sidelines. Jack Lambert went up to each one and shook hands with them. Later on I found out that he told each of them, "Thank you for making this game what it is today and giving me the opportunity to be part of it." I thought that was just a super thing for him to do.

THE LOUSIEST SEAT IN THE HOUSE

CY FRASER

HALFTIME DIRECTOR

New York Giants 1936–

It would be very difficult to imagine a Giants' home game without Cy Fraser. He's truly one of kind.

—Raymond Walsh, vice president, New York Giants

This will be my fourteenth season with the Giants. Over that long span of time, the one pleasant constant has been Cy Fraser standing in the player's entrance tunnel with that big smile and his words of encouragement.

—George Martin

WE had a band coming down from Providence, Rhode Island. They were going to perform at halftime and play the national anthem. Because of all the traffic, they were late getting to the park, so I went over to look up the leader as soon as they arrived. I told him where he should have the kids just before I gave him the cue for the anthem. He looked at me and said, "Mr. Fraser, this is a fife-and-drum corps—we can't play the anthem."

This meant trouble because the stadium was filling up and we were running out of time. I had to do something and that's when I remembered that the Giants had a band that played during time-outs, things like that. They were all union guys, professional musicians, and could play just about anything. The only problem was that their bandstand was located on top of the bleachers. I ran across the field, and now I've got some pretty stiff stairs to climb. In Yankee Stadium the bleachers go up pretty high, and when I got up to the top Herb Steiner, the band's director, said, "Cy, what are you rushing for?" I explained what the situation was and he said, "No problem, we can play it blindfolded."

I couldn't hang around because I had to get word to Bob Shepard, the announcer. Otherwise he's going to say, "Now, ladies and gentlemen, St. Marys' band from Providence, Rhode Island. Will you join them in the national anthem?" The only phone at that time was in the dugout, so I had to run down the stairs, across the field, and it was touch and go, but we made it. You can rest assured that from then on I always asked if the band could play the national anthem.

Speaking of the anthem, it got me in trouble with Allie Sherman. We were playing Cleveland at Yankee Stadium, and for some reason the Browns were late coming out of the dressing room. The Giants were already in the dugout, and some of them were starting to come up on the steps and out on the field. I have a background in the theater and think things should be done dramatically. One guy standing here, another couple over there—that doesn't look good.

One of the clubhouse boys came over to me and said that Sherman wanted to know what was going on. I told him, "Cleveland is a little late coming out." He said, "Allie doesn't want his club standing around. If you don't get the introductions done soon, he's going to bring them out on the field." I said, "If he does that, they'll come out right in the middle of the national anthem." We managed to get everything done and I went over to the Giants' bench. That's where I sit during the game. A couple of minutes later Sherman comes up behind me. "I want to see you in the clubhouse after the game, Fraser. Nobody is going to treat my ball team like that."

I didn't pay much attention to him, but it really burned me up. When I got home, I wrote a letter to Sherman and explained the situation to him. How Cleveland was late coming out, which held up the introductions, and ended it up with: "I have spent my life making friends. I hope I didn't lose one Sunday." I didn't see him until the next Sunday, when I had to get the lineup from him. He gave it to me, and I said, "Allie, did you get my letter?" He said, "Oh, yeah," and put his arm around me. "Cy, forget about it. I was up for the game and took it out on you." I said, "I forgot about it when I wrote you the letter."

I'm originally from Philadelphia. My father was a railroad engineer on the Pennsylvania Railroad, and he was the one who gave me the exposure to the theater. Keith's Chestnut Street Theater was a two-a-day vaudeville house in our neighborhood, and on many occasions my father took me with him. Like most kids growing up in those days, I liked sports and was really more of a baseball fan. My aunt took me to see my first big league game, and I was so thrilled and impressed by the game that I wrote a nine-stanza poem. In fact, I can still remember the lineup of that game and Grover Cleveland Alexander was pitching for Philly. The Philadelphia ball park was like the Polo Grounds; the dressing room was in center field. When the game was over, instead of going to the dugout, the players would have to go out to center field and the fans would pour out of the stands to say hello to them. Alexander was running across the field, and I managed to rub my arm against him. My brother Jimmy used to love to tell people, "Hey, Cy, show everybody your arm that rubbed up against Grover Cleveland Alexander."

After I graduated from West Philly High, I worked for the Texas Oil Company in their credit department. I also worked a couple nights a week for Coleby Custom Tailoring Company. They decided to open a New York office in 1926, and I came here to head up the operation. That was a great time to be in the City. I lived in the Forrest Hotel, which was on Forty-ninth Street between Broadway and Eighth Avenue, and worked at Forty-ninth and Seventh Avenue. Sports and theater were my bag and at Times Square was the place to be. If a guy said, "Do you want to meet the president of First National City Bank?" it wouldn't have meant a thing to me. On the other hand, if somebody wanted me to meet a young fighter, I was in heaven.

I got married in 1931. Anne, my wife, was Helen Phelan's first cousin. Helen's father was General John J. Phelan, chairman of the New York Athletic Commission. Helen was married to Jack Mara, whose father, Tim, owned the New York Football Giants. We would always go over to my mother-in-law's house for Sunday dinner, and one afternoon Jack Mara asked me, "Cy, I need somebody to represent the Giants at the front gate on Sundays. We get a lot of flak and headaches out there. Lost tickets, deadbeats, and I need somebody who can smooth things out." I had been a Giants' fan, even before the family relationship, and it sounded like a lot of fun, so I told him I'd do it. That was 1936.

My job was really to sort out the phonies from people with a legitimate problem. That wasn't too hard for me to do because, living in Times Square, I could have been a postgraduate student in spotting phonies. A guy would come up to the gate and give a big story to the guy taking tickets. He'd say that he was a great friend of Steve Owen, the Giants' coach at that time, and how his good friend, Steve, would want him and his friends to get in for free. While this was going on, I'd be sizing the guy up. The more phony a guy is, usually the more indignant he gets. Finally I'd step in and tell him, "Sir, there's no problem. You go up to the Giants' dressing room and knock on the door. Tell your good friend, Mr. Owen, to come down and we'll take care of everything." Most of the time they'd find some excuse and you wouldn't see them again.

This was before television, and the only way a team made money was by selling tickets. My wife and I would go to games at the Polo Grounds in those days and you could put your feet on the seat in front of you and throw your coat on the next seat. It was always comfortably well filled downstairs, but upstairs you could get lonesome. Now, of course, they have that gag about the couple that get divorced. She gets custody of the kids and he gets custody of the Giants' tickets. You know what I tell my friends when they ask me for tickets? The only way you can get a seat for a Giants' game is to get a cabinet maker to build one for you. Put it under your arm and carry it over to the Meadowlands. That's the best I can do for them.

We also had a lot of trouble with scams. There was a broken-down refreshment stand across the street from the main gate of the Polo Grounds. Somebody who worked there had a racket worked out with a guy on the gate. You'd go over to the hot dog stand and give the guy two bucks. He'd tell you what gate to go through. The signal was to go to the ticket taker who wasn't wearing his hat and he'd let you in for free. We got wind of it and the next Sunday I went over to the gate and told the ticket taker, "You know, you'd look better with your hat on. Mr. Mara wants all the men at the gate to wear their hats." He started whining, "Oh, Cy, it's too hot for a hat," but he couldn't do anything but put his hat on. Shortly after that the problem dried up.

Another problem I had to deal with were people who either lost or forgot their tickets. One Sunday the guy at the press gate called me over. A lady with a party of four had forgotten her tickets. It turned out that her name was Mary Sotos, and she was Ford Frick's secretary. He was the president of the baseball National League at that time. I wrote out a card, "Seat this party in so-and-so. Cy Fraser for J. D. Mara," and had an usher take them to their seats. About a week later Mary wrote me a very nice letter saying she had never been treated so courteously at a ball park. You know, ball parks are usually the worst—lots of "dese" and "dems" and "dose guys." "Get your cold beer here." I'm not criticizing them for that—

they're an important part of the game—but there wasn't much class or culture involved. Especially then. She told me that the Giants were so nice, and that was the way Jack Mara wanted me to handle things for his club. Treat a legitimate problem in a courteous way, but if you spotted a phony, give them the brush.

Another incident comes to mind. It was a cold, bitter day at the Polo Grounds. That was an open stadium, and you could go up to the top row and look right down on Coogan's Bluff. No protection from the weather whatsoever. This guy was sitting up there and he came down to the main gate. He was mad. "I can't sit up there. The wind is hitting me right in the back of my neck." I tried to calm him down, but he wasn't having any part of it. Finally I told him, "There's nothing I can do about it. I can't change your seat and we can't play football in your living room." This was before television, of course. "But I do have a suggestion for you. Turn your collar up."

There was a Dr. March who had an office at 101st and Broadway. I can't authenticate this, but I believe he put up some of the money to buy the Giants' franchise for $2,500 in 1925. Dr. March's office was the most cluttered office you ever saw. I don't see how anybody could go to him as a doctor, but Steve and Bill Owen were very good friends with him. Bill was Steve's brother and he played for the Giants in the 1930s. Dr. March's office was sort of a headquarters for the Giants outside of the ball park. I became good friends with Dr. March and Steve Owen, and as a consequence, I got close to a lot of the Giants. Cal Hubbard played for both the Green Bay Packers and the Giants during the 1930s, and we became very good friends. He was a tremendous athlete and is the only man in both Hall of Fames, baseball and football. When he was playing for the Packers and they were in town for a game with the Giants, he used to march five or six Packers down to my store to get some clothes. I'll always remember the time he brought Champ Seibold in there. Seibold was a defensive lineman, a big, raw-boned country boy, and Cal said to me, "I want you to make a suit for this big son-of-a-bitch.

He hasn't a coat and pants that match." In those days they didn't wear sport coats with odd pants like they do today. You wore a three-piece suit and that was that. Cal brought in a lot of guys. Clark Hinkle, Milt Gantenbein, Don Huston—I'm grabbing names out of the blue—and I got to know some of these guys, too.

In those days I would say you had rougher guys playing pro football. They might have gone to college, but probably mainly to play football. That's like a lot of them today, but they had more of an "eat you alive" complex than I see in the fellows today. They play hard, but it seemed to be a rougher game in those days. There was a guy who played for the Packers named "Buckets" Goldenberg. If you can believe it, he played quarterback and guard. The fans in New York really disliked him, and they'd be yelling, "Let's get Goldenberg. Kill Goldenberg." There was another guy named Glenn Campbell who played for the Giants. I think he played end and he never wore a helmet. You have to remember that those guys also played sixty minutes a game.

To give you an idea of what kind of guys we're talking about, "Tex" Irvin came into the store to get some clothes. He was a big tackle who played for the Giants in the early 1930s, and he and a couple of other players were driving down to Texas because the season was over. On his way out of the store, he asked me if he could have one of the big, brass cuspidors that we had for decoration. I asked him what in the world for. He said, "All of these guys are tobacco chewers. If we can put one of those on the floor of the car, we won't have to spit out the window." The outstanding one in my mind, however, was Cal Hubbard. After he retired from football he became an umpire in the American League and remained a close friend until he died.

The Giants moved to Yankee Stadium in 1956, and when we got over there Jack told me, "Cy, I don't want you wasting your time on the gate anymore. Things have smoothed out pretty well. I'd like you to coordinate everything that happens pregame and halftime on the field." I started doing basically what I'm still doing today: checking the lineups with the coaches, getting the clubs out of the dressing rooms on time, getting the band in place, and telling them what to do. I also coordinate everything with Bob Shepard, the P.A. announcer, so he can give the player introductions, make the announcement for the anthem, cue the band for the anthem—all of those things.

It was just about the time we moved to Yankee Stadium that television came in, and that has really become an ogre over everybody's head. Television runs the game today. We used to blow it once in a while in the old days, but today we can't afford to. Everything has to hit it right on the money because of those commercial breaks. Years ago they picked up the anthem. You saw the people singing, the players on the sidelines, the flag flying over the stadium, and then they would introduce the offensive and defensive teams. Now, all of that is over and done with when the game comes on the air. I can realize the commercial value of that time, but it was nice to see that before a game.

I get annoyed when I stand on the sidelines and see these players not opening their mouths during the anthem. I'm still a red, white, and blue American. I love patriotism and I love the national anthem. I always sing it like crazy, as best I can, whether I'm at Giants' Stadium, Shea Stadium, whatever. Once in a while I'll see some of the officals singing, but the players very seldom sing.

As soon as the anthem is over, that ends my duties and I head over and say hello to Martha Wright and Mel Broyles. She sings the anthem and he accompanies her on the trumpet. The bands don't play the anthem anymore because a lot of them can't play it in her key. She does it in B flat. Besides, she's in good hands with Mel. He's the first trumpet with the Metropolitan Opera Orchestra.

I've got the lousiest seat in the house. If the action is down at my end of the field, I can see it, but if it's in the center for the field, forget about it. When the weather is inclement and those big guys put on those hoods it's worse. I sit on the same end that the defense sits on. I hear a lot of talk, but I never talk to them. The players are very intense during a game and are concentrating on what they're doing. Somebody who hasn't been around the game as long as I have might want to say, "Nice catch," or something like that. They don't want to hear it, especially from me. One afternoon I was standing near the phone and Leonard Marshall was sitting on the bench by himself. He looked at me and said, "I bet you've seen a lot of ball games." There had been an article in the program about me and I guess he had seen it. Other than something like that, I stay out of their way.

I must be lucky because I've only been run into by a player once. We were playing Pittsburgh. Bob Schnelker was a wide receiver for the Giants, and I think his number was eighty-seven. He caught a pass and started running full speed up the field. A defensive player came across and pushed him out of bounds. I saw him coming, and that eighty-seven on his chest looked as big as this room. At that time the benches were very low, and running full speed, he vaulted over the bench. His knee hit my shoulder and over I went. I was stunned and Doc Sweeney came running over and asked me if I was all right. He said, "Don't sit down, Cy. Get up and walk around." If Schnelker's knee had been a little bit this way, I would be talking out of the side of my face.

One of the few days I left early was December 7, 1941. As I said, I'm involved with the theater, and I was doing a play in Jackson Heights, a Sunday afternoon matinee. When I got to the Polo Grounds, I asked Jack if I could leave right after the kickoff. He said, "That's all right, Cy. Most of the fans are in by that time, and we'll have somebody else down there just in case." I took a taxi over the Tri-Boro Bridge, and when I got into the theater, one of the guys who was in the play said, "Did you hear the news? The Japs bombed Pearl Harbor." Can you believe it? I missed that big dramatic moment that everybody talks about.

It's tough to pick the best football player I ever saw, but it might have been Gifford. I still remember that catch he made against Pittsburgh. It was just fantastic. He caught it on the run and didn't lose a step. Jim Brown was another one, and so was Del Shofner. Their positions have a lot to do with it. The linemen are all in a bunch, and you never get to see that much, but you've got to give them a lot of credit; they're in the trenches taking it on every play. If you'd like my opinion of who is a class guy, one of the finest gentlemen I've ever met, it would be George Martin. He's close to my number one guy. I went over to his locker the day they clinched the title, and I waited until the reporters were done talking to him. I just wanted to tell him that I was very happy for the team and especially for him. At one point I had written a poem and had someone print it up for me. I said, "George, I want to give you something to remember me by," and gave him a copy. He looked at me and said, "Cy, do you think I need anything to remember you by?" That was the nicest thing he could have said to me. Then he put his big arm around me and hugged me. His eyes filled up and mine did too. It was such a nice gesture coming from him, and I was so glad for him after all the frustrating years that the Giants had gone through. It just hit me in the soft spot, I guess.

As far as my full-time work, I'm on the beach. After I left Coleby, I went to work in the airline uniform business and did that until last August when the company shut down their New York operation. I never wanted to retire, and if it hadn't been for that, I never would have. At this stage of the game, I'm not going out and look for a job. I'm eighty-three years old, and when I wake up in the morning I figure I'm ahead for the day. As far as the Giants go, I don't like to jinx myself and say I'm going to do this or that. I'm superstitious about that kind of stuff. It's a *schlepp* over to the Meadowlands, and I have to be in the dressing room by ten in the morning. As long as the Giants want me, I guess I'll be there.

Up until last year, I had a great string going. In the fifty years that I've worked for the Giants I had never missed a game. Not at the Polo Grounds, not at Yankee Stadium. When we played at the Yale Bowl and Shea Stadium, I made every one and I hadn't missed one at Giants Stadium. Last December I got in my car to drive to the stadium, and when I got a block from my home I heard a thumping noise. I stopped the car and looked underneath, and this green fluid was flowing out of it. I don't know which end of a hammer to pick up, so I couldn't figure it out. When I called road service, I realized that there was no way I was going to get there on time. It was such a frustrating feeling because I'm the only one who does my job.

I called up Tom Power, the Director of Promotions, and told him that I was in a bind. He said, "Don't worry, Cy. We'll manage." I told him that I'd call him at halftime and see how they were making out. When I got him on the phone, the first thing he said was, "Cy, we have to have reliability."

"LISTEN, MY BOY"

MILLARD KELLEY

TRAINER

Detroit Lions 1955–67

In 1958 I was traded to the Detroit Lions by the Cleveland Browns. During that first year with Detroit, I had the opportunity to meet and work with Millard Kelley, or "the Great Duck"—duck as in "mallard." I quickly came to realize that Kelley was "the best trainer in the NFL." He always had the energy to give treatment and take care of every player or coach, not just the stars. He had time for everybody, even an occasional injured wife or two during the year. The players had complete faith in him and he never let us down.

—Jim Gibbons

I grew up in Pittsburgh, Pennsylvania. My dad was a salesman and never was much of an athlete. My mother, on the other hand, was a real good basketball player in high school. When I was about six or seven years old, she developed a heart problem and the doctor put her in bed. She didn't even get up to go to the bathroom and stayed in that bed until the day she died. I was nineteen. It's sad, but that's how they treated heart conditions in those days. Today heart patients run marathons.

While I was in high school, I played basketball and football and when I graduated went directly into the Navy. That was 1942, and I didn't get out until 1948. I was a gunner's mate and started out on a destroyer escort and ended up on an aircraft carrier, the *Coral Sea.* When I got out of the service, I went to Purdue University and played freshman football until I got hurt. Then I went out for basketball and got cut. At that time I wanted to be a math teacher and was also interested in coaching. I knew that if I was coaching at the high school level, I would have to do my own taping and take care of injuries, so I went down to the training room to see if I could pick up some skills. It was also a way for me to keep my involvement with athletics. The guy who ran the operation, Bill "Pinky" Newell, was only a few years older than I was, and he said he could use a student trainer.

Pinky was a great teacher, and I worked in the training room the entire time I was going to Purdue. I really enjoyed the environment and decided that I would try for a career as a trainer. I asked Pinky for some advice, and he suggested that it would behoove me to go to physical therapy school. The extra training would make me a better trainer and also help me get a better job. I took his advice and went to Stanford University for a year and received a certificate in physical therapy.

When you're working in the training room, you get hands-on experience. Actually treating the athletes for sprains, pulled muscles, any problem they might have. You apply the different types of treatment: heat, cold, massage, and exercise. In physical therapy school you get the theory behind the treatment. You work with a cadaver and learn what the bones, muscles, and nerves look like and how they function. You take a very comprehensive course in kinesiology, which is the study of muscle action. If you tell a player, "Bend and straighten your elbow," you know the muscles that are being used to bend the elbow. You also know the nerves that are involved and where the blood supply is coming from. All of that information can be used to help figure out why an injury hurts. All of that information makes you a more complete trainer.

My first job after I graduated from Stanford was with a Triple A baseball team, the Sacramento Solons. The team's trainer had gotten sick, and I took over in midseason. They were a good group of athletes because in Triple A they're usually on their way up to the majors or on their way down. The real world took a little getting used to. I had a real small training room, and some of the players liked to hang around in there. As you probably know, baseball players chew tobacco and they were spitting on the walls. I had to put a curtailment on that immediately. That brings up the only problem that I can think of when I was working with athletes. Some of them weren't very considerate. When somebody gets to that level of proficiency, there's a chance that he's gotten spoiled. If you had a big group, they could start with a little one-upsmanship with each other and anybody who was around them. If you got them one on one, however, they were pretty decent. They soon learned the rules, and they didn't come into my training room unless they were clean and dried off. That's where I had to work, and I wanted it shipshape.

After that season at Sacramento, I went to Michigan State and worked there as an assistant trainer. That was Duffy Dougherty's first year at Michigan, and they had a select coaching staff—guys like Bill Yoman and Dan Devine, who went on to great success as head coaches. Dealing with coaches has always been like anything else in life. You have to gain respect from the people you work with. They have to respect you, and once you've gained their respect, they'll accept what you tell them. It's just like changing your barber or dentist. You don't like to change if you like the one you've had. Even though the new guy may be better, you're involved emotionally with his predecessor. Whenever I came into a new job, I found I had to sell myself to the coaches, players, and management. That's why it's a challenging and fun job.

Sometime during that year I was at Michigan the assistant trainer at Purdue died, and Pinky asked me if I wanted the job. I always enjoyed working with him, so I told him I'd be interested. In the meantime we had a fellow who used to come around at Michigan State to sell us equipment, and the two of us got to talking one day. He said, "Do you know the head trainer's job is open with the Detroit Lions?" I said, "Yes, I've heard, but I'm not ready for that yet. Besides, I'm planning on going back to Purdue." I hadn't been in the field that long and didn't think I could handle anything like a pro football team. He said, "Why don't you just go up to the Lions and try. It would be a good experience for you." The two athletic directors at Purdue and Michigan hadn't gotten together yet about the job at Purdue, and while I was waiting for that, I said, "What the hell, I'll go interview."

Buddy Parker was the Lions' coach at that time, and I went to see him and his assistant. We talked for a while, and then Parker said, "Why don't you go and see Nick Kerbaway," who was the general manager. During our conversation Nick started to talk about money and contracts. I told him, "Wait a minute. I don't know if I'm ready for this. I just came up here for the experience, and it sounds like you're offering me a job." He said, "I am." I asked him if I could make a phone call, and when I got hold of Pinky, I told him they had offered me the job and asked him what he thought I should do. He said, "Go right ahead and take the job. It's a hell of an opportunity, and you can do it."

My first experiences with Buddy Parker were a little rocky. We had our training camp in Ypsilanti, on the campus of what is now Eastern Michigan University. The field was out in a little valley, and there must have been 99 percent humidity. Horrible conditions to practice in, and Parker wouldn't let the players have any water. He thought that made a guy tough, but I've found that you can kill people getting tough. I finally convinced him that it wouldn't compromise their basic meanness to have some water during training camp.

Buster Ramsey was our line coach, and he was another one from the old school. He had been a tough football player in his time; he played guard with the Chicago Cardinals and was an excellent coach. He liked people to hit, and at that time Doak Walker played for us. He was our big point getter. He did everything—he scored touchdowns and kicked field goals and extra points, but Ramsey used to get furious because Walker wouldn't try to block some 240- or 250-pound lineman. Walker weighed 165 pounds, and he might block somebody if he had the angle on him, but he wasn't about to pit himself against some monster who weighed seventy-five pounds more than he did. Buster would get mad and start yelling. "Doak, come on. Knock somebody down." Parker understood, of course, and didn't expect him to do anything of the sort.

I had a great deal of respect for Buddy Parker and kind of quaked in my shoes around him that first year. He demanded a lot from his people, and the Lions had won the championship in 1952 and 1953. In 1954 they played in the championship game and Cleveland beat them. When I got to the Lions, a lot of those guys from the championship teams had retired and we lost our first six games in 1955. We had played on the West Coast and those were the days before jets. If there was a headwind, it would take us a good bit of time to get back to Detroit.

Parker was an extreme introvert, except when he got a little Jack Daniels in him. Then he was an extreme extrovert. On that trip back from Los Angeles, he was walking up and down the aisle of the plane, and when he thought of something he would stop and get on somebody in no uncertain terms. He never really yelled, but when Buddy said, "Listen, my boy," you knew you were in big trouble.

There was only one real problem that I had that first year. We had an outstanding player, Jack Christiansen, and he had a knee problem. Many times a player would get hurt, and he wasn't sure how it happened. We would always break down the films and try to find out how the injury was sustained. By looking, frame by frame, you could usually get an idea of what happened, but the only thing we could figure out was that Jack got kicked in the knee. He was going to make a tackle and when the guy changed direction, he ended up getting kicked. His foot wasn't even-planted, so we couldn't understand why he was having so much pain bending and straightening his knee. He was a tough kid, so we sent him in for a consultation with the doctor, and he couldn't find anything wrong structurally. At that point I decided that he might have a torn cartilage and didn't even realize he had done it.

We went down to Baltimore and took Christiansen along, even though he wasn't going to play. Just after we got to the hotel, Coach Parker called me up to his room and asked me, "What do you think is wrong with Christiansen?" I said, "Well, talking with the doc, we think he may have a torn cartilage." Parker looked at me and said, "That's what I heard. Listen, my boy, you don't make the diagnoses. You put that boy on the next plane back to Ann Arbor, and let's find out what's wrong with him."

At the second consultation they gave him a local anesthetic and found that he could bend the knee easily. As long as he couldn't feel it, it was just fine. The final diagnosis was that he had suffered a severe bone bruise. It was in such a place that when he tried to bend his knee the muscle would put pressure on the bruise and it would be very painful. That was a good lesson for me because it taught me two things. You can't be hesitant and you also have to learn to say you don't know.

Working with athletes, especially at the professional level, is much different than working with lay people. Many times people are not interested in how quickly they get back from an injury. If it's a workman's comp case, they don't have to go to work and they're still getting paid. When a physical therapist sees a patient, he doesn't have to make a decision right away. "Let's see if this works. If we don't see an improvement in a week, we can try something else." A professional trainer is working with people who are motivated differently. An athlete is very anxious to get back because that's his livelihood. He's also a prime patient because he'll do what you tell him to do.

Everybody that I've talked to in the business agrees that the doctor-trainer relationship is usually an outstanding one. Both the doctor and trainer know what their role is, and it's not unlike a surgeon and an operating room nurse. The relationship was always very close and a great experience for me. The Lions' team doctor was Dr. Richard Thompson, and he was just a ball of fire and a great guy to work with. He was always on call and would always drop in to training camp on his way to the office. If anything happened that needed his attention, I would call him and we'd send the player right over to his office. There was no sitting in the waiting room for an hour and a half; he would take him right in.

After William Clay Ford bought the Lions, we had a big problem. Before he came into the picture, we would send our players to the University of Michigan at Ann Arbor for consultation. They were familiar with athletes because of the school's athletic programs. Now we had to send our players to Ford Hospital. The facility wasn't the problem. It's a big, beautiful teaching hospital, but they didn't have much experience with athletes. We would send somebody there for consultation, and a doctor would tell him, "You can't play for six weeks." When I heard that, I'd get on the phone to them. "How can you tell that player he won't be able to play for six weeks. You don't even know what we're doing for him." Our situation was unique in that we didn't just see a player one or two times a week. I would see him seven days a week, three or four times a day, and set up a program designed especially for him. He's motivated to get back and works as hard as he can to get back in condition. We weren't going to have a man play until he's ready to play, but you don't want to plant the seed in his mind that he's not going to be ready to play for six weeks. We were sending players to Ann Arbor behind management's back, and when they found out about it, they gave us hell.

There were players, and they were in the minority, who would get hurt during a game and then wouldn't come in for treatment. Anyone who was hurt during the game on Sunday had to be in on Monday for treatment. That was their day off, so you would get a few guys who didn't want to lose their free time, and they'd wait until Tuesday. Sometimes they would try and hide the injury and try to tell us that they got hurt during practice on Tuesday. You can't very well hide anything like that when you're playing pro ball. We'd look at the game films and usually find out how and when the injury had occurred. They didn't do that very often because it didn't go over too big with the coaches or myself.

One of my big fears when I took over at Detroit was whether I, a relative babe in the woods, would be able to live up to all the other trainers the players had in college. We had thirty-three players, and since it was very rare to have two men from the same school, I'm working with players who had had thirty-three different trainers. That situation actually ended up working to my advantage because I found out how good or bad their college trainers were when they came to me with an injury. A guy would say, "My trainer back at Notre Dame used to do this." If I thought it had merit, I would try it. If, on the other hand, it was absolutely wrong, I would say, "Let's try my way first. If that doesn't work, we'll try your man's treatment." By doing that, I got feedback from all the players, and that gave me a wealth of knowledge. I also learned to listen to the players and it all worked to my advantage.

There were some great players at Detroit while I was there. Bobby Layne was the quarterback. All I can say about him is that in my experience, working with athletes, you run across some who are outstanding athletes and others who are outstanding leaders. Bobby was one of the most take-charge guys I've ever been around.

You always knew who was in charge on the football field; there was never any question about that. Face masks were just starting to come along when I went with the Lions, but Bobby would never wear one. He said they got in his way. If he had something wrong with him, it was hard to get him to come in for treatment. He was so sure of himself. In other things, his personal life, he was pretty excessive. Bobby liked his extracurricular activities, and he partook of them whenever he wanted to. I'll say this for him: he was always ready to play on Sunday, and he gave everything he had.

McMahon is a Bobby Layne type. He's a leader who goes out there and takes control of the game, but he has to learn to protect himself. During one game the ball was fumbled by the Bears, and McMahon was diving for the ball with his arm outstretched. It was a dumb move to make, and to me, observing, he should have let them pick up the fumble. He's been injured a lot, and I think it's because he tries too hard. He's not built like a defensive lineman and has to use a little discretion. The players who last know how to back off, when to save themselves. You'd see a player like "Hopalong" Cassady. A guy would get him by one leg, and he'd drop to the ground because two or three other guys were going to land on him. The good ones just seemed to know when to stop running, and that seems to be something you learn by yourself.

Leon Hart, Jim David, Tobin Rote, Hopalong Cassady—we had some great ones, but two players really stand out in my mind. People are always interested in my experiences with professional football players. Whenever I talk to youngsters, or older people for that matter, I always talk about Joe Schmidt and Jim Gibbons. Both of them were fine football players, but they were also fine family men, businessmen, and Christians. Everything they do they work at to the best of their ability and they've put their football careers into the proper perspective. Both of those men are well-rounded individuals, and they didn't spend more time at one thing than they did at another.

Joe was the one who always came up with the nicknames for the other players. Wayne Walker played with us for fifteen years. He was a fellow linebacker with Joe and a very vain guy. Joe named him "Victor Vain." Jim David was an outstanding defensive back out of Colorado State and a pretty tough guy. His nickname was "the Hatchet." Then there was Alex Karras. He had the upper body of a 250-pound guy and short stubby legs. They weren't anywhere in proportion to his upper body, and when he ran he took very small steps. Joe used to call him "Tippy Toes."

While I was working with the Lions, I wasn't getting paid during the off-season, so Dr. Thompson and I set up a sports medicine clinic. Business was pretty good, so at some point I hired a physical therapist and made him my partner. Every year I would go to training camp and leave him with all the problems. I kept telling him, "One more year, just one more year," but finally the practice was getting so lucrative that I had to make a decision. My time with the Lions had been very enjoyable, but I decided to concentrate on physical therapy. I resigned in 1967 and moved out here to Aspen in 1969.

Aspen is a very young community; I'm an old man out here. The people who live here find all sorts of ways to hurt themselves. Skiing, of course, is the big one, but there's also mountain climbing, bicycling, rafting; you name it, they do it. Most of my business comes from physicians referrals for postsurgical or posttrauma therapy. I have three children—two sons and a daughter—and both boys played football at Aspen High School. I worked with the coach for eleven years, and among other things, we had an excellent weight and flexibility program. The trainer's big job is really to prevent injuries. It's a lot easier to prevent an injury than heal one, and one of the ways to do that is with a flexibility program. Lots of stretching. They've really done some good things here in Aspen's program, and I think some of it is starting to catch on nationwide. For one, blocking below the waist has been eliminated on kickoff and punt returns. Also, if the ball is run outside the tackles, there's no blocking below the waist. During my tenure with the school, we only had one knee injury that required surgery, and I think that's a pretty good record.

I don't know if the NFL or colleges will take any steps to move backward, but some things seem to have gotten out of hand. A player today is like a warrior going into battle with the gear they wear. The man from Texas who made the first flak jackets is now making other types of pads. With all that stuff on, a guy will be able to run through a wall. I don't think the game was meant to turn into something like that.

The guys are bigger, faster, stronger, and they can deliver a devastating blow. Steroids have helped make them bigger, and I have been away from Detroit for at least over twenty years, and they were saying the same things about steroids then that I'm hearing today. We never dispensed any because they were supposed to have side effects, but they didn't know what they were. They still don't have any hard-and-fast answers. It's time somebody did some extensive studies because nobody seems to have any conclusive proof one way or the other.

As far as drugs go, the only problem we had was with amphetamines, and that didn't really amount to much. A few guys who came out of the World War II era thought they were getting old, and I think they felt the pills would keep them from losing a step or two. Our first-string players never even thought about using them. As for myself, I've never even had a joint and have never been around an athlete who offered me drugs of any kind. I'm not a saint, and I enjoy an occasional beverage at the same time, realizing that alcoholism is one of the worst drug problems there is. We never figured that drinking was a problem, but now, when I talk with trainers, they tell me they do a lot of counseling. Even with all the publicity they get today, I still have to think that it's a real minority of the players that are into drugs. Sure, they make a lot of money, and that's a place to spend it, but I think the problem has been blown way out of proportion by the media.

As far as diet goes, at that time the pregame meal was still steak and eggs. You can't use any of that for energy during the game, but that's what the old coaches thought a football player needed. They started to refute that when they did some testing at the University of Nebraska. Instead of having steak and eggs or ham and eggs, they'd have four peach halves, two pieces of toast, and some tea. It wasn't hard to convince them because I took some players during training camp and asked them if they wanted to be in a test group. If you create a group like that, everybody else wants to know why they can't be in the group, and pretty soon they all tried that meal and found out it worked.

We'd give them the pregame meal four hours before the game, and then, maybe an hour or so before kickoff, I'd give them a big glass of my "magic potion." That consisted of Sustagen, cold water, and some chocolate syrup. Sustagen was a product hospitals gave people intravenously who couldn't feed themselves. It had a lot of nutrition in it, and a player could use everything that was in that potion during the game. Our preseason games were going pretty good the year I started using it, and the guys were joking at practice one day about the "magic potion." The sportswriters picked up on it and started asking me, "What's this we hear about a 'magic potion'? I said, "Wait until we test it a little while longer; then I'll tell you all about it." The next week we played San Francisco, and that was the year they came up with the shotgun defense. Nobody had a defense for it, and they beat us 49–0. So much for the "magic potion."

THE MIDDLE MAN

JAMES GALLAGHER

PUBLIC RELATIONS

Philadelphia Eagles 1949–

In the most positive sense, Jim Gallagher is an anomaly. Nearly forty years in the same organization, no less than four changes of ownership, a dozen or more head coaches, and a variety of responsibilities. Fair testimony, I would say, to his credentials as the consummate public relations person. He is blessed with an uncanny memory concerning people and events and quietly goes about getting the job done. Easily one of the most competent, unassuming, respected people I know.

—Pete Retzlaff

I was a young stenographer just out of business school when I went to work in the University of Pennsylvania's athletic department. That was the fall of 1948, and Penn had real good teams in those days. Chuck Bednarik was the captain, and they'd get seventy-eight thousand people at a game. After a couple of months I left Penn and went to work for the Pennsylvania Railroad in the main terminal at Thirtieth and Market Street. The railroad had that seniority business, and six or seven months after I started, another guy pushed me out because I was low man on the totem pole. I went back to the employment office at Pierce Business School, and they told me the Philadelphia Eagles were looking for a stenographer.

We all knew about the Eagles in those days, but pro football wasn't that big in Philadelphia. Like most major cities at that time, Philadelphia was a big college football town. Penn was always good. Temple and Villanova had decent teams, and the Philadelphia Catholic High School League games were very, very popular. I went to North Catholic, Bucko Kilroy's school, and that's where we always went on Sundays, not the Eagles' game. Portable radios were just starting to come out then, and somebody might have one and you'd hear a holler, "Hey, Tommy Thompson threw a touchdown pass," or something like that. When pro football started to get popular, high school football began to suffer. Just about the only people at the games were the mothers and fathers of the players.

I started with the Eagles in September of 1949. Then the Korean War came along and I was drafted, spent two years over there driving jeeps, and when I was discharged the Eagles wanted me to come back to work for them. My dad told me, "You take advantage of the GI Bill and go to school." The Eagles said that would be fine, and I could make my own hours. I enrolled at Temple, and as soon as classes were over I hopped on the subway. Our offices were located in Center City in those days.

There were only a handful of people in the office at that time, and I did a little bit of everything. If they got swamped in the ticket office, I'd hustle tickets. If the switchboard got jammed up, I'd answer the phones. Looking at the setup we have today, most people wouldn't believe the offices that we worked out of in those days. The president had an office the size of the one I'm in now. We didn't have much of a personnel department, but I kept the records of the college players, mostly seniors. We had a few scouts around the country, and they would send information back to the office. I'd make a card out for Joe Doaks from SMU or Vanderbilt, whatever, and keep it up to date—what kind of statistics the guy had, outstanding games, any information that would help the coaches with the draft.

At that time the Eagles were owned by a group called the One Hundred Brothers. They were all Philadelphia businessmen. Each man threw in $3,000, and they bought the franchise from a New Yorker named Lex Thompson for $250,000. Jim Clark, who owned Highway Express Lines, was the guy who got them together, and he was the president of the club. Frank McNamee, Paul Lewis, Joe Donoghue, and Vince McNally actually ran the club. The rest of the stockholders didn't have anything to say about how the club was run. That would have been a mess. Clark, McNamee, and Lewis all had other jobs, but they stopped in during the week and put in their two cents' worth. Vince McNally and the head coach ran the football end of it. Joe Donoghue was in charge of the day-to-day business activities.

Bert Bell was the commissioner, and he ran the league with an iron hand. There were only twelve teams, and he was very close to the owners. Bert used to hire me to take the minutes of the owner's meetings. Today they have the meetings in Hawaii and nice places like that. We always had them in Philadelphia because the commissioner's office was right around the corner from the old Eagles' office. One year we actually got to go to Los Angeles, and we had to take the train because Bert Bell didn't like to fly. There were eight of us—a couple of NFL office people, a few owners, Bert, and myself. We took the Broadway Limited to Chicago, which was the Pennsylvania Railroad's version of a Cadillac. We had a six- or seven-hour layover in Chicago, and everyone went over to George Halas's office to say hello. While we were there, we hired a coach. Jim Trimble had been fired after the 1955 season, and the Eagles were interested in hiring Hughie Devore. He was the head coach at the University of Dayton and wasn't sure he wanted to leave the collegiate ranks. Bert Bell got on the phone and convinced him to take the job. Bert was a very persuasive guy. We took the Super Chief out to Los Angeles, and Devore met us when we got there.

The trip itself was terrific. We had a suite and Bert Bell had one bedroom to himself. Another guy and myself shared the other room and our room doubled as the hospitality room. We had a big trash can full of ice and beer. That was our bar. The writers who were covering the meetings would stop in, and Bert just loved to talk. We'd all open a bottle of beer—there were no cans in those days—and would sit there chewing the fat.

There were some very interesting people at those meetings. George Preston Marshall, who owned the Redskins, was along on that trip, and boy, was he a heck of a speaker. He'd get up and make these inspiring speeches about the future of the NFL. I remember him talking about charging ten dollars for the championship game. Half the guys in that room almost fell off their chairs. They couldn't believe it because the best seats in the stadium were going for three or four dollars. Marshall said, "We have a great game and it's worth ten dollars." That was in 1954 or '55, and today they don't bat an eye charging a hundred dollars for a Super Bowl ticket.

It was the proverbial smoke-filled room in those days because just about everybody smoked something. A lot of them were cigar smokers, like Art Rooney and Joe Donoghue. Bert Bell was a cigarette guy, and he also used to take his teeth out, wrap them in a napkin and start gassing away. Art Rooney always liked to tell how Bert would go to bed while the owners were arguing about things, and in the middle of the night he would come back into the room, all groggy, wanting to know if they were getting any place.

When the discussions started about television, it was Bert Bell who insisted on dividing the money up equally between all the teams. That was one of the most important decisions he ever made because otherwise New York, Chicago, or Los Angeles would get all the money. A team like Green Bay would have been literally left out in the cold. He insisted on that and it's still that way today.

I've been here through four ownerships. Jerry Wolman bought the Eagles in January of 1964 for five and a half million dollars. Each of the One Hundred Brothers got sixty thousand dollars for his original three-thousand-dollar investment. Then, when he went bankrupt, Leonard Tose paid sixteen million for the club in 1969. The present owner, Norman Braman, bought the team two years ago for sixty-five million. I'm sure with inflation it's worth a little more than that now. When Jerry Wolman bought the team, Joe Kuharich was the coach. Eddie Hogan was the public relations guy at that time, and he and Kuharich didn't get along. Joe was kind of a hard-nosed guy, and he rubbed people the wrong way. Jerry asked Eddie to step aside, and then he called me into his office. "Jimmy, I want you to take over the public relations job until the end of the year." I said, "Jeeze, I don't know anything about that job." He said, "Oh, you can do it," so I faked it for a year. I had never been into publicity. Most public relations guys had been in the newspaper business. I had no training or background, and here I was tossed into this job.

At the end of the year there were rumors that somebody was going to come in from Washington and take my place. That's where Jerry Wolman made his money. Three or four names were being kicked around, and then Jerry took me aside one day. "Don't pay any attention to that shit, Jimmy, you're the guy. Let them talk all they want." He even gave me a few more bucks, and I've been here in this job ever since.

The public relations person in the football business is the middle man between the club and the media. The fans pick up the information by reading, listening to, or watching the media. We have to get the information out to everybody, set up press conferences, and arrange for interviews. Years ago a sportswriter would come in and want to talk to somebody. You'd get the guy, sit him down, and they'd do their interview right there. Today it's turned into a major event. *Sports Illustrated,* NFL Films, or one of the networks may want to come down and do a big splash on our quarterback or coach. You can't do that at the last minute, and it has to be all set up. You have to have a couple of days notice so you can alert the player or coach. The coach will say, "I can't do it at ten o'clock. We're in team meetings." That has to come first because you can't stop the meetings and pull a guy out for an interview. The media has to work around our schedule today. Years ago, it was just show up and do it.

Everybody and his brother has a tape recorder. You see them out at training camp. They've got their notebook in one hand and the tape recorder in the other. My job is to help the media guys do their job. We were at home playing the Steelers in the 1960s. The Steelers' public relations man had to go back to Pittsburgh, and this radio guy wanted to interview him for his show. He just wanted his voice, of course, so he said, "Why don't you be him?" I pretended to be the Pittsburgh P.R. guy, and I did the same thing I would do for the Eagles, but just changed the names.

The coverage today is incredible. It's like living in a fishbowl. Back in the 1950s we had three newspapers in Philadelphia, and they each had a beat man who covered the Eagles. They didn't come around that often because they were also covering other sports. Today they have a guy who is assigned almost exclusively to the Philadelphia Eagles. The television guys won't come down every day, but they call. "Anything going on today? Who's working out?" I'll say, "So-and-so is an interesting story because he's trying to get that knee back in shape." Sometimes you have to say, "I can't help you out," but that's also part of the job.

I've grown right along with the sport. Every year we've done things a little bit bigger. We have public relations meetings where all the guys like myself from the different teams get together. There used to be twelve or thirteen men at the meetings, fourteen counting the NFL representative. Most teams only had one person doing the job. Now you have at least two or three, sometimes more. Only a few years ago I can remember sitting in a meeting, and NFL Films made a presentation about videocassettes. I had no idea what they were talking about. They said, "You'll see, this is the thing of the future." They were right. We've got a 16-mm projector over in the corner, and we haven't used it for ages. You'd have a big reel and that would hold a half-hour highlights film. Now you can get the whole year on a casette. I have had all the film transferred onto casettes, and I don't have to fool with screens and broken film, thanks to the modern world we live in.

Statistics is another area. Everything used to be done by hand; now we put it on the computer. The hometeam is responsible for running the game, and we hire the stat crew. One guy is a CPA; another one is a lawyer. Most stat crews are like that—sharp guys with the numbers who also have good eyes. When the ball is marked, they know it's on the forty-two, not the forty-three. The punt wasn't thirty-six yards; it was thirty-five. We depend a lot on those guys because statistics have become so important. We didn't have as many statistics when I started. There wasn't any such thing as a sack. They had something called "tackled while attempting to pass," but nobody paid any attention to it. Now a sack is a big thing. It's good because the defensive lineman gets a little publicity. On the other hand, I like enthusiasm, but all that dancing around is rather silly.

We play a game here on Sunday afternoon, and it's over at four-thirty. We sit down at the computer at six o'clock, and by a quarter of seven, the whole thing is finished. We send the sheet of stats to the mailing house along with a release, and they run them off, stuff them, and get them in the mail the next day. Our mailing list of somewhere between nine hundred and a thousand sportswriters and radio and television sportscasters all over the country.

Nobody likes it when the media starts to get on your back, but you have to expect it. If the team is losing and the fans start calling the talk shows, you can't say, "Hey, stop it." That's the nature of this business. We've had some turmoil over the years, and when that happens, they'll let you have it. But we've also had some real glory days, too. It works both ways. When the team is playing well and winning, week after week, you get glowing articles. It's all strawberries and cream. When we start to louse up, they get on us. We have to fight back, but you're never going to win the battle. You can't beat the press.

Joe McGinniss was a young guy when he first came to Philadelphia and he was covering sports. He wrote some nasty things about the coach or somebody like that and a couple of the players said they didn't want to talk to him. I talked to the guy at the NFL office and he said, "Jim, you can't keep him out. That's his job, to cover the Eagles." I told the players that they couldn't keep him out, but they just shouldn't talk to him. It worked itself out, but they refused to talk to him for quite a while.

Another guy who got a lot of people mad at him was Larry Merchant. He was one of the first reporters to start putting teams and players under the microscope. Not just the game story, but why it happened, where were the players last night, all that crap. Larry stirred up a lot of B.S. The Eagles were playing the 49ers out in San Francisco and a couple of the players threw him in the swimming pool with all his clothes on. I'm not sure, but I think Van Brocklin and Bednarik were in on that one.

We get a lot of requests for photographs of the players. As far as the older players go, Bednarik, Van Buren—they're the ones we get the most requests for. There's a terrific shot of Bednarik walking off the field at Yankee Stadium. It was snowing and it was his last year in the league. The photo won first prize in the annual photo contest here in Philadelphia. Tommy McDonald, Pete Retzlaff, Bill Bergey—we get requests for them, too. Sometimes it's fans; other times it might be a guy writing an article for a magazine. I had a call from a guy yesterday who owns a bar. Clarence Peaks was in his place, and he wanted a picture of him to put up on the wall. I don't get that many requests for Clarence. One photograph I do get a lot of requests for is the 1960 team. It's a different type of photograph because the guys are wearing green blazers and gray pants. That was the championship team, but we didn't know we were going to win the championship because the picture was taken in October. Tom Brookshier was on that team, and I get requests for his picture because he's a popular player. When those guys are around, we always end up talking about 1960, and Tom told me, "After we beat somebody that year, they'd say, 'You weren't that great,' and I'd say, 'You're right, but we beat you.' " Everybody was putting us away that year, saying things like, "You only have Van Brocklin" or "You only have Bednarik," but the entire team played great that year, and we beat Green Bay for the championship when Chuck Bednarik stopped Jim Taylor in the last seconds.

Every year we have an Eagle Alumni Day during training camp. The ex-players come back and watch practice. Then we introduce them to the crowd and allow the fans to come out on the field and mingle with the players, the current ones as well as the guys from years past. Some of the fans have no idea who Steve Van Buren or Mike Jarmoluk are, but a lot of the old-timers get a kick out of it. We have one fellow, Joe Pilconis, who has been there on Alumni Day the last three or four years. He lives up in the coal region and played during the 1930s. Joe probably played for eighteen dollars a game.

The year 1986 was Buddy Ryan's first with the Eagles, and there were a couple thousand fans at the Alumni Day. After the morning workout, he got up and thanked everybody for coming. Then he said, "We're going to go undefeated in our division." When the season was over, they threw it right back in his face. He thought he could do it, and you can't crucify a guy for that. A coach like Ryan is good for me because he's colorful and alive. He might step on a few toes, but that's life. Everybody's not a soft-boiled egg.

They're lined up out there today for a public relations job. We get mail in here every day. "Hi, I'm Joe or Jane Doe. I went to Dartmouth and I would love to get into public relations. I worked for the school newspaper." They think it's glamorous and colorful and forget about the long hours and the Saturdays and Sundays you're not home. A couple of years ago I had lung cancer, but up until then I traveled with the team and did all the advance work. If we played a team like Dallas or Los Angeles, I'd go early in the week. Sometimes I'd come back to Philadelphia and then fly back with the team on Saturday. If we're playing the Bears, we'd leave on Saturday. It's only a two-hour flight, so we get to the hotel in the afternoon. We get up the next morning and take the bus out to the stadium. We play the game; then it's back to the airport and home. We're in the city less than twenty-four hours. Starting last year I have started to handle the team travel. Go down to the airport and make sure that the bus and equipment truck are on time, make the hotel reservations, and book the media rooms—that sort of thing. To show you how big pro football is today, we're going to play at Green Bay this year. I called one of the fellows at the Packers, Tom Miller, and he told me the name of the hotel they stay at. I called them and they were sold out. After calling three or four more that were sold out, we're staying in a Howard Johnson's. Nothing fancy, but there's a bed. Those fans come from three hundred miles away and we're lucky to have that.

We've got great fans in Philadelphia. When we were at Franklin Field in the 1950s and '60s, we sold out almost every year. That stadium held sixty thousand. We moved here to Veterans Stadium in 1971, and last season we sold fifty-four thousand season tickets. Our capacity is a little under seventy thousand. A lot of cities would love to have the attendance we have. The fans are known to boo once in a while. They call us the King of the Booers, but I don't blame them. If they're watching lousy football, they want to let you know. You're not kidding them because they've been around for years. A lot of those fans know as much about the game as we do.

We started drawing the big crowds in the late 1950s, when Van Brocklin came to town and the Eagles started winning. Even before that, if the Cleveland Browns came in, there was always a big draw and we always had a hell of a rivalry with the Pittsburgh Steelers. We've never had too much trouble with the fans, but if there was a fight in those days it seemed that the people took care of it themselves. You didn't have everybody running around like you do now.

One of the big problems is drinking. This year the sale of beer is going to stop at halftime. We check packages at the gate, and we catch a lot of fans trying to take booze into the stadium. But that's hard to control. We had a case here recently where a guy was in a wheelchair, a handicapped fellow. He had a little cabinet under his seat and there was a keg of beer in there. Another group used to throw a rope over the side of the stadium and hoist up a keg of beer. That's a hell of a way up, but some guys will do anything for a drink. Aside from a few things like that, our fans are very well behaved. The only time I can remember having a little trouble was when some of the fans started throwing golf balls down onto the field. The officials stopped that in a hurry, but they were complaining after the game. Some of them are golfers, and they were mad because the fans were throwing cheap balls.

A FEW YEARS OF HAPPINESS AND MANY YEARS OF SORROW

CHARLES BARCLAY

FAN

New York Giants 1937–

I don't know if I'm making a mistake, but I'm raising my son as a Giant Fan.

—Toots Shor

I'M not a gambler. Oh, I'll take a pool for two dollars because I figure it's me against the bookmakers, and I even win once in a while, but I won't bet on a particular game because I believe that a person who bets on sports roots for his money, not for his team. Don't get me wrong; I'm not putting gamblers down because most of them are extremely knowledgeable about the game. They have to be if they're going to put their money on the line, but their attitude is cold.

When I was a kid, I was a baseball Giants' fan. My best friend was a kid who had moved to the Bronx from Brooklyn, and he was a rabid Dodger fan. One afternoon a Dodger pitcher threw a no-hit game, and I decided to show my buddy what a big sport I was. He worked downtown, and when he came out of the subway I went over to him. "Jack, I heard that Ed Head pitched a no-hitter. Congratulations." He looked at me with a long face and said, "I had Boston."

Like most New York kids, I was attracted to sports, mostly baseball and football. This is my fiftieth year of Giants' football, and the combination of the baseball and football Giants has given me a few years of happiness and many years of sorrow. When the Giants won the Super Bowl, it surpassed anything that I can remember and made up in some ways for fifteen years of terrible football. The unhappiest moment, of course, was when the baseball Giants left New York for San Francisco.

Sports and wars have a lot in common in that we tend to dwell more on lost causes then the ones we won. I don't think that often about the World Series of 1954 when we cleaned house with the Cleveland Indians. On the other hand, it rained on a Sunday during the 1951 World Series when we played the Yankees and our pitching rotation was thrown off. I've never forgiven the elements.

I was born in my parents' bedroom in the Bronx. My dad was a working man all his life who came to the United States from Austria in 1904 and worked as a waiter until he was seventy-two years old. He wasn't much of a football fan; he liked professional wrestling. In later years, when it came on television, I'd tell him, "But, Pop, it's not real." He didn't want to hear it, so I went to most of the games by myself.

The first game I saw was in the Polo Grounds. The Giants played the Detroit Lions, and I was just amazed at the high level of play. The only football I had ever seen or played were some pickup games in the park. They weren't using the T-formation at that time, just variations on the single wing, and the tailbacks were the key men. They were the fellows who ran the ball, threw the ball, and often kicked. The thing I remember most about that game, Detroit had a back, "Dutch" Clark, number seven, and during pregame warmups, Clark stood on the fifty-yard line and drop-kicked the ball through the goalposts. Then he turned around and drop-kicked a few through the other goalposts.

That was in 1937, and I saw the last four games of the season. The last game was horrendous. The Washington Redskins came to town, and in those days George Preston Marshall owned the team. They would show up with their whole entourage, including the Washington Redskins' Marching Band, and would make a great deal of noise. At halftime the band would really put on a great show. Today at Giants' Stadium, they usually have a high school band from some place in New Jersey put on the show, and that's generally when I eat my sandwiches. Sammy Baugh was a rookie that year, and they also had a running back named Cliff Battle, who took the Giants apart. The Redskins used an unbalanced line, and wherever "Turk" Edwards, their big tackle, lined up, that's where they ran. He just knocked people ass over teacup.

It used to cost me fifty cents to go to a game, a dime carfare, and you bought a card at school for twenty-five cents that let you in the Polo Grounds for forty cents. I would bring along a sandwich because a hot dog cost a dime, and I just didn't have it. In those days they let youngsters sit in a special section in the upper left field stands. I never bought a program, that was out of the question, but I'd sometimes pick one up after the game. I still have a few of them at home including one for a game in 1938 between the Giants and Pittsburgh.

In those days Pittsburgh was known as the Pittsburgh Pirates, and they had signed the best collegiate running back that year, "Whizzer" White, the same Byron White who today is an associate justice of the Supreme Court. The Pirates paid him what was an incredible amount of money in those days—$15,000. The Giants and Pirates were going to play on Monday night. Why they scheduled it on Monday night, I don't know because that was a long time before "Monday Night Football."

One of the leading New York sportswriters, Jimmy Powers, who wrote for the *Daily News,* had written an article that suggested Whizzer White's teammates were so resentful of the money that he was making that they were slipping blocks and allowing him to take some shots. The Pirates were so incensed by this that they offered to bet any amount of money that they would beat the Giants. Their offer may have been more figurative than anything else, but they beat the Giants and White was outstanding that night. The Giants went on to beat the Packers for the NFL championship that year.

I graduated from high school in January 1940, and spent one semester at CCNY before I dropped out. I really wasn't up to the pressure of heavy study at that point and looked around for a job. I took a course in radio and television repair, and my last job before I was drafted was working for the Lighthouse for the Blind, fixing their recording machines. At that time I would go and pick up tickets at the Giants' ticket office. It was located on Forty-second Street, between Sixth Avenue and Times Square, and you could go there on a Wednesday and buy a couple of seats for that Sunday's game. As I recall, prices were around two bucks for general admission. But at the beginning of the year you could buy what the Giants called a courtesy card, and with that card you could buy the same seat for a buck and a quarter. I would pick up my fiancée at her parents' apartment, and we'd take the subway down to the Polo Grounds and see a game for $2.50.

We were there at that famous game on December 7, 1941. I'm just going by my memory, but I don't remember any announcements being made until the end of the game. The Giants had won the eastern championship the week before; they beat the Redskins and were playing their arch rivals, the Brooklyn Dodgers, in the last regular season game before they went to Chicago to play the Bears for the title game. The Dodgers were beginning to build a decent team at that time; they had players like "Ace" Parker and "Bruiser" Kinard, and the giants knew that the Bear scouts were in the stands, so they didn't use any of their regular plays. The Dodgers beat them 21–7, or something like that.

During the game, it was a full house; there were all kinds of whisperings and hubbubs in the stands, and my wife and I had no idea what was going on. Portable radios were extremely rare in those days. When the game was over, the P.A. announcer made the announcement that all leaves for servicemen were canceled and that all members of the armed services were ordered to return to their bases. We walked down the ramp and came out on the street, and the newsboys were hawking the papers with the story about the attack on Pearl Harbor.

For a few years my wife came to all the games with me. Then one Sunday we were heading to the subway with snow up to our navels. It was freezing cold and we were all bundled up, and halfway to the subway she turned and looked at me, said, "I don't know why I'm doing this," and turned around and went home. She's seen very few games since then, but I'm blessed with a couple of sons, so I started taking them to games when they were about nine years old. My older boy was just about that age when we played the championship game against Green Bay in Yankee Stadium, and I think that was probably the worst weather I've ever experienced at a football game. The wind chill factor was so low I don't think they could measure it.

When I was ready to leave the apartment with my son, my wife stood at the front door with her arms out and said, "You're not taking that child out in weather like this." He began to cry and said, "But I want to go." We went, and at halftime I bought him a hot dog. He was sitting next to me, and after a few minutes he said, "Dad, could you please help me?" He had so many clothes on that he couldn't bend his elbow to bring the hot dog up to his mouth.

The field was, of course, natural turf, but there was practically no grass left and the ground was frozen to the consistency of concrete. Today some of the players wear gloves of some sort, but in those days they didn't have anything like that. Players had blood running down the backs of their hands from sliding on that frozen surface. The game was close, and at halftime you could feel the excitement in the air. The Giants came back out on the field, and there was a cry that began with just a few fans and finally became a full-throated roar: "Beat Green Bay! Beat Green Bay!" It impressed everybody but Vince Lombardi and the Packers because they beat the Giants 16–7. What can I tell you?

I was drafted in 1943, and after basic they put me into a college training course and I ended up in the signal corps. I was stationed at Fort Monmouth in New Jersey for most of the war. I missed most of the 1943 season, but I would go and see a game whenever I could. The Giants did have freebee seats for soldiers out in either the left or right field stands, I forget which.

After I got out of the service I went to work at a radio station for three years and did a little bit of everything—disc jockey, engineer, and I also was the sports editor of this little peanut whistle station. It was an FM station at a time when very few people knew what FM was. During the time I worked for the station, I had a press pass, but when we went off the air, I had to go back to buying my tickets. You could still buy them at the ticket office without much trouble, but in 1951 I was working as a recording studio technician and we were doing Wheaties commercials with Mel Allen, the broadcaster. I asked his intercession to get me season tickets in a decent location, and he got me seats on the eight-yard line in the upper stands of the Polo Grounds. The following year, again with Mel's help, we moved to the thirty-yard line and then in early 1956 the Giants moved to Yankee Stadium. They sent me a notice asking me how many seats I wanted and where I'd like them. I wound up in my present location, upper stands at just about the thirty-five-yard line and retained them through all the moves, Yankee Stadium to the Yale Bowl to Shea Stadium and finally, to Giants' Stadium.

As long as I've had my seats, I've been sitting with just about the same people. There's a very lovely family, a man, his wife, and their daughter who sometimes brings her friends. I remember when the man's father used to bring him to the games when he was just a child. His father is a little bit older than I am, and he went to Florida and retired. There was another gentleman who had just one seat next to my three. His name was Jerry and he always had the newspaper with him and would give the comics to my son. Jerry was a cab driver and I saw him once in the city. He passed away about six years ago. The fellow who sat on my left was a criminal court judge; he died just recently. My sons are both lawyers, so there was a little bit of mutual interest there. The judge had a son who is just about to graduate from Stuyvesant High, and we've seen him grow up over the years. I seem to remember that his seat at one time may have belonged to Gene Rossides, the great Columbia football player who became an attorney, but I have no idea what happened to him.

I think my seats are a little bit high up, and I probably could have improved them, but I didn't want to leave because I like the people around me. However, I do have to say this. Sometimes people can't go to the game and will sell their tickets. That's fine, I've done it myself, but tickets will find their way through three or four hands to people who are not really fans, and some of them don't know how to behave at a ballpark. It's been in the news and on television, the fact that you have some rowdyism at the games, but I think we've been lucky and had less at Giants' Stadium than at some of the other ballparks. I can only recall one incident and that was at Yankee Stadium—that's how long ago it was. We were playing the Cleveland Browns, the last game of the season. It was down to the last minute and a half, the Giants were winning, and the fans in the center field bleachers poured out onto the field. Paul Brown took his team off the field, and finally the announcement came that the Giants were going to forfeit the game if the people didn't get off the field. If that happened the Giants would have been out of the playoffs, so everybody went back to their seats. It did, however, take a long time to get them off the field, and I think that was a display of excess by those fans.

They've begun to stop selling intoxicating beverages a little earlier in the game, and I see nothing wrong with that. I've never forgotten a definition of freedom they gave us in elementary school. "My freedom to swing my arm ends where your nose begins."

We've had some situations of people throwing beer cans, that sort of thing, but it happens infrequently. I do see an idiot every once in a while stand up without his shirt on, when the wind chill factor is minus eight and scream, "Go, Giants, go," and I don't know where he wants to go with them.

The Giant who was the absolute best player, considering all his talents and length of service, was Frank Gifford. He could do it all and had an indomitable spirit. He wasn't a flashy runner, he was an efficient runner, and at the end of every run he would stretch out and give you two more yards. He had that horrible injury when Bednarik hit him—a fair shot, by the way—and he stayed out for a year and couldn't stand it. He had to come back and played well for a few more years. Following Gifford, I would have to mention Mel Hein. He made quite an impression on me because I saw him when I was very young. He played both ways, center and what we call a linebacker today. I really believe that the team that won the Super Bowl, especially at the end of the year, was as good a team as the Giants have ever had. They were extremely good at every position and only a handful of Giants out of the past would have made that team. I think Frank Gifford could have played at any time and anywhere. Tittle too. Mel Hein would have made the team as a terrific linebacker.

One of the things I've always enjoyed is following a college star and wondering which team will sign him in the draft. If he signs with another team, you look forward to seeing him in action when he comes to town. I recall "Biggie" Goldberg, who came out of Pittsburgh and played for the Chicago Cardinals. He ran back punts, and the thing I remember most about him was that he achieved full speed in his first step. I hear fellows talk about O. J. Simpson, and he was a tremendous back, but watching O.J. run always reminded me of another great runner, Ollie Matson, who was an Olympic star and also played for the Cardinals. He got around defenders with such grace and ease, and yet he had tremendous speed. O.J. had that kind of stride. Jimmy Brown was a case unto himself, and I don't think I can find enough superlatives to describe him. You can't say he did it all because he wasn't called upon to do it all, but Paul Brown certainly asked him to do a great deal. I can recall a game at Yankee Stadium during the few years when the Giants dominated the Browns. Jimmy Brown had been hurt early in the game, but Paul Brown kept sending him in and sending him in. At one point late in the game, it was out of reach for the Browns. Sam Huff walked over to the Browns' bench, and we learned later that Huff was berating Paul Brown for exposing Jim Brown to so much danger. The Giants knew Brown was hurt and tired, but if he was in the game they had to hit him. Paul Brown didn't look away; he just gave Huff that icy stare of his. I think that action by Huff was an indication of what a professional ball player is really like.

There are loads of fine players today—all you have to do is watch the Pro Bowl. The broadcasters like to tell us that the players are bigger and better, and I think that's only partially true. Many are just bigger, not better. In fact, a lot of them are worse. The owners, players, advertisers, and broadcasters look at the fans as an opportunity to make money, and because of that attitude they've overexpanded the National Football League. There are, in my humble opinion, not enough adequate players to staff a lot of these teams and provide the fans with a good football game on a given Sunday. I'm glad that they've reached out to parts of the country that didn't have pro football before and brought the game to fans who were never interested or exposed before, but today you've got guys who can't block and tackles who can't tackle and receivers who can't catch the ball. I think we're being fooled when they tell us this is the best football we've ever seen.

At one point, many years ago, I was privileged to do a test cassette program for Time-Life with Johnny Unitas. I was working freelance, and we went to Baltimore and put a mike in front of Unitas, and he said some things that were very interesting. He felt that expansion diluted the game when the Colts went from thirty-three to thirty-seven players! I mean, there are forty-five now and some coaches are talking about forty-nine. He explained that the Colts had eleven guys on offense, eleven guys on defense, and eleven guys looking for their jobs. Players would go to Coach Webb Ewbank and ask to be on special teams because they didn't want to give anybody an opportunity to show he could run faster or block harder than they could. Unitas divided the players into two groups: the superstars and those with lesser abilities. Superstars will always give you a good game by the very nature of their superior talent. Even if they're hurt, they'll play well. Lesser players may have an occasional game where they exceed their limitations, but they're not going to do that consistently so the level of the game depends on your journeyman ball player. If that player feels that in order to keep his job he's got to give one hundred percent, you're going to have an excellent game. Today, with the expanded squads and greater number of teams, a player knows there's nobody who's going to take his job, and he's not pressed to play his best. There're a lot of big fellows out there who can't play, but the teams have to fill the uniforms.

As far as owners go, I think the Mara family, Wellington, and before him, his father, are excellent businessmen and also as much fans of the team as I am. They probably reflect whatever are the best qualities in football team ownership. The only contact I have ever had with Mr. Mara was on the few occasions when I have written directly to him to express a criticism or doubt. On at least two occasions I received a handwritten reply, which is evidence to me that the Giants have an interest in the fan. It's true that they've had a sellout since day one, and the Maras have been accused of not being concerned with the success of the team. Why spend money if the fans are coming anyway? I think to a certain extent that might have been the attitude at one time, but the turning point was bringing in George Young, who is the man responsible for where the team is today.

When the Giants announced that they were going to build a new ball park in the Meadowlands, I felt, as a season ticket holder, that I should go over to their office and take a look at the artist's rendering. I couldn't believe it. Here's a modern stadium being built in the northeast where games are going to have to be played in December and January. Not only was there no dome, there wasn't any cover. At the Polo Grounds I used to sit under cover, and Yankee Stadium had cover for most of the fans. At Giants' Stadium I doubt that more than 20 percent of us have any kind of protection. I wrote to tell Mr. Mara that I thought the new stadium was obsolete before it was built. I recall one Sunday when we had a terrible day. It was sleeting, the kind of day you suffer through. The weekend before, on TV, I watched the Lions playing in their new Silverdome. It was wintertime in Michigan and people were sitting in their shirtsleeves. The bottom line is that it's an exhibition, entertainment. I wouldn't want to go to a Broadway play where the roof was leaking and the actors were uncomfortable.

The most atrocious development of all is AstroTurf. The owners spend all kinds of money on a player, take a kid out of college who is a high draft choice, give him a nice bonus and a big contract, and he'll run across that stupid carpet and get turf toe or something else that will cripple him. Everybody sees it and knows about it, and I can't believe, with the technology that's available, that they can't build a stadium with a retractable dome and play on real turf. It's October 3, the sun is shining, it's a bright crisp day, leave the dome open. But if it's December 3 and there's a freezing rain coming down, close the thing and give everybody a break.

John Madden, whom I admire tremendously, is always saying that the ball players have to be in the mud to really play the game. Maybe they like that sort of thing, but I don't. It could be because I'm not seventeen years old anymore, but I don't see that as good football.

"HAIL TO THE REDSKINS"

HARRY HINKEN

BAND MEMBER
Washington Redskins' Band 1939–

Everybody knows Harry and he's extremely popular with all of us in the Redskins' organization. It's a two-way street because Harry is very important to the Redskins and to be honest, the Redskins are his life. Harry's wife would be the first one to tell you that.

—Billy Ball, Director of Entertainment, Washington Redskins

HAIL TO THE REDSKINS

Hail to the Redskins.
Hail Victory!
Braves on the warpath.
Fight for old D.C.
Scalp 'um, swamp 'um, we will
Take 'um big score.

Read 'um, Weep 'um, touchdown,
We want heap more.
Fight on, fight on, 'till you have won.
Sons of Wash-ing-ton.
Rah! Rah! Rah!

Hail to the Redskins.
Hail Victory!
Braves on the warpath.
Fight for old D.C.

—Corinne Griffith/Barnee Breeskin

IF you've been to the Pro Football Hall of Fame, you saw that the Redskins Band is part of their exhibit. They've got one of our bass drums and a full dress uniform, complete with Indian headdress on display. There are also pictures of us marching down Broadway in New York City. One of the members of the band went out to the Hall of Fame this summer with his family, and as he was about to buy his tickets, he showed them his Redskins Band card. They told him he didn't have to pay because the band was inducted into the Hall of Fame the first year they were eligible and inductees get in free. The Redskins Band has played a very important part in the promotion of professional football right from the band's beginning.

George P. Marshall brought the Redskins down from Boston in 1937. There's a lot of guessing about the name, Redskins, and I don't think there's anybody living today who really knows where it came from. At one point Boston had an Indian for a coach, "Lone Star" Dietz, and the city also had a baseball team called the Boston Braves, so it could have come from either of those. The attendance at the Redskins' first game in Washington drew more fans than the team had attracted in Boston the entire year before. In fact, the Redskins had won the Eastern Division in 1936, and George Marshall refused to play the championship game in Boston because of lousy attendance. Instead, they played in the Polo Grounds in New York and Green Bay beat them, 21–6.

The philosophy of the Redskin organization has always been to provide entertainment from the moment a ticket holder enters the stadium until he walks out. The fans are going to be entertained by the teams, music, dancing, and a great halftime show. Marshall wanted women to come to the games because he thought they brought class to the sport, and he also thought a football game should be a pageant. That's why we've got the marching band, the pro band, the Redskin singers, and the Redskinettes. The Redskinettes aren't like other cheerleaders because everything they do is choreographed with the band. There are thirty-two girls, and they're spread around the field. At the end of each quarter they do a special routine when the teams are changing ends.

I think Marshall thought more about the band than he did about the football team. He was an entertainer who loved show business, and his thinking has been passed down to the present owners, the Cook family. The first year the team was here, Marshall hired a local dance band and had a big teepee erected on top of the bleachers. That was the era of the big bands, Benny Goodman, Glenn Miller; and the band would play that kind of music during the game. There was also a bunch of fellows who worked for a dairy who formed a marching band that performed at halftime. They weren't called the Redskins Band, it was something like Thompson's Chevy Chase Dairy Marching Band. The official Redskins' Marching Band, with the Indian outfits, didn't come along until the next year.

When the band was formed, Marshall and his wife, Corinne Griffith, who had been a silent screen star, met with the members and asked them to suggest a team song. There were about 150 men in the band, and they all voted for "Onward Christians Soldiers" because it was the one song that most of them knew by heart. Marshall wouldn't have anything to do with that because he wanted his own song, so Barney Breeskin, the director of the pro band, wrote the music and Corinne Griffith wrote the lyrics and they called it "Hail to the Redskins." That was how the Redskins' fight song came into being, and we've been playing it ever since.

You'll never hear us play college songs because we never wanted to give the edge to the other guy. Hell, in the later years we had Joe Theismann and he came from Notre Dame. You might say, why not play the Notre Dame victory march and inspire Theismann? The problem with that is, there might be some big linebacker on the other side of the field who also went to Notre Dame, and he might hear the old school song and come out and try to win it for his alma matre. The only college song that I can recall being played since World War II was the University of Georgia fight song, and that was in honor of President Carter when he came out to see a game. We had to borrow the music from the University of Georgia band.

The Redskins band has always been a volunteer organization, and we have quite a few professional musicians in the outfit. Initially the compensation was a ticket for each member that he could give to his wife, or whatever, and today each band member gets two tickets. The band was all men until eleven years ago. We didn't have anything against women; it was just that when they built RFK Stadium, there was no place for potential female band members to change. The director and myself got together and decided that we were going to figure out a way to get women in the band. We set up some lockers so they could have their own little cubbyhole, and today we've got several female musicians. In fact, we audition everybody who trys out for the band, and the first person to score 100 on the test was a woman.

At the present time we have at least seventeen directors of high school bands in the group. The Assistant Secretary of Education, CIA people, members of the White House staff—you name them, we've got them. We've got lawyers sticking out of our ears and a lot of schoolteachers. There are six fellows from the Army Band and two out of the Marine Drum and Bugle Corps, as well as three from the Air Force Band and a couple of former Navy Band members. Some of our people have thirty or forty years' experience, and they can play anything.

We try to give people a variety of music, and right now we're in a period of transition. Instead of playing a lot of Broadway show tunes, we're leaning more toward marches. We never play anything in the Top 40—that's the kind of music the pro band plays. They've got synthesizers and electric guitars, so they can handle the new music. All of the groups alternate songs. The marching band will play something, then the pro band will come next, and then the Redskin singers. There's about twenty singers and sometimes they will also sing with the bands, depending on what the tune is. There are times, too, when our percussion section will get those drums beating, and that really riles up the fans. It has an influence.

Four or five years ago I met Howard Cosell coming into the stadium, and we started to talk about the band. He told me, "It's not printed anywhere, but usually when we come into Washington we figure the band is worth one point on the scoreboard." He wasn't being facetious because you can go to a football game where there isn't any music and you don't have the type of atmosphere we have.

If a player is injured, the marching band always plays an up-tempo tune to bring up the spirits of the people. We had a situation one time when I was putting up the music for the next song. Pittsburgh was playing here and a black ball player had been injured. I didn't know what was going on, and the band by chance started playing "Bye, Bye, Blackbird" as they were carrying this guy off the field. The phone rang in the bandstand, and when I picked it up, George Marshall was on the line. He was screaming, "Stop the band! Stop it! Stop it!" and I couldn't figure out what he was talking about. But when he said stop it, I stopped it and came up with the next number. It was going out on television all over the country, and so help me God, it wasn't intentional.

I grew up in Alexandria, Virginia, which was a segregated society, but I think I've changed like most intelligent people. I've made an effort to recruit black members for the band, and at one point I wrote to every school in Washington and didn't get any response. It was years before blacks forgave the Redskins because we were the last team in the NFL to hire a black player. The Redskins were the first team to go on regional television, and we went all over the South. Marshall took advantage of that, and we had the whole South behind the team. Even today there are fans who come to the games from as far as North Carolina, places like that. At one time the interlude in "Hail to the Redskins" was "Dixie," but at one point we were forced to get rid of "Dixie." A fellow in the band wrote a new interlude called "Warpath," and that's what we play today. We did have some trouble with the Indian thing, during the civil rights movement, but it wasn't the band so much as the Redskinettes. They wore black wigs with a ponytail, and they came down on us for that so the girls went back to their natural hair.

When I was a young kid, I played football and was in one band or another all the way through high school. I have pictures of myself drum-majoring the Sons of the American Legion Drum and Bugle Corps when I was ten years old. I was a big fellow for my age and played offensive center and defensive linebacker. Fridays I would play for the high school and then on Saturdays I'd play for a semipro team. I got five dollars a game.

My father owned a furniture store founded by my great-grandfather, who came over from Germany. Originally they made their own furniture and sold it door to door from a cart. My father was in World War I and had a bayonet wound that gave him trouble until the day he died. He was a big sports fan and was the one who took me to my first Redskins game. From that moment on, I knew I wanted to play pro football, and because I wasn't old enough to do that, I joined the Redskins Band. I started playing trombone as a reserve in 1939 and have been a regular member since 1940 except for World War II.

Right after Pearl Harbor, I went down and enlisted in the Marine

Corps. I was called up in March, and when I got out of boot camp, they put me in the post band at Parris Island. I drum-majored the band until my father died in July 1942. When I got back to Parris Island, I told them I wanted to go into combat, so they put me into the First Marine Parachute Regiment, which was involved in the invasion of Guadalcanal. We were a specialized group and never did get to make a combat jump because they didn't have the planes. When they disbanded the paratroopers, we became the 28th Marines in the 5th Division. At one point we were dumping supplies out of a C-47 over Bougainville for a unit that had gotten itself in a jam, and I was hit by ground fire. They brought me back to the United States, and right after I came back the 5th Division shipped out for Iwo Jima. That's where I lost all my friends. I didn't want to come out of the Corps, but they set me loose with an honorable medical discharge and I came back to Washington.

Before I joined the Marines, I had nine scholarship offers to play football, including one with Ohio State, but my injuries created problems and I couldn't go on with it. I went into sales or one thing or another, and then I went into the insurance business in the late '40s. I've had my own agency ever since. After the war I took over as drum major of the Redskins' Band and did that until 1953, when I got polio. I was in the V.A. hospital for almost two years, and it left me paralyzed from the waist down. When I got out of the hospital, the Redskins sent for me and they brought me out on the fifty-yard line at halftime. I got a standing ovation, and I don't mind admitting I was crying like a baby.

We were one big happy family at that time because there were only thirty thousand seats in Griffith Stadium, and everybody knew everybody. This team, and the environment they play in, is entirely different from anything else in the NFL. It's been said, and it's probably true, that there are enough senators and representatives at the game to have a quorum of the Congress of the United States. All of your top news people and government officials go to our games, and they're just as loyal as the guy pumping gas. It's not the blue-collar crowd that you get in other stadiums like Pittsburgh or Philadelphia. We don't have the fist fights that you have in other places, but you're still going to have those few odd characters in a crowd of fifty-five thousand. A drunk is a drunk, and maybe in Pittsburgh he gets drunk on Iron City beer. Here they're drinking Jack Daniel's, but in general we have a very well-behaved crowd. When our fans go up to Philadelphia, they will invariably end up in a brawl, and we had to stop going to Baltimore because the last time the band went over there they were throwing whiskey bottles at us.

We don't go on trips anymore, and that policy began when the team started flying. It costs too much money to fly that many people. The last train trips we made were when Jerry Wolman owned the Eagles, and the last bus trips were to Baltimore. The band used to go to Cleveland, Pittsburgh, and New York. In New York we would go to the Polo Grounds, Yankee Stadium, and Ebbets Field. We went to Brooklyn one time, and the fans were booing the band when we came out on the field. At that time we had a drum major who had been a national collegiate twirling champion. We started to play the "National Emblem March," and this drum major, Eddie Sacks, got out there and started to twirl. It was as if a cardinal had walked on that field to give a benediction. I mean, that crowd quieted right down. We were playing soft. He stood out there twirling, and you could hear a pin drop in that stadium. Eddie left us and went into automobile racing. He won the Indianapolis 500 and was later killed driving in that race.

After I was paralyzed, I stepped down as drum major and "Buck" Wright took over. He's a former World War II drill instructor and is now in charge of field security. I never thought about it until I started to talk to you, but it's been a tradition right from the start that there's always been a former Marine involved with the band. Our first director, John D'Andelet, was a former director of the Marine Band. The Redskins' Band has always been a disciplined group, and it's not an excuse to get together to drink beer or party. Today I'm the personnel director of the marching band and assistant director of entertainment for the Redskins. That includes the band, the Redskin singers, and the Redskinettes, as well as booking the singers for the national anthem and the entertainment for the half-time show. I don't do everything myself; we have a committee that helps me.

There are some great stories that go along with the Redskins, and I've been around for most of them. There was the time they lost 73–0 in the 1940 championship game against the Bears. We had beaten them just two weeks before, and you're not going to find anybody who will tell you exactly what went on, but there was a big party the night before. George Halas put all of his players to bed at ten o'clock, and the Redskins left the party to go to the stadium. Enough said. George Marshall almost had a phobia about having the band march down the field at the end of the game playing "Hail to the Redskins," and it wasn't any different that day. The Bears had just beaten us 73–0, and they were announcing over the P.A. system that season tickets would go on sale Monday morning while we were marching down the field playing "Hail to the Redskins." You should have heard those fans—it was unbelievable.

We always had a parade when we got into New York. There would sometimes be as many as fifteen special trains, full of fans, that would come up to New York from Washington, and when everybody got off the trains at Penn Station, we'd march up Broadway with the band up front. New York had never seen anything like it. At ten or eleven o'clock on a Sunday morning, here came fifteen thousand football fans down the street!

One Sunday evening we got back from New York at about eleven o'clock after playing the Giants up in the Polo Grounds. We'd beaten them, and I don't remember if it was a championship game or not, but it was a big win, and there must have been ten thousand fans waiting for us in Washington at Union Station. Marshall had decided on the train that we were going to have a parade when we got back, so the band got all lined up and the fans were ready to go when the police department said no because we didn't have a permit. Marshall was trying to talk to the cops, and there were thousands of fans milling around, so the cops arrested the drum major because they didn't know who else to arrest. They took him over to the First Precinct and set bail at twenty-five dollars. Between Marshall and Corinne Griffith, they had just enough to get him out. I think Marshall had twenty and she had five, or vice versa.

After I was paralyzed, I got into swimming. It's good therapy for polio patients because gravity and resistance are eliminated. During the '60s I started to get serious, and somebody suggested I try the English Channel. My coach was a former Olympic swimming coach, so I asked him. He said, "Why not?" We didn't know what we were getting into, and by that time it was too late. The wire services all over the world were writing me up, and if I hadn't been getting so much publicity, the first time I went in for a training session I'd have come back home. The Channel is a very fickle body of water. It's so damn cold, the currents are terrible, and the weather can turn bad before you know it.

I attempted the Channel three times. The first time I went twenty-five miles and hit an oil slick, and had to come out of the water. The second time I made it, and on my third try I hit a boat and broke my back. A force-seven storm came up with twenty-two-foot seas, and a wave threw me upon the deck of a boat. I'd just been greased, so when I hit the deck three people jumped on top of me so I wouldn't be washed overboard. The official word from the Channel Association was that it was an act of providence, and they asked me if I would allow them to put it in the record book as the shortest attempt, fifty-seven minutes.

One of the reporters who accompanied me on the three trips was a fellow who wrote for the Washington papers and had covered the Redskins, it seemed, forever. In 1945 the Redskins played the Cleveland Rams for the championship. The next season the Rams moved to Los Angeles. I wasn't there, but people have told me it was so cold that the band's instruments froze up before the game started, and the wind was blowing something terrible. During the first quarter Sammy Baugh dropped back and Steve Bagarus was in the end zone, wide open. The wind blew Sammy's pass into the cross bar, and the rule was that if the passer hit the goalpost, it was a safety, and we ended up losing the game by one point, 15–14. They changed the rule after that, but I was telling you about this reporter.

The press area had no protection, so all of the reporters were boozing it up pretty good to stay warm. This fellow called in his story after he got out of the stadium, and he told me, "I didn't remember what the hell I wrote because I was so drunk I blacked out." When he got back to Washington, he was afraid to go in to the paper because he was sure he'd been fired, so he waited until the last minute, and when he got there everybody started congratulating him on the great story he had written. He ended up winning the sportswriters' award for that year, 1945.

The majority of fans today don't know anything about the early Redskins. It's kind of scary, expecially as you grow older, how much people don't know about the past. There are schoolkids around here who don't know who Churchill was, and if I mention Guadalcanal or Iwo, people have no idea what I'm talking about. I was having lunch with a couple of the current Redskin players before training camp started this year, and one of them is a defensive back. I was talking about the old Redskins and the fact that Sammy Baugh is remembered by most people as a great passer, but he was also a hell of a kicker and held the record for the most tackles made by a defensive back in one season. This guy said, "Well, I'm going to break that record this season." He has no idea how great those guys were.

I've seen so many players over my fifty years of watching pro football, and I just can't remember them all, but there are always those who stand out. Jim Brown. I have never seen anything like him running with the ball. He never went out of bounds. It was always straight down the field. Marion Motley was another great one. It didn't make any difference if a man tackled him, you had to have some help to get him down, or he would just keep on walking to the goal line. As far as the Redskins go, Eddie LeBaron was a great quarterback, and he really earned the title of magician. The way he could hide the ball, nobody knew where it was. Steve Bagarus, old double zero, who played for us in the late '40s, was one of the best open-field runners I've ever seen. He was also a real good-looking guy, and there would be four or five thousand women waiting for him to come out of the stadium. As for Sonny Jurgensen, his record as a passer stands for itself, and he was a great ball player to watch. We also had Gene Brito, a defensive end and one of the great Redskin ball players.

According to the record book, he was good. But I was never one of Joe Theismann's fans. Now, Billy Kilmer was one of those guys who could fit in the '40s and '50s just as well as he did in his time—a rough, tough kind of guy. John Riggins is another tough guy who would have fit in the earlier era. John was a real character. I know John's father and mother very well, and I sat through a couple of games with his father. You would never know that John is his son. Duane Thomas was another one. He'd go by me before every game, and I'd always say hello to him. He'd just walk by and ignore me, act like I wasn't even there. But after a while he started to search me out, and he'd say, "Good morning, Mr. Hinken." I guess I just wore him down.

If you asked me who's the greatest ball player I've ever seen, I don't even have to stop and think—Sammy Baugh. There's a famous story told about how Ray Flaherty, the Redskins' coach, told Sam when he first came to Washington in 1937, "Sam, you're not in college anymore. You have to put that ball right in their eye." Sam said, "Which eye, Coach?" He could do everything and was also a hell of a nice guy. Sam was a modest guy. Certainly professional football is exactly what the word means—you're getting paid to play football. But those guys in Sam's time weren't getting the kind of money we see today. It seems that a lot of players today are making the big money and don't want to act like human beings. They're in the minority. We have a hell of a lot of good guys on the Redskins.

Doug Williams is the nicest guy you would ever want to meet, and Dave Butz is another good one. I could name a lot of them.

Along with all of the other things I do, I'm in charge of the players' gate, and I see these guys acting like they're doing everybody a big favor by signing autographs. I think about all the players I've seen who were in this position ten, fifteen, thirty, forty years ago. All I can think of is: "The wheel is going to come around, and their day will come."

STAN, WHERE DO WE GET THESE GODDAMN OFFICIALS?

STAN JAVIE

OFFICIAL

1951–81

One time Stan was on his way to the airport after working a game. He was late and rushing to make his plane when he was pulled over for speeding by a New Jersey state trooper. The trooper asked to see his license and told him to get out of his car. Meanwhile, Stan is explaining to him who he is and why he is in such a hurry. The trooper looks up from the license and says, "I know who you are. I listened to the game and I didn't think too much of your officiating. I couldn't do anything about it then. But I can now." The trooper tells Stan to get back in his car and to drive backwards for fifteen yards. Stan did what he said, then the trooper hands him back his license and says, "That was my penalty on you. Drive more carefully in the future."

—Norm Schachter, former NFL official.

STAN JAVIE

VAN Brocklin and I carried on beginning with my rookie year. The Los Angeles Rams were playing the Giants in New York, and Bob Waterfield, the Rams' quarterback, got hurt so they put Van Brocklin into the game. Near the end of the game, Los Angeles had about half a yard to go on fourth down, and instead of punting they tried a running play. I marked the ball. They measured for the first down and were short. I was a back judge, a sideline official, and since I was close to the bench they would always let me have it. The Rams were going off the field letting me have it, and the Dutchman had a vocabulary of four-letter words that you can't believe. Now I was a rookie, and this was a crucial game, so I kept backing up and backing up, but finally I'd had enough. "Knock it off," I told them. With that Van Brocklin started in again, so I flipped the flag. "Van Brocklin, you're gone."

Charlie Berry, our head linesman, came over and wanted to know what was going on. Mike Wilson, who was also in our crew, said, "The kid just threw Van Brocklin." Charlie looked at me and said, "You had a good reason?" I said, "Yes." He said, "Good. Get his ass out of here." By now the whole Rams' bench was going goofy, and Joe Stydahar, their coach, said, "What the hell am I supposed to do now? I don't have another quarterback." The Giants took over, kicked a field goal, and that put them ahead with only a few seconds left to play. The Rams ran a few plays without a quarterback, and you can imagine how they were letting me have it, costing them a game.

The game was about to end, and Wilson had the gun. The Rams called time-out, and Charlie came running over to me. "Javie, you start running when Mike shoots the gun, and don't stop until you hit the dressing room. We'll hold them off!" We were playing at the old Polo Grounds, and I was thinking to myself as I was running across the field, "Wonder what Bert Bell is going to say about this rookie?" Sure enough, Bert called me the next day. "What the hell happened, Stan?" I told him exactly what Van Brocklin said, and Bert told me, "Way to go, kid."

Bert Bell was a fabulous person. He just had a knack for doing things the right way, and his belief in professional football helped make the game what it is today. You just had to sense that he understood everything that was going on around him. Bert was loved by everybody in the league, and he had an amazing personality. He could deal with all the strong personalities in the league and tell them what to do without antagonizing them. They'd listen because he had his special way of doing it. He'd tell the officials, "Let's not have any trouble out there. Make sure you conduct yourself the right way because we want to put on a good game for the fans." He didn't worry about what the owners or coaches said. If it was good for the game, that's the way he wanted it done.

Jim Lee Howell was the Giants' coach in the late '50s. Howell was the kind of guy who would complain before the game, at halftime, during every time-out, and when the game was over. Dick Lynch was a defensive halfback for the Giants around that time, and I used to call him "Fast Hands" Lynch. He would bat the ball away, and it would look great, but at the same time I'd catch him using his other hand. I'd throw the flag, and the crowd would go nuts and Lynch would start in on me. I'd say, "Don't do that to me, Richard." I called him Richard, and he called me Stanley. I told him, "You'll get me in trouble with the coaches and fans with that sneaky stuff."

They said I set a record that day. I think I had fifteen fouls against the Giants—eight for interference and half of them were on Lynch. Howell was beside himself after the game. "I don't want to see you anymore. I'm going to report you." Bert asked me what happened, and after I told him he said, "Jav, you're going back up to Yankee Stadium next week."

Lou Palazzi was working with me that next weekend, and he had heard what was going on. Lou had played for the Giants before he became an official, and he and Jim Lee Howell had been roommates. Palazzi told me, "Jim's my old friend, my old roommate. When we go out on the field, I'm going to be with you." We get out on the field, and Howell looks at me. "What the hell are you doing here?" I said, "What am I doing here? What's it look like I'm going here?" Lou said, "Now Jim . . ." Howell looked at him and said, "Shut the hell up, Palazzi, I'm talking to him." I said, "Lou, that's your dear friend, your old roommate, Jim Lee." Howell walked away mumbling. It was almost the same kind of game, not as many fouls, but he was on me again, and when I talked to Bert on Monday, he told me, "You're going back this week."

You know what Bert was doing? He was telling Howell that the coaches don't run the league, Bert Bell runs the league. The third week I walked out on the field, and I had to go over to Jim because I have to get the names of the captains. He just threw up his hands. "I give up. I'm not going to complain. I ain't going to say a goddamn word. No more, no more." Years later I met Jim Lee Howell at a Giants' preseason game. He was retired by that time, and we both had a laugh about Bert's reaction to his complaints.

Howell had an assistant coach working for him by the name of Lombardi. You've heard the name, Lombardi? I can still hear that voice, just screaming at me. At one point it got so bad I went over to Howell. "Jim, are you the head coach or is that guy the head coach? Tell him to shut the hell up, or he's going to cost you some yardage." Howell said, in that Arkansas drawl of his, "Awl right, Vince, now you just gotta keep quiet." Lombardi would mumble something, and pretty soon he'd be screaming again. You can't believe how many times that would happen, and finally I said, "All right, Lombardi, you're the head coach. What do you want to know, Coach?" Jim Lee would start yelling, "Cut that bullshit out, Stan. I'm right over here."

Time went by, and I read in the paper that the Green Bay Packers had hired one Vince Lombardi as their head coach. Aw hell, here we go. You know, he was just the opposite when he became a head coach. However, he never got any quieter, and I will always remember his favorite expressions. *"Stan, what the hell is going on out there?"*

I'd say, "Well, Vince, I don't know. I'll find out for you." *"Stan, where do we get these goddamn officials from, Stan?"* "Well, Vince, I don't know. I don't have anything to do with that."

I will always remember his favorite expressions. We had a game in Milwaukee, and I stuck Boyd Dowler for fifteen. Vince wanted to know what the penalty was for. I said, "You ask Dowler what he said to me." We had a time-out, and Vince came over to me. "Dowler said he didn't say anything." I said, "Vince, is that what he said? I told you what he said, now you don't have to talk to me anymore because I lied to you." He started in on me. I told him, "Vince, I told you if I lied to you, you don't have to talk to me anymore," and I walked away.

The game went on, and we had another time-out. Vince walked over to me. "Stan, I want to apologize." It turned out that he had asked somebody to go over to Dowler and ask him what he said. The guy said, "Dowler didn't say anything." Vince went to Dowler himself after he talked to me, and that's a man. That's class. Vince was a tough guy. He was very demanding, but never abusive. There was always respect between us. I had Vince in his first game at Green Bay and his last at Green Bay, in Super Bowl II, his first in Washington and his last at Washington. I remember him on the sidelines in Dallas, the last game of the season. Washington hadn't had a good year and he said to me, "Stan, this is no good. This is never going to happen to me again." It was as if he knew what was going to happen. That was the last game he coached.

Don Shula is another good one. When he was coaching the Colts, they had this kid from Syracuse, a big end who could run like a racehorse: John Mackey. I got him for holding on two consecutive plays, and as you probably know, Shula is a very excitable guy. There were a lot of photographers around, and he chewed me up and down. I walked over to the sidelines and said, "Don, that took a lot of guts to do that in front of all those people. That's showing a lot of class." After the next play he came over to me. "Stan, you're right. I'm sorry," and that's the real Don Shula. You can be upset, it's part of the game, but it takes a man to admit he's gone too far. I know a lot of coaches who wouldn't and didn't, even though they knew they were wrong.

Another time we were in Chicago and Baltimore ran a play. This guy went around end for maybe eighty yards and I had a clip. I was coming back and Johnny Sandusky, a good friend of mine, he was Shula's assistant, let me have it and stepped out on the field. *Boom!* Down goes another flag. Johnny went crazy and by that time Shula was over there yelling at me. "I don't want you talking to any of my players or coaches." The game was going along and something happened out on the field and Johnny asked me, "Stan, what was that?" I didn't say a thing. Shula was standing right there and he got into it. "Goddamn it, Stan, what's going on out there?" I turned to Sandusky and said, "Would you please tell the coach that he told me not to talk to any of the coaches or players." Shula looked at me. "What the hell are you talking about?" That was another quality the good ones had. Different ways of telling you, "Hey, forget about it, everything is all right."

I grew up in a section of Philadelphia called Manayunk. My mother and father both came from Poland, and my dad went into the soda-bottling business. The family name was Jaworowski, and my dad shortened it to have a business name. My older brother Joe still has the business and it's under the name, Javie's Beverages. I had five brothers and three sisters. Three of my brothers were involved in high school sports, and I played football while I was going to St. Johns High School. After I graduated, I went to Georgetown University and majored in economics. I played football while I was in college, and there were some games that I started, but I was never what you would classify as a first-stringer. I was, however, good at one thing: I could block anybody.

When I was a sophomore, Al Blozis was a senior and a big star at Georgetown. (Not only was he a great football player, he was also the world's shotput champion.) The seniors were the meat grinders and we were the meat during practice. It was block this guy, block that guy, and I must have impressed Al somewhere along the line. After Al graduated, he went to play for the Giants, and when I was a senior he came to see me. "I've talked to the Giants about you, and they're going to contact you. They need guys who can block." Al was a great human being. He's in the Giants' Hall of Fame, and when he couldn't get into the service, because he was too big, he demanded an exemption and was killed in action. God bless him, what a man.

Sure enough, somebody from the Giants contacted me and I asked them what I'd be paid. He said, "$350 a game." Then the draft came along and I never expected to be drafted, but I showed up on the Eagles' list. They sent me a letter that said I had been drafted by them and a card to fill out if I was interested. The letter said, "If you sign and make the team, you will get paid $150 a game." I called the guy at the Giants and he said, "Ask the Eagles if they will release you. What the hell, you're fifteenth on the list." I thought, "If I'm going to get my brains beat in, it might as well be for $350 a game." I wrote a letter to Vince McNally, the general manager of the Eagles, and he said no. Do you know, for three or four years I kept getting this card from the Eagles. "Do you want to sign?"

After I got out of Georgetown, I started working at Honeywell, in Philadelphia, doing production control. The coach at my old high school, St. Johns, needed an assistant. Honeywell had a shift that started at seven and ended at three so I could hustle over to the school after work. I helped him for a year. At the end of that year, he got an offer from a bigger school, and when he took it, St. Johns asked me if I would work full-time. I took the job at half of what I was making, but what the hell, I was single and really enjoyed the work. Besides, I was going to be the next Knute Rockne.

I coached three sports—baseball, basketball, and football—and taught two subjects, so I had a full schedule. After four years at St. Johns, Malvern Prep, a private prep school, offered me a job. I had gotten married by that time and it meant a little more money, so I took it. I always felt that if I was going to be a good coach I needed to know the rules. When I first started out it was, "What's the rule on this?" and "What's the rule on that?" so I joined the local football officials' group. On my off-days I would officiate, and I really got to like it—junior high, intramural, anything I could get. You worked those games all by yourself and got five dollars for it. After a while I progressed to junior varsity and then varsity games, finally doing small colleges in the Middle Atlantic Conference.

One day I was sitting at home and my wife, Stella, answered the phone. She said, "Mr. Bert Bell of the National Football League wants to talk to you." I thought, "All right, who's the wise guy?" Holy Toledo, there was Bert on the phone. He told me, "We're looking for another official out of the Philadelphia area and Jack Glascott and Mike Wilson recommended you highly." Glascott and Wilson were working both college and pro ball because in those days you could do that. Work a college game on Saturday and do the pro game on Sunday. It was a lot simpler in those days because, for one thing, we didn't have any films to review. How well you did was determined by Bert saying, "Did you have any trouble?" You'd say, "No trouble." He'd say, "Good." Coaches could complain, and it didn't do them any good. Then the teams started to take films and the league office started to take films, and if there was a controversy you didn't know about it until the league office called you in. When Mike Wilson was the supervisor, they started to fool around with films and when Joe Kuharich, former coach of the Redskins, took over, they finally got involved. I can't complain about the use of films because I think it improved the quality of the officiating, especially under Art McNally.

I told Bert that I'd be interested in the job and went down to his office and filled out an application. Bert said, "You're on. We'll pay you $500 a year to start." In my last season, 1980, I was getting $1,200 for a regular season game, $3,000 for a Super Bowl. There were a few fellows who were working in college ball and they told me not to do it. Pro ball wasn't what it is today, and they were telling me that it wasn't going to last. I liked the idea of professional football and I liked Bert, so I told him I'd take the job.

There were some problems my first year, throwing guys out of games for roughness or swearing, things like that, but at the end of the year Bert called me into his office and said, "I'm giving you a raise, $800 a year."

I was always the kind of guy who tried to use common sense. If somebody started to give me a lot of B.S., I would take it up to a point. You've got your thirty seconds—get it off your chest. But if you keep it up, we've got trouble. If you use the wrong words, then we've really got trouble. Every club had a team leader, and they often were an official's best friend. I don't care what you call them—the protector, enforcer, godfather—many times they were the captain and usually the toughest guy on the team. Philadelphia's Mike Jarmoluk was that type. I'd make a call and everybody would be arguing and carrying on. Big Mike would come over and say, "Everybody shut up. He called it. You can't change it. Let's play football." Mike is a fine human being, and I always called him the "Gentleman Enforcer." Tom Brookshier, who played on the Eagles with Jarmoluk, was a tough individual and could handle himself one on one with anybody. However, when Brookie got involved, it was usually with more than one guy. He'd get in trouble and you could hear him yelling, "Yo, Mike, over here." Jarmoluk would come running. "Hold on, Brookie, I'm coming."

My younger son Steve is an official in the NBA, and we often talk about the philosophy of officiating. It's really a matter of understanding and handling people. You can't start to get involved with the personalities on the field. You have to let them play the game. Sometimes an official will get a big head and fail to realize that he can't let himself become more important than the game. When my son was starting out, he would say, "This guy did this and that guy did that . . ." I told him, "Look, it's not your job out there to change those guys into what you want them to be." Then I told him what I always told rookies I worked with. The league gives you the right to throw a guy out of a game anytime you think you have the proper conditions, but it's a right you shouldn't abuse. Some officials lose their perspective and forget that they don't own the game. We're just part of it and we're not the owners. I've also talked to my son about criticism and how to accept it, how to use it the right way to make you a better official. Again, you might be egotistical and say, "Hell, I'm an official and I'm always right." Tell everybody to go to hell and insist you're right when you're wrong. Or you might learn from your mistakes and try to avoid the same situation in the future. Those are some of the things we talk about.

You remember when you first saw a player. How they developed. From the time they were rookies until the day they retired as veterans. Some of them went on to become assistant coaches and guys like Landry, Noll, Reeves, and Shula became head coaches. I saw them all through that. Joe Schmidt was one of them. The Players' Association used to have an annual meeting in Florida. It was at the Hollywood Beach Hotel, one of those old-time hotels. The rooms and the beds were big. They invited any of the officials who wanted to come down, and since it was off-season, what the hell. This one year I was standing with my wife and Sam Huff after dinner and he was telling her, "Oh, Stan, he's one of the best," and all of this B.S. Sam was a great player and a real con artist. My wife was beaming and I told her, "Don't feel so good, Stel. He's planning for next season."

Doc Thompson, the team doctor at Detroit, was there and we were talking. Detroit was looking for a coach after Harry Gilmer left, and there was talk about Joe Schmidt getting the job. Doc said, "Joe just got a call. I think it's from Detroit." Joe came back and told Doc that he got the job and everybody was saying, "Congratulations. Good luck, Joe." He came over to us, and I said, "Congratulations, Joe. Now things are going to change between us." He said, "Not us, Stan." I said, "Joe, there's a big difference between me and you as a player and me and you as a head coach." "No, Stan, we're going to stay friends." I looked at Doc. "Now remember, Doc, you heard it here."

That year I had a game in Detroit where I threw out Mike Lucci, and I threatened to throw out the trainer and my friend Doc Thompson. Joe Schmidt is screaming his head off at me. I said, "Joe. Remember Florida. We're always going to be friends." He said, "Horseshit on that friends stuff." I said, "But, Joe, remember the handshake." He said, "Handshake, my ass!"

The players today are bigger and faster than they used to be, but I don't think there are any greater runners than the great ones of twenty or twenty-five years ago. The best of them today aren't better than Jimmy Brown or Gale Sayers or Ollie Matson. Jimmy Brown was the all-around best runner I've ever seen. He was the best because he was a fullback who ran like a halfback. They were also just as rough, if not a little more so. I can't tell you exactly what game it was, but Green Bay had an extra point coming up. They put these wingbacks in to block, right along side the ends. The ball was snapped, and this damn wingback wound up and took a swing. I never saw one like it, but he missed. I threw the flag and, as the penalty was being marked off, Vince was screaming, "What the hell is going on, Stan? He missed him." I said, "Yeah, and he's lucky he did. I gave him fifteen yards. If he'd hit him, he'd have gotten fifteen years!" The wingback was a rookie named Ray Nitschke.

There were a lot of players who impressed me over the years—Unitas, Jim Brown, Dick Butkus, Bednarik, O.J., it's almost unfair to pick out any one player; Kyle Rote, Lenny Moore, Bobby Mitchell, Ray Berry, Bobby Layne, the list goes on and on. My God, I couldn't believe the things they could do out on that field. One guy who always impressed me was Emlen Tunnell. He played for the Giants in the Polo Grounds, and he was a great athlete and a hell of a gentleman. It was a pleasure to watch a guy like Bart Starr come out of nowhere and become one of the greats. Larry Csonka was another one. He was a hell of a runner and a real character. I worked Super Bowl VIII, when Larry was tearing the Vikings apart.

He went in for a touchdown and just lay there. I yelled to another official to come over and see what was wrong. Just as we got over to him, he looked up and said, "What's wrong? What's going on?" I said, "What's going on? We thought you were hurt." "No," he said, "I'm just resting."

They were different. The guys who played in those years were in it for the love of the game. You could feel it out there on the field. Those players weren't pampered, and there was a lot of mutual respect. An official wasn't an enemy. You were there to officiate, and they respected you for the job you did. Sure, they yelled at you, but I yelled back and they'd back off. In modern times somebody yells at you and you yell back, they'll report you. Hey, you're an official. It was easy for me to figure that one out. If a guy wants it that way, I just kept throwing the flag. You can't be a star if you're sitting on the bench. Many times I'd throw the flag and somebody would say, "Aren't you going to throw him out of the game?" I'd say, "No, he's the best player the other team has on the field. Every time he opens his mouth, he 'gains' fifteen yards for them."

When the time to retire came, I always hoped I would recognize it and wouldn't have to be told to get out. I wanted to leave the game with the feeling that I had done the best possible job right up to the end. I was prepared to retire after Super Bowl XIV, but Art McNally asked me to consider one more year. That next year, 1981, was thirty years for me, and my last game was the Pro Bowl in Honolulu.

Oh, yes, I was telling you about Van Brocklin. Our relationship smoothed out at one point, and then he became a coach. We reverted immediately to our old ways. Every official in the league knew what was going on. "Oh, oh, Javie's got Van Brocklin this weekend. This is going to be something." We had our own private war going on.

One weekend I was going down to do a game in Atlanta, and I ran into John Hentz, who at that time was the executive producer for NFL Films. We were talking on the trip down, and he tells me that they're going to put a mike on Van Brocklin. I said, "You're kidding." He said, "No, he's one of the real personalities in the game today, and we thought this would be great for the fans." I didn't say much but was thankful that he told me what they were going to do.

That Sunday I was a perfect gentleman. No matter what Dutch said, I would say, "Yes, Coach. No, Coach." He'd be screaming, "Coach, my ass. What is this 'Coach' shit? Javie, you're screwing up this game." I'd just stand there and say, "Coach, I know." Coming back from Atlanta, I ran into John again and asked him how it went. He said, "Stan, that guy's incredible. I don't think we'll be able to use any of it. I've never heard anything like that in my life." Then he added, "But, Stan, I want to tell you something. You did a hell of a job controlling your temper. It must really be tough being an official." I said, "Yeah, John, nobody gives us credit for what we go through out there." I can just imagine Pete Rozelle and Art McNally when they saw that film. "Boy, the way Javie is controlling himself. How about that guy." They would have had an entirely different kind of film if I hadn't known what they were up to. That film is still around and it's hilarious. There must be eight minutes of Dutch and at least six minutes of it are bleeped out.

A couple of years before he passed away, Dutch and I got together at an NFL Alumni dinner and I'm glad we did. We got to talking and I thanked him for all the memories. He actually smiled!